Tom Graveney

Also by Christopher Sandford

THE CORNHILL CENTENARY TEST 1980

GODFREY EVANS: A BIOGRAPHY

TOM GRAVENEY

The Biography

CHRISTOPHER SANDFORD

H. F. & G. Witherby Ltd

First published in Great Britain 1992 by
H. F. & G. WITHERBY LTD
14 Henrietta Street, London WC2E 8QJ

A CIP catalogue record for this book is available from the British Library

ISBN 0 85493 211 9

Typeset at The Spartan Press Ltd,
Lymington, Hampshire
Printed and bound by
Butler & Tanner Ltd,
Frome, Somerset

To
Malcolm Galfe

Contents

Acknowledgements

My thanks to those who, even inadvertently, enlightened me about Tom Graveney: David Allen, Keith Andrew, Tony Brown, Denis Compton, David Dalby, Basil D'Oliveira, Godfrey Evans, Gloucestershire CCC, Alf Gover, Jackie Graveney, Ken Graveney, Tim Graveney, Stephen Green, the late Sir Leonard Hutton, Brian Johnston, Don Kenyon, Keith Miller, John Murray, Eric Russell, Bobby Simpson, Sir Garfield Sobers, Brian Statham and Derek Underwood. MCC and the Cricketers Club of London kindly provided facilities. On a personal note, my thanks to Malcolm Galfe, to whom the book is dedicated, and the staff of Charing Cross Hospital, in whose wards much of it was written.

C.S.
1992

1

Introduction

After 1966 a quarter-century passed before England beat West Indies at The Oval. In both cases the home sides were led from the front; in both they bowled and fielded like dogs fresh from the leash. The differences lay all in the batting. In 1966 the England innings was threatened by collapse; at one point it read 166–7. It survived through the heroics of Murray and a century last-wicket stand; that and the matter of 165 by a batsman recalled that summer at the age of thirty-nine. The innings was pure Graveney – not only in the elegance and power, reminiscent of Hammond, that characterised his strokeplay, but for the extraordinary circumstances surrounding his return. Against the same opposition in 1957, Graveney ended the series with an average of 118. In 1963, Frank Worrell was said to have asked each time the England side was announced: 'Is Tom playing?' The answer, with equal consistency, was no. It remained so through seven further series, home and away, until the second Test at Lord's, 1966. Graveney scored 96. In the next, at Trent Bridge, he made 109. The ways of selectors have been mysterious since the game began, and few cricketers can be said to have enjoyed the support at times conferred on them by public and press. Even so, to ignore a man for two seasons in which, member of a Championship-winning side, he averaged 54 and 49, suggests intransigence. To recall him then, at the ebb of his career, smacks of perversity. That Graveney responded as he did says volumes for his ability to surmount disappointment and despair. But to Tom Graveney disappointment was almost an old friend.

*

There are differing views of Graveney, though not of his skill as a player. To E. W. Swanton he remains 'the best professional batsman produced since the War'; to Brian Johnston, 'a man who compelled you to watch and enjoy the manner of his batting'. Of his peers, Trevor Bailey found 'few, if any, players more attractive to watch', while Sobers considered him 'the best front-foot player' of his generation, seeing no cricketing reason for Graveney's periodic absences from the Test team. 'It must', says Sobers, 'have been something he said.'

The last remark is revealing. If not volatile in the way of Trueman, histrionic like Evans or given to interior moods such as Laker or Wardle, there was a suspicion that Graveney's temperament failed at times to display the obduracy expected of it. In short, Graveney was laid-back. Others to whom the accusation has applied include David Gower, in whom there are additional touches of Graveney's character. One can speculate on the nature of a society that neglects the artist in favour of the artisan, but it was Graveney's peculiar misfortune to play his early Test cricket under a man who, above others, personified the austerity of the post-War era. When, in Coronation year, Len Hutton presented the England team to the Queen at Lord's, he looked at Graveney, in the latter's words, 'as if surprised to see me there'. Later that winter Hutton greeted two flowing drives by the younger batsman in a Test at Barbados with the phrase, 'We don't want that. We're going to grind this out.' Graveney, for this and other reasons, ended the series in a state of quiet despair, having been in the centre of an umpiring controversy at Port-of-Spain and returning, in his captain's words, 'a disappointment'. On that tour he averaged only 56.

Graveney's career, too, had a tendency to the accident-prone. Whatever the merits of his case, in 1960 he left Gloucestershire acrimoniously after thirteen seasons; in 1969 he was banned and effectively sacked by England. Even his curtain-call, as player-coach of Queensland, ended in dispute. The three events are unconnected and reveal no single flaw in Graveney's character; only the suspicion that, at times, the man was not as seemingly tranquil as his cricket. Beneath the benign, almost avuncular exterior, Graveney retains the tenacity of a northerner, native of Northumberland, taught never to squander his gifts. Lest those gifts seem to have been granted without condition, it should be remembered that he began his professional career with a nought.

In the 1890s the Palairet brothers distinguished Somerset with the power and grace of their play. Of a later generation, Woolley was regarded as elegant a batsman as ever donned pads; Cyril Walters as a genius who combined almost fluid style with earthy determination. It is not the least of Graveney's achievements that, at its best, his strokeplay could be compared to theirs, yet be considered by a very different exponent, Geoffrey Boycott, as 'the technique I most admired'. Even at the end of his career, Graveney showed what remained of himself from the 1950s. He flowed into the drive like no one since Hammond. The bat was an extension of his nervous system. Cricket, to Graveney, was never a compulsion – merely what he did. He had talent that could have led to a career in golf, or even accountancy; but for the influence of his brother he might have remained in the army. Graveney may have disappointed some by playing in Graveney's way, which retained vestiges of the amateur's. Cricket was central to his life, but, like Compton, Miller or Evans, he had interests outside it. Like them, those interests were sometimes held against him; a fleeting cameo of an innings as evidence of frivolity. Like theirs, Graveney's answer lies not just in the achievements of his career – 47,793 first-class runs, average 44.91 – but in the enjoyment he provided over a quarter-century. If, as Swanton has written, 'In the era of Hutton and May, it was the grafter who was apt to be preferred', then, in Graveney's case, it was to the loss of cricket lovers everywhere. As Compton, not the least fluent of batsmen, has said: 'Tom was, without doubt, the most stylish of his day. Only England could ever have considered dropping him.'

Graveney's first-class career extended from 1948 to 1972; from Bill Edrich to John Edrich, from Bradman to Boycott. It encompassed the dawn of one-day cricket; abolition of the amateur; creation of the TCCB and other changes; D'Oliveira and South Africa. He played 79 Tests, scoring eleven hundreds, 4882 runs; captained and even kept wicket for England. Wherever cricket is played his name is synonymous with grace, with control, with style. Batsmen may have scored more runs, or batted with greater tenacity; few have given such pleasure to so many. If such is Graveney's legacy, then cricket owes him its gratitude.

2

'Things can only get better'

In May 1927 Walter Hammond scored 1042 first-class runs; that summer New Zealand, for the first time, toured England; Cardiff City won the FA cup; for six weeks England simmered in reams of sun. Some time in June the weather broke in a shawl of rain. That season five County Championship matches were never started and in 28 others less than a day's play was possible. In Sydney there was talk of a teenager called Bradman.

On 16 June, in the village of Riding Mill, Northumberland, Mary Graveney gave birth to her third child, a son, Thomas. A farmer's daughter from nearby Newcastle, Mary married Jack Graveney, an engineer, in 1920. The family came from London and the south-east; a road in Tooting bears the name; the River Graveney lies tributary to the Thames. Jack's work was armaments. His passion was sport. Cricket, golf, football and tennis were about him in London and, later, as a manager of Vickers Armstrong in Newcastle. His oldest son, Ken, remembers, 'Games were everything to us. They were in the blood.'

When Tom was five he was taken with his elder brother to play golf at Ryton. Clubs were specially designed. He recalls the sensation of swinging, eye on the ball: a natural. That summer, 1932, he received his first cricket bat, reward for courage in the face of the dentist. It was signed by Bradman. He saw India at Jesmond. In the sole Test they lost to Jardine's England. That winter Jardine and Bradman were, for a time, the most celebrated names in part of the world. At home Jack arranged 'Tests' of his own, with his sons in the guise of Hobbs and Sutcliffe. The Master's role was Ken's: 'We shared a birthday,' he says.

Jack Graveney died in 1933, barely 51. In addition to the normal effect on any six-year-old, the event presaged a crisis in Graveney's life. That winter, the family – Mary, Ken and Tom, their brother Maurice and sisters Margaret and Dorothy – left Riding Mill for Fleetwood, where in time the children acquired a stepfather, Bob Gardner. While life continued to be 'comfortable', Gardner's job with the construction firm of Sir Lindsay Parkinson was not one to encourage thoughts of idleness among his new family. In 1934 Tom and Ken were boarded at Arnold House, Blackpool, where unknowingly they would acquire a Lancashire qualification. Cricket continued to play a part in Graveney's life, although only, as he puts it, 'as one of half a dozen sports that attracted me equally'. According to Ken, at this stage his brother was 'talented . . . without showing any great flair for batting. If anything, he had more skill as a medium-pacer'. Graveney, like many a schoolboy, lost that skill with time – but continued to bowl leg-spinners and googlies with pleasure and occasional effect throughout his career.

In 1938 Gardner was assigned to a project in Avonmouth Docks, Bristol. The town was teeming. Mobilisation was at hand. In Gloucestershire the county (and now Test) captain had metamorphosed from Hammond W.R. to W. R. Hammond; that summer he scored 240 against Australia at Lord's, an innings, said *The Times*, 'which can seldom have been surpassed'. 'Right from the start,' says Graveney, 'I admired Wally more than any other player.'

Graveney himself was beginning to blossom. At Bristol Grammar School he played scrum-half, then, with the onset of adolescence, centre and full-back. He took to squash and fives; 'Still keeping his options open,' says Ken, 'as we all did.' Then, in 1939, he came under the influence of a master, M. A. Tulloch. He was a club cricketer with a basic knowledge of the game, yet possessed, says Graveney, 'of the gift to bring out whatever natural ability existed'. A twelve-year-old ought to be coached in such a way that he never forgets that cricket is a game to be enjoyed, and, in Graveney's words, 'that the ball is there to be hit'. Tulloch was such a coach. Under him Graveney was encouraged to develop what was natural and to discard what was not. With which in mind, Graveney cites 1939 as the year in which he began to think seriously about sport (the word still generic). That summer Hammond's England beat the West Indies by one Test to nil; the captain himself scored 138 at The

Oval. In the same match Learie Constantine played a role possible to no one else; 5–75 in England's first innings and a cameo 79 in better than even time. Graveney saw both players in the tourists' match at Cheltenham and, under Tulloch's influence, determined from then on that 'cricket would be a part of my life, if not my living'. It was July 1939.

The following two summers brought steady success. Against Weston County School he took 9–5, bowling, as he says, 'without style – none'. As for batting, Tulloch and another master, Alan Carter, encouraged without nagging, inspiring that priceless commodity in any sport, enjoyment. In 1941 Graveney encountered another influence: Jack Bessant, a Gloucestershire player on either side of the First World War, later groundsman at Bristol University. With the family home abutting the college, the teenage Graveney was soon a regular helper, spectator and finally player, as Bessant encouraged him to 'make up the numbers' in visiting sides as diverse as the Bristol Police and Home Guard Elevens. It is worth remembering that, at this time, Graveney was still regarded as a medium-pacer who could bat; not once in his schooldays did he score a century and, until at least 1943, he was thought too slight to be more than a glider and pusher of runs. His captain at the Grammar Preparatory School in 1939 remembers him as 'thin as a rake . . . with a cap almost concealing his head'. Despite which, he notes that 'Even then, Tom "had" something. You could tell he'd go on in the game.' The captain, David Dalby, went on himself, becoming a distinguished secretary of Kent.

What, meanwhile, of school? Both Graveney and his brother recall their reports as being 'strangely better in the winter terms than summer', for which an explanation suggests itself. Summer, too, was the season for golf, Graveney's second abiding passion. It was mitigated somewhat in 1942, when, playing a game in which the brothers would chip a ball to each other while on the move, Tom was struck by a swinging drive and needed half a dozen stitches in an eye. That finished his golf for the year, the same in which Ken left school for the Royal Marine Commandos, where in time he was commissioned lieutenant. The separation crystallised life for Tom, who realised that 'schooldays were running out and more serious things were being mooted'. In 1943 he sat, and missed, his School Certificate, on the basis of a single failure in English Language. That summer he continued his schooling at the hands of Bessant and George Duffield, the ex-Sussex bowler, on the University ground. By now he had grown to incorporate the reach essential to the front-foot player he became. 'Everything changed when Tom grew,' says Ken. 'A lot of the coaching by Tulloch and Carter made sense.' Still a career in cricket, or any sport, was unthinkable.

In 1944 Graveney re-sat and passed his School Certificate. That autumn, aged seventeen, he was faced with the bleak prospect of finding a job. Bleak because his first choice, accountancy, revealed such 'dingy, miserable conditions' that he was forced to reconsider. After consulting his mother and stepfather, Graveney (not for the last time) followed his brother's lead and in spring 1945 joined the army. There followed six months of basic training at a Young Soldiers Battalion, after which came pre-OCTU, and OCTU; finally in May 1946 he became 2nd Lieut. T. W. Graveney 364610 of the Gloucestershire Regiment with a posting to the Middle East. He set sail on his nineteenth birthday.

Immediately, at transit camp in Cairo, he found himself immersed in cricket. Earlier, in OCTU, he had added boxing to his sporting interests, making use of his newly extended reach. This and the life that greeted him in Egypt convinced Graveney that the army was for him, and, in sixteen consecutive days that summer, fourteen were spent at the wicket. Playing on hard, even pitches encouraged, Ken believes, the confidence to play straight; and both brothers agree that by 1946 Tom's primary instinct was for batting. He himself calls this 'a natural development . . . without a conscious decision on my part'. Ken's view is more prosaic: 'He dropped bowling because it was too bloody hot overseas. The Other Ranks did the bowling.'

From Egypt the Regiment embarked for Greece, where Graveney played more cricket on rough coir matting, an experience later to stand him in good stead on tours of India and the West Indies. Eventually the Brigade broke up. Graveney and five others were posted to the Royal Artillery, which in turn suggested he transfer to the unit permanently. Graveney's refusal was as much in deference to his original commission as to the ordeal of cleaning and loading heavy guns. The army's response was decisive: Graveney was ordered to a transit base in Suez and thence to a camp for Jewish terrorists in Kenya; 'Not', he says, 'the most enticing prospect in the world.'

Here events took a turn as fortuitous as any in Graveney's career. At Suez the commanding officer greeted him with the phrase, 'You're the one who scored those runs in Cairo. Would you like to be sports officer?' Graveney took all of a second to agree. For the next six months he was assigned to organising and playing cricket, football, rugby, golf, tennis, hockey; a child let loose in a toy department. It was almost an anticlimax to return to England when granted leave in August 1947. One reason he did so was to establish contact with Ken, who had left the service in 1946 but without taking to civilian life. He was restless and talking of rejoining the army. Having played as a batsman and change bowler for Stoke Bishop, the elder Graveney applied for a trial at Gloucestershire. During it he strained his back so severely that, throughout his brief career, he played in near-constant pain. Impressed by his persistence, the county offered a contract which was accepted with alacrity. In 1946 the great Hammond, 50,551 runs, 819 catches, had retired; to general surprise the following year the county climbed three places to be runners-up. On 9 August they were entertained by Yorkshire at Bradford. Gloucestershire made 182, Emmett 64, whereupon the home side recovered from 45–5 to 228. The visitors declined to 142–7 – 96 ahead – before Emmett (who next year would represent England in place of, of all people, Hutton) went on to make 113. Yorkshire were left a target of 236. That they failed to reach it was due largely to the bowling of Tom Goddard, who took the last three wickets for 1 run. Gloucestershire won by 8 runs and led the Championship.

Such was the prelude to a match at Cheltenham which, in John Arlott's words, 'whatever the mathematical possibilities decided the pennant'. For two days the home team struggled in heat that at times seemed to tire even the spectators; the opposition, Middlesex, harried like a pet dog; Jack Young took 5–27 in the second innings, Goddard fifteen wickets in the match; the ball burnt to the boundary with convulsive speed. At this very moment, on a troopship in the Mediterranean, Tom Graveney was hanging on Arlott's distant commentary in the radio room. When he reached Cheltenham on 21 August, Middlesex had prevailed. The Championship was decided. That night his brother made the suggestion that would change his life for ever.

*

Charlie Barnett played twenty times for England, the last in June 1948 against Australia at Nottingham. Barnett holds the record for the highest score for England on the first day of a Test. In 1934 he scored eleven sixes in an innings of 194 for Gloucestershire at Bath. In 1947 Barnett was thirty-seven. On 31 May the county hosted a match for his Benefit at Bristol, Yorkshire being beaten by nine wickets. On six of eight Sundays thereafter Barnett organised, played in or attended similar matches. Ken Graveney describes these as 'fun, but played in the knowledge that spectators expected us to perform. There were no punches pulled.' Graveney's own place on the fringe of the First Eleven made him an automatic choice, and by mid-season he recalls both Barnett and the Gloucestershire captain, Basil Allen, deferring to him to some extent on the composition and logistics of the games. Thus it was that, on the Thursday following the fateful fixture at Cheltenham, Ken Graveney – in his own words, 'wholly innocently' – approached the beneficiary with the news that his brother Tom, recently arrived from Egypt, would henceforth be available to make up the numbers if required.

'He's playing Sunday,' said Barnett.

Given little or no choice, Graveney played on Sunday, and the one that followed, terrified, he says, of occupying the very dressing-room of Neale, Crapp, Emmett and Goddard. In Graveney's own assessment, he was 'nothing special' as a batsman in such company, and his first two innings in Gloucestershire colours ended in single figures. In the third, against a Kent XI, Godfrey Evans remembers him as a 'tall, emaciated-looking youth' who, after a nervous start, gave evidence of a technique which left the England stumper no doubt of his potential: 'He had a top-of-the-handle grip, high backlift, and because of his height was always on the front foot. He loved to drive. The bat went in a complete arc as he made the stroke, finishing almost on his shoulder . . . Even then it was obvious he had something.'

Both Ken Graveney and David Dalby agree that 'he loved to drive', the result, they say, of Tom's early coaching by Tulloch. According to Dalby, in 1939 the motto at Bristol Grammar School had been to 'take the game to the bowler', a maxim adopted by Graveney 'the second he had the height to do so'. In Egypt, too, colleagues remember him driving on the flat, arid pitches 'with the precision of a machine', if somewhat more style. The combination of ability, aptitude and strength seems to have contributed equally to Graveney's development, which in 1947 lacked but one essential for success: competition.

In the second week of September, Barnett's team faced Essex at Stinchcombe. Among the opposition was T. N. Pearce, whose own *annus mirabilis* would come the following year. Opening the innings with Billy Neale, Graveney scored 32, including six off-side boundaries. His brother remembers it as the day 'Tom, for the first time, gave notice'; Graveney himself as 'the moment I was accepted.' So much so that, after the match, Barnett sought out the twenty-year-old with the suggestion that the two 'have a few' before the return drive to Bristol. It may have been then, or on the journey itself, that Barnett asked the batsman his plans. For once Graveney was at a loss for words.

Shortly before leaving Suez, overtures had been made to appoint him a staff officer in physical training. The prospect was an attractive one. No less averse to the Dickensian gloom of accountancy, Graveney viewed a life of near-continuous sport, all found, as 'a dream come true'. The army is a very different matter when one excels in a given field. Still Barnett's offer intrigued him, and when in the following days it was reiterated by Colonel Henson, the county secretary, and Allen, the captain, Graveney promised to consider it. He consulted Ken, whose own position on the staff helped decide the issue. 'I told him the army would still be there if it didn't work out. County cricket, on the other hand, only knocks once.' That September Graveney chose cricket.

A love of the game may not have been his only motive. That autumn Graveney had met Jackie Brookman, cousin of the Gloucestershire off-spinner Monty Cranfield. While his first memory of her is as 'noisy', their relationship was to continue, first at long distance, then, on his return to Bristol, resulting in their wedding in 1952. When Graveney returned to Suez it was with the dual prospect of first-class cricket and marriage to sustain him. Immediately on landing he tendered his resignation from the army.

It was a greater risk than he knew. In 1947 the Gloucestershire top order batting read: Barnett, Allen, Neale, Crapp, Emmett; Andy Wilson, the wicketkeeper, was good enough to score 1,000 runs in a season. A sixth batting place was contested between Graham Parker, the former Cambridge Blue and rugby international; reliable Cliff

Monks; and Ken Graveney. The last was restricted largely to Second Eleven and Benefit games, and remembers the county side that season as 'full of wily, seasoned pros, all capable of making 1,500 runs or more in a year'. Even Allen, the Cambridge Blue in his first post-war season as captain, scored 1716. In short, the county, if lacking a player of the decisive genius of Hammond, was well served by those who had learnt their cricket under his influence in the 1930s, and the suspicion must be that a twenty-year-old, signed on the basis of a handful of charity appearances and the recommendation of his brother, was seen at best as a long-term option. Ken Graveney confirms that '. . . while Tom was favourably noted by men like Barnett and Neale, the county was far from awestruck at the prospect of signing him . . . If anything, he was regarded as cover for a number of players then in their mid-thirties, not as a star in his own right.'

For the last three months of 1947 and the first of 1948, Graveney continued his life in Suez. On 31 January he received his separation papers from the army. For the remainder of that winter he returned home to Bristol. He renewed relations with Jackie Brookman. He played golf. He waited. On Thursday 1 April 1948 Graveney became a professional cricketer when he reported to Colonel Henson at the County Ground, Bristol. Throughout that month he engaged in the cursory training then characteristic of first-class cricket, training replete with the baggage carrying, tea making and other duties characteristic of the junior pro. His salary was £200 p.a. On 30 April Graveney learnt that, along with Emmett, he would open the county batting in their fixture next day against Oxford at The Parks. May Day was raw and dripping; raw as Graveney's hands as he dropped the Oxford batsman Donald Carr on the cover boundary. That was bad enough. When Gloucestershire's turn came the twenty-year-old went to the wicket, in his own words, 'like a condemned man approaching the wall'. Execution at least was quick. Graveney departed, c. Travers b. Whitcombe, for nought; and few of the handful of spectators present could have guessed they were witnessing the début of the supreme stylist of his generation. In the dressing-room the Gloucestershire coach, Charlie Parker, sought out Graveney with the assurance 'things can only get better', and outside the pavilion a small boy asked for his autograph. It was a start.

3

Recognition

When Graveney was signed by Gloucestershire, it was on condition that the committee increase his salary when results merited it. The way he played in May 1948, he thought they might reduce it. Immediately after his début Graveney scored 4 and 4 against Worcester, then 8 and 25 versus Sussex at Bristol. In the match against Yorkshire he learnt still more of life in his new profession when Brian Sellers, an outspoken critic of Hammond's captaincy of England, was himself raucously booed by the Bristol crowd. Barnett and Emmett added comment of their own by scoring 226 in two hours to win the match. It was one of only nine Championship victories all season.

'The county suffered after the success of 1947,' says Graveney. 'A number of batsmen were, frankly, past their best and there was no new blood in the side'; himself excepted. For nearly six weeks, a triumph of hope over experience, he remained *in situ*. On 16 June he was dropped. It was his birthday. A fortnight later the Australians appeared at Bristol. This was the match, says Graveney, when he 'knew England were in trouble'. Australia compiled 774–7 declared, in so doing destroying Goddard, who returned figures of 0–186 and was never the same bowler again. In the pavilion, as twelfth man, Graveney overheard the Australian captain, Hassett, ask Morris if he could 'go after' the off-spinner. Morris could, to the tune of 290. The tourists went straight from Bristol to the third Test at Manchester where, incredibly, England omitted Hutton. In the previous matches, at Trent Bridge and Lord's, the opener had been the target of almost personal abuse from Lindwall and Miller, the latter of whom admits to 'trying to bounce Len out of the series'. In consequence England's most distinguished batsman was dropped and George Emmett chosen for his first and only Test. The decision returned Graveney to the county eleven and, having made 26 and 2 not out against Lancashire at Bristol, he then distinguished himself against Derbyshire at the same venue by making nought in each innings. In the first he was caught by Pope in the leg-trap; in the second, left in dwindling light facing twenty minutes before the close, he lasted five. Allen promptly returned him to the Seconds and Graveney himself returned to golf. At Old Trafford England managed a draw.

How good was Graveney at this stage of his career? According to his brother, 'basically orthodox, with a strong preference for the front-foot play he learnt from Tulloch . . . All he lacked was confidence.' In Graveney's own view, his chief technical flaw was the high backlift, which, while responsible for the flowing drive that became his trademark, contributed equally to his demise against fast bowling. Like his brother, he cites 'inexperience' as his main drawback. The bowling of men like Pope and Coxon – to say nothing of Lindwall and Miller – was a class above anything encountered in the army, while the wickets that summer did nothing to encourage positive strokeplay.

Graveney returned to the first Eleven against Nottingham at Cheltenham. He scored 64 not out, his first Championship half-century, on a sodden pitch. It was the start of a four-week period in which he made 600 first-class runs; he cites it as the moment his batting 'clicked'. Against Hampshire on a turning pitch he scored 47, thanks in part to the kindness of Barnett. Earlier in the season the opener had examined Graveney's bat and declared it 'no surprise' he remained virtually scoreless. 'Try mine,' he suggested, and for the rest of that season Graveney enjoyed probably the most beautifully 'alive' blade he ever possessed. As well as the confidence it gave him, the gesture proved that, even at this stage of his career, Graveney was considered an investment. More than forty years later, Denis Compton stated that 'you knew, right away, Tom was a genius. Gloucester were on to a good thing.' It says much for the county, and Barnett, that they were prepared to wait for it.

Evidence of Graveney's potential followed in a match against the Combined Services in late August. Of a first-innings total of 234 he scored 89. On the last day he went one better and, according to *Wisden*, 'hit well all round' to make 114, his maiden first-class century. There were, as he puts it, 'rough edges' about his innings, and the Services' attack was no more than university or club standard. Yet it confirmed Graveney as a player of or near the highest class, and Compton, for one, claims that 'to have scored a century on any pitch that summer was an achievement'. (He scored nine.) As the season drew to an end, Graveney believed he was at last acclimatised to the higher grade of cricket, and that he no longer felt 'an intruder' in the Gloucestershire dressing-room. 'There was a feeling that I might, after all, make it. Two months earlier, I wasn't so sure.'

To confirm which he scored 52 against Kent at Gloucester, described by Evans as 'masterly' and by Graveney as 'probably the high water-mark of the season'. On the last day, 31 August, he was awarded his county cap. In early September he represented, improbably, the North versus the South at Hastings. The South prevailed and Graveney contributed nothing. None the less, on the evidence of his form since late July, *Wisden* noted the presence 'of a newcomer . . . who showed graceful right-handed strokeplay', and Graveney ended the season with 973 first-class runs at an average of 28.61. That winter the county arranged for him to coach at the indoor school at Bristol. It was a low-lit building whose facilities bordered on spartan. Still, in the company of the county coach, Parker, and men like Emmett and Crapp, Graveney learnt as much as he taught, particularly the back-foot strokes to reinforce his driving. As spring dawned he felt in 'the best form' of his career. He was ready.

He was ready. Against Oxford at The Parks, Graveney improved on his previous nought by scoring 108, described by *Wisden* as 'stylish' and 'splendid'. The early season was played in damp, dripping conditions such that the county never established a rhythm; not until the fifth match did they appear on a home ground. Against Nottinghamshire Graveney added a second century before sitting out the Combined Services match at Bristol. Appearing for the opposition was a frail, coltish teenager who scored 80 in the first innings and 90 in the second. 'We were all impressed by his composure,' says Graveney: Peter May. Graveney himself scored 63 against Sussex, then, on 22 June, reported to Bristol for the match that brought him to national attention. In scoring 96 against

Middlesex, Graveney impressed men like Young and Edrich, who knew a prospect when they saw one, and Compton himself, who notes that this was the moment that 'Tom arrived . . . It was only a matter of time before he played for England.'

Graveney had the chance to assess his Test potential when, on 2 July, the touring New Zealanders arrived at Bristol. He scored 38 and 1, falling to the left-armer Tom Burtt, a man who 'closed down' batsmen at will. Burtt's ascendancy led directly to the demise of three-day Tests; of the four played in 1949 all were drawn. Of New Zealand, Graveney notes that 'being subjected to more "scientific" bowling and field placing was valuable experience', and the tourists' captain, Walter Hadlee, adds that 'even then . . . you could see the essence of his technique. None of us had any doubt Tom would make it.'

Confirmation followed in a match with Somerset in late July. Against an attack including Hazell, the left-armer who that year took 106 wickets, Graveney scored 159. According to his brother, it was now that 'more than one observer' was heard to speculate on Graveney playing for England, who had established a precedent in 1949 by selecting the eighteen-year-old Brian Close. Bailey, too, made his début that season and believed that 'Tom was on the verge of selection'. Few in Somerset would have argued.

Cricketers in their second season frequently suffer from being 'found out' by other players. The corollary is that they themselves have the ability to find others out. In 1948, both Graveney and his brother cite inexperience as a factor inhibiting his play. As a result, much of that season was spent in reconnaissance of the sights and sounds of his new profession. In 1949 things were different. Graveney emerged from the indoor school with the determination to establish himself as quickly as possible, and the few present at Oxford on 3 May witnessed the result. Not only was Graveney more attuned to bowlers like Jackson, Coxon and Pope, he now actively relished his encounters with spin, not least as provided by Jack Young at Bristol. Laker, who finished the season with 122 first-class wickets, was another on whom (encouraged by Emmett) Graveney was severe, believing that 'at this stage, you could destroy Jim's confidence'. Goddard, too, had appeared in the indoor school, the dim light concealing the baldness and decay of the matting on which, over after over, he instructed his young colleague. There has seldom been a more generous cricketer. The results were self-evident from the first match, and from it Graveney drew confidence.

After the monsoon conditions of 1948 the weather improved to encourage positive play, and batsmen, among them Hutton, Hardstaff, Langridge and Simpson, dominated the ball; a measure of the conditions is that Glamorgan, who won the Championship in 1948 largely on the strength of their bowling and fielding, fell to eighth. Under the circumstances batsmen could hardly fail to prosper, and Graveney notes that conditions could hardly have been better. *Wisden* agreed, adding that, of a Gloucestershire team rising one place in the table, not the least of 'several causes for satisfaction' was 'the work of the brothers Graveney. In his second summer . . . T. W. Graveney put together four centuries . . . His elegant strokeplay stamped him as one of the best young batsmen in the country.' Significantly, his average had risen to 33. Note, too, *Wisden*'s description of Graveney's strokeplay in 1948 and 1949 as 'graceful' and 'elegant'. It was echoed by Parker in the indoor school that winter: 'We know you can play,' he bellowed. 'Now let's see you *graft*.' Even style had its limits.

Graveney began 1950 as though the previous season had not happened. In the traditional opener at Oxford he reverted to his 1948 persona and scored 12 and 19. It was the beginning of a bleak year for the county and himself. Gloucestershire remained seventh in the Championship, yet won only six matches and contributed, in Graveney's words, 'towards the aura of unpredictable charm surrounding West Country cricket', in contrast to the 'ruthlessness' of a Surrey or Yorkshire. Against Warwickshire Graveney scored nought; versus Kent nought and 23. Salvation came, as in 1948, against Nottinghamshire at Bristol, where Graveney scored 197. Two matches later he made 115 against Glamorgan at Gloucester, where, says *Wisden*, 'during a stay of two and three-quarter hours, [he] continually penetrated a packed off-side field'. To emphasise which, in the following month he made 201 of a total of 383 against Sussex, 'overshadowing his colleagues' (the *Post*), and recording the first double-century of his career.

And that was that. From early July the runs dried up. Graveney himself believes that now, more than in 1949, he was 'found out' by opposing bowlers, who in turn benefited from more helpful conditions. None more so than 'Sonny' Ramadhin and Alf

Valentine, who arrived in England unknown and left it four months later with a total of 59 Test wickets between them. From June to August the country's attention focused on the extraordinary events that saw West Indies win the series three-one and alter their status in world cricket for ever. To Graveney, Ramadhin 'possessed all the virtues' – length, direction, variation – 'with an ability to spin the ball either way with an action that was unreadable'. By the time the tourists appeared at Cheltenham on 19 August, the bowler's reputation, already celestial, was extended when he took 8–15 and 5–36 to defeat Gloucestershire by an innings. Graveney was one of the relative successes (19 and 23), despite which he admits to 'not reading the bowler at all'. More pertinently, this was the moment when he felt 'a touch of realism entered my dream of playing for England', not least because in 1950 no fewer than twenty-five players did so. 'With respect to Dewes, Parkhouse and the rest,' he says, 'I knew I was on – or above – their level.'

For Gloucestershire Graveney scored 1772 runs at an average of 36, seen by *Wisden* as 'not making the progress anticipated, possibly because soft pitches told against his forward strokeplay'. That winter he returned to the indoor school, where Parker and others strengthened his technique, and, as before, developed his back foot. Facilities at Bristol were bleak. The matting was rough and aerogated; above it shafts of light filtered through the dusty beams. Still, confronted with ball after repetitive ball, Graveney learnt the virtues of the cut, the sweep, even the hook. The man emerging in 1951 would, in all but experience, be complete.

Rarely can a season have begun so well. Against Oxford in early May, Graveney scored 201 of a total of 361 for four declared, 'driving and hooking powerfully' (*Wisden*). Immediately afterwards he made 50 at Taunton in a match dominated by the ball. His brother recalls the 'transformation', noted also by Emmett and Parker, of Graveney's play, and Bedser, who encountered him later in May, was conscious of a player 'with all the strokes'. In mid-May Graveney reported for the fixture against South Africa at Bristol believing that he was playing as well as he ever had.

This was the match, played in dripping weather in front of capacity crowds, that determined the two Graveneys' careers. In the nets prior to the start, Ken, still suffering from the back strain incurred at his trial, broke down and took no part in the match. At season's end he announced his retirement. Tom, meanwhile, proceeded to score 37 in the first innings and 93 in the second. The South African team featured the raw power of Cuan McCarthy – considered by Hutton 'as fast or more so' as Lindwall – the off-spin of Rowan and slow left-arm guile of Mann; as balanced an attack as then existed. Graveney considers his second innings, in arctic weather, the ball seaming in the leaden atmosphere, as 'under the circumstances, outstanding'. For good measure a back-foot drive saw Nourse, the tourists' captain, struck by the ball on the left thumb, which was subsequently revealed to be broken. Nourse later appeared in the first Test at Nottingham, scoring 208 and helping South Africa to their first victory in sixteen years. At Bristol he offered rueful congratulations.

On his twenty-fourth birthday Graveney reported for a fixture against Derbyshire at Gloucester. He scored 89. Bets began to accumulate on his being chosen for England. The following week, at Bristol, he made 128 against a Warwickshire attack including Eric Hollies, who finished the season with 145 wickets and helped his county to their first Championship in forty years. More pertinently, Graveney confirmed his new-found ability to adapt to conditions, *Wisden* recording that 'in the interests of the side [he] curbed his desire to hit'. At the end of June, England defeated South Africa at Lord's, thanks to the bowling of Roy Tattersall; the batting again looked invertebrate. The press descended on Graveney and demanded, rather than suggested, he be considered by the selectors. More than one had appeared at Bristol.

On 1 July 1951 Graveney heard that he was in the England twelve for the third Test at Old Trafford. Amidst 'near-hysteria' in the family he reported to Manchester, convinced that his sole responsibility would be 'collecting the autographs'. On the morning of 5 July he learnt otherwise, when Freddie Brown approached him with the news that Compton was unfit. The great man had been injured by, of all things, a full toss, and – by his own admission – lacked his previous appetite for the game, following a disastrous winter tour of Australia. No sooner had the news sunk in than Graveney was on the field at long-leg. In the first over Eric Rowan edged the ball to slip and Bedser was on his way to figures of 12–112. In wet, wind-racked conditions, his use of the leg-cutter suspended belief; the South Africans batted as if in a trance. By the end of that day

Graveney was perched on the balcony as Hutton and Jack Ikin opened the England reply. The second day was washed out. The first ball of the third, from Rowan, turned, bounced and struck Hutton on the chest. The England players exchanged glances. At the fall of the second wicket Graveney came to the crease. His innings of 15 was praised by *The Times* for its correct technique; in the context of the match it was neither disastrous nor distinguished. South Africa collapsed in the second innings and England were left needing 139 to win. At lunch on the final day they were 135–1, Hutton 91 not out. Prior to the Test the opener had scored his ninety-eighth and ninety-ninth first-class centuries and arrived at Old Trafford amidst agitation for the hundredth. *The Times* remarked that 'pantomime stalked the field' as, the outcome decided, McCarthy bowled a series of donkey-drops to advance the issue. Hutton eventually reached 98, finishing the match with a four rather than a six; England won by nine wickets; and Graveney, at the crease or in the field, had done nothing to disgrace himself.

Godfrey Evans, who was omitted from the team for the fourth Test, remembers Graveney as a 'quiet' débutant, uneasy in the company of men like Hutton, Bedser and Brown. All that changed when Graveney was at the crease. Even his cameo of 15 was, says Evans, 'evidence of things to come', and Bedser himself states that 'Tom, under the circumstances, did well'. From Manchester Graveney drove to Bristol where, on 11 July, a Championship match began against Northamptonshire. He scored 103 and 105 not out, recording a century in each innings for the first time in his career. In the Gentlemen v Players fixture that followed, Compton returned to make 150 in three and a half hours; May, still a Cambridge undergraduate, scored a century; Graveney contributed 37 and 3; and the Players won with three minutes to spare. For the fourth Test at Leeds, May was included and Graveney not. 'Rightly,' he says, particularly when the débutant scored 138. Graveney fielded as twelfth man when Bailey collapsed with a strained back (despite which he scored 95), and the match itself lapsed into a draw. The Headingley crowd jeered Compton when, off Bedser, he twice dropped Eric Rowan, providing further evidence of the 'ruthlessness' of Yorkshire cricket. A strong distaste for 'softness' (as represented by the south) would, in time, be directed at Graveney himself; 'There was a feeling that everyone should bat like Hutton,' he says. Others demurred and, in an article in *Wisden*, Cardus challenged any modern cricketer 'to command the guaranteed appeal' of a Hammond. In time one did.

May retained his place for the fifth Test, which England won by four wickets to take the series three-one. Graveney emerged with his reputation intact. If not the overnight success of May, his performance at Old Trafford had none the less met expectation. *Wisden* noted that he displayed a cool head, while a mark of his progress was that the Almanack believed 'no one executed the square cut and drive with greater technical perfection', which was high praise for one previously thought 'limited' in his strokeplay. For Gloucestershire Graveney scored 2139 runs at an average of 53.47; in all first-class matches 2291 with eight centuries. For the first time his name appeared in the leading averages, among those of Compton, Hutton and Robertson; *The Times* spoke of him as 'a batting star in his own right'. He had arrived.

Graveney's triumph was offset by two departures from the county side. In September Tom Goddard, who had taken 2979 wickets in a career spanning thirty years, announced his retirement. When he missed much of the season with pneumonia and pleurisy, it was feared that, at fifty, the end was nigh – and so it proved. In a tribute to the bowler's career in *Wisden*, David Moore wrote that 'for him no day could be too long, no captain's demands too great'. Nor those of his young colleagues: Graveney considers Goddard, 'fingers the size of bananas', the consummate off-spinner; direct, deft, determined. Nothing was too much trouble in the interests of the side; it was Goddard who forged much of Graveney's technique by endless practice in the nets and indoor school. As a man he could be tetchy. When, in 1948, Australia set out deliberately to destroy Goddard at Bristol, it was agreed that, in turn, the bowler should be 'given one' off the mark. Ian Johnson duly bowled a full toss which Goddard sighted, struck . . . and edged for a catch behind. The comment was unprintable.

For Ken Graveney, too, the close season brought retirement. Early in May, against Somerset, he took five wickets and held three catches in the second innings before scoring an improbable 25 to win the match. It was, for more than a decade, his last. After breaking down in the nets he never played competitively again. Earlier in his career, Ken had achieved a splinter of cricket history by taking all ten wickets in an innings against Derby at Chesterfield. He was, in his own words, an 'up and down' cricketer, capable of outstanding success, yet lacking his brother's capacity for genius. He notes this without bitterness or self pity, and over the years few were to serve Gloucestershire or England more diligently. In 1952 he joined the Sutcliffe Catering Group (formed expressly to give employment to former Marines), rising in time to managing director, and in the early 1980s served as chairman of Gloucestershire and a member of the Cricket Council before emigrating to Florida. Forty years on, he retains the 'numbing loss' of his retirement, offset by the knowledge that, sooner or later, his brother would succeed. 'After all, Tom was a genius. For him it was a matter of time.'

4

'Like Hammond himself'

The SS *Chusan*, an almost implausible luxury after the deprivations of war, arrived in Bombay on 2 October 1951. On board were the sixteen members of an MCC team unrecognisable from the previous tour of Australia: Hutton, Compton, Bailey, Bedser and Evans were all rested in favour of players of whom only Graveney and Brian Statham would be retained. The captain was Nigel Howard of Lancashire, who finished the tour with a total of 86 runs in four Tests. They were his last. Graveney, on his first overseas tour, and Alan Watkins, on his last, were the major successes, while with the ball Roy Tattersall took 21 wickets. The series contained all the usual charm of the sub-continent.

In the first match, against Universities of India, Graveney scored 101 of a total of 340, including a six and fourteen fours. The pitch, in *Wisden*'s words, was 'perfect'; the bowling, in Graveney's, 'ordinary'; the batting a triumph for one arrived two days before. Throughout October Graveney became acclimatised to the sights and smells of his new surroundings – the pitches, umpires, the almost manic passion which left every discussion a potential row.

At Amritsar Graveney was woken before dawn by the call *Allahu akbar* ('Allah is most great'), repeated with the insistence of an alley-cat. At the ground, one end of the wicket was found to be damp and dripping, while the other retained the texture of sand. It seemed the residents of nearby Patiala had taken offence that Amritsar had been chosen for the match. Graveney watched in amusement as arguments overlapped and became the same argument; in bemusement as local officials became confused in their efforts to mark a new pitch, causing it to look like a giant chess board. When play got under way he scored 79 and, the following week, at Dehra Dun, 101 against a Services Eleven in less than three hours. When the team for the first Test at Delhi was chosen, Graveney was among the first names announced. Unfortunately, at that very moment, Brian Statham was approaching Howard with the news that 'Tom doesn't look right. He's got something.'

He had dysentery. While England spent the next week grinding out the Test, Graveney ground his teeth in hospital. Reports from the ground did nothing to cheer him. Merchant and Hazare scored centuries of such tedium that at times Graveney welcomed the distraction of his illness. In reply Watkins batted for nine hours and the match expired, rather than concluded, in a draw. Following the Test MCC, including Graveney, played Pakistan in Lahore. Still morbid and groggy with fever, he made 26 in the first innings and 109 not out in the second. For Pakistan, who would play their first official Test a year later, a sixteen-year-old called Hanif scored 26 in two and three-quarter hours.

At Karachi MCC found yet more exotic conditions. The playing area was a forty-yard square in an outfield of sand; the pitch itself coconut mat on cinder. Between turf and sand was a drop of eighteen inches. In the distance the groundsman ambled distractedly with an ancient roller pulled by two bullocks.

The bowlers had the time of their lives; MCC the fright of theirs. The tourists were out for 123, after which Statham restricted the home lead to 7. In the second innings the pitch was merely devious. More than one batsman detected unevenness in the matting, which broke like the roll of incoming waves. Graveney scored his second successive hundred against Pakistan and the home side were left needing 285 to win.

Had Statham not been the character he was, the match would have finished him. In the second innings MCC shouted for lbw thirty times, thirty times refused. The Pakistani tactic, according to Graveney, was to 'move back on to the stumps, covering them with both pads, and push the bat down the line. It worked.' Pakistan won on the final morning and MCC returned to Bombay, and relative sanity, for the second Test. Relative; being in a dry state, Graveney was forced to sign a form confessing to being a hopeless alcoholic before buying a beer. After Karachi he would have admitted to anything.

The Test itself was drawn. It started under scudding cloud, the heat fumes swathing the players like a towel. On winning the toss Hazare spent fifteen minutes before deciding to bat; the team, twelve hours in scoring 485. Hazare himself edged a bouncer from Ridgway on to his forehead and was never the same player again. In the England reply Graveney scored 175 in eight and a quarter hours. His innings, then the longest of his career, was punctuated by a drink and salt tablets every hour. When he left the crease on the fourth morning he walked like a shadow. To those who found – and still find – Graveney lacking in resilience, his answer was unanswerable: for four sessions he defied all that India could offer, leading *Wisden* to praise his innings as 'subdued' and 'displaying concentration and selection of the right ball to hit'. For the record, Graveney was on the field for twenty-four and three-quarters of a total twenty-seven hours' playing time, and Statham considered his innings among the very best he saw. It remained the highest by an Englishman against India overseas for fifteen years. The match lapsed into stalemate, as did Graveney into the medicinal beer that night.

Christmas and New Year were spent in Calcutta. Howard, in the way of captains immemorial, ordered the England side into their rooms before midnight. Graveney is adamant he was in bed before breakfast, and three hours later he was on the field for the third Test, which subsided in another draw. To Graveney, the match was 'about the best argument against timeless Tests' ever; it might still be going today had the clock not intervened on the fifth day. The tedium was relieved only by the riot of sounds and colours – faded, like flowers wilted in the bulb – of the crowd. Mankad batted with terrible concentration, like the most advanced pupil in a class of under-achievers. At one stage play was delayed as a child, no more than eight, marched gravely across the outfield to present an ice cream to Alan Watkins. Watkins in turn offered it to the umpire, who placed it in his pocket where it dripped for the rest of the day. In the half-built stand the crowd flapped and darted, braying, screaming, fighting, pausing occasionally to watch cricket. The cricket continued.

Graveney prepared for the fourth Test by scoring nought against East Zone (Robertson 183). At Kanpur the Test was played on a brown, arid pitch on which India bowled two leg-spinners. England included Hilton, the Lancashire left-armer. For forty minutes Statham and Ridgway bowled as if in another dimension; neither could raise the ball bail-high. Hilton appeared. His first ball turned square, and from then India collapsed. Only Roy kept his head while the batsmen, and crowd, lost theirs. England were eventually left needing 76, and reached them easily enough, Graveney contributing 48 as the Test was won by eight wickets in three days.

At Madras it was India's turn. The match was decided on the first day, when, after winning the toss, England were bowled out for 266, on a wicket that should, thought Graveney, have produced 500. India reached 457–9 before declaring, at which point the pitch, ominously, was turning. England scored 183, of which Graveney made 25. India won by an innings, recording their first Test victory. The series was drawn, as were the tourists who sailed to Ceylon in mid-February. Already five months abroad, MCC reached Colombo hopeful of finding 'a quiet end' to the tour. Instead they found a Commonwealth side including the Australians Miller, Harvey and Hole, and their nemeses Fazal Mahmood and Mankad. The ensuing match was played in searing heat such as caused the wicketkeeper, Brennan, to collapse with sunstroke. For the Commonwealth XI Miller took 3–20 and 2–4, which would have been more but for an incident in the second innings when Graveney was caught behind. The fielding side erupted with the exception of Miller, whose 'Not out' swayed the issue. According to Graveney: 'He wanted to have a longer look before bowling at me in a Test. Typical of Keith.'

In the representative match that followed, MCC humbled a Ceylonese team of club standard. Graveney scored 102 in that last first-class fixture of the tour; followed by 120 against a Central Province XI, before sitting out the final fixture in early March. From his four Tests in India he had 363 runs at an average of 60.50, on the tour as a whole 1393 at 55.72. *Wisden* considered him and Watkins to have been 'the only batsmen to enhance their reputations', describing Graveney as scoring mainly in 'an arc between extra cover and wide mid-on, usually off the back foot'; the last, incredibly, thanks to George Duckworth, the pre-war England wicketkeeper and manager of Commonwealth sides to the subcontinent. Before boarding the *Chusan*, it was he who approached Graveney with the advice, 'Don't be hit on the pads.' The batsman's response was to determine never, unless forced, to play forward, a denial of his reputation as a front-foot batsman. Such was Graveney's technique that it survived and even prospered from a reversal of instinct. The man returning in April would be steeled to face his Test opponents that summer: India again.

1952 was a turning-point in English cricket. Not only was the Test side to enjoy a half-decade of world supremacy, but England entered the era by appointing Hutton their first professional captain. The selectors (Yardley, Brown, Wyatt and Ames) agreed that to consolidate on the 1951 series and the last Test of the 1950–51 tour of Australia (won by eight wickets) required a captain sure of his place in the side. Compton, vice-captain in Australia, heralded it as 'a triumph of common sense'; Evans as a 'natural' selection. Sensible it may have been, but to Hutton – for whom the splintered seats of the professionals' room had been as near as he came to the Lord's pavilion – the appointment was anything but natural. Throughout his tenure doubts were raised about the captain's fitness. They found expression in the fact that, unbeaten in six series and victorious in four, Hutton believed to the end that 'My face never fitted'. Two years later he would be appointed to defend the Ashes by a single vote.

Little more than a month after his return, Graveney re-acquainted himself with India, playing for MCC at Lord's. He made 158. *Wisden*, not untypically, noted that he 'excelled with the drive', adding darkly that he 'enjoyed much good fortune'; the batsman himself admits that the tourists were 'ordinary', particularly in the absence of Mankad, who was representing Haslingden in the Lancashire League. A week later Graveney scored 171 for Gloucestershire against Sussex, playing all the strokes. His winter overseas had given him confidence, as had the proof of 1951 that he was 'worth or better' his place. Graveney recalls the season as one of unprecedented optimism, based partly on Hutton's appointment and dimmed only by Statham, his room-mate on tour, failing to appear in a single Test. England had a replacement.

Fred Trueman, bowling up the Headingley hill, had figures of 3–89 and 4–27 in his first Test. The press were ecstatic and Graveney, for one, believed the praise affected the bowler's equilibrium. Compton, too, wrote: 'Some can stand success, others cannot; at that time I don't think Trueman could.' Even Evans says that 'he would in no way have been harmed had Len applied more discipline'. Whatever the cause, the effect was a bowler who, for more than a decade, remained etched in the public imagination. Almost lost in the eulogy was Graveney's 71 in the first innings, including a stand with Watkins which brought together the two batting successes of the tour to India. England won by seven wickets and Hutton, according to *Wisden*, 'did not falter, while his astute leadership, perhaps, guided future policy', a reference to the captain's faith in bowlers with pace and batsmen without. Graveney himself concluded that 'Much as I admired Len as a player, it was impossible to get on his wavelength as a person . . . One moment he would disarm you with his dry humour, the next look through you as if you were a pane of glass.' In the nineteen Tests in which he captained him, Hutton never fully mastered Graveney's name.

For the second Test Mankad returned. He scored 72 and 184, taking five wickets between. In the England first innings Graveney made 73, indulging in a century sixth-wicket stand with Godfrey Evans. Indulging because Evans – who had steeled himself by spending the previous evening in a night club – scored 98 between the start and lunch. The wicketkeeper to this day praises Graveney's 'selflessness' in allowing him the strike. Graveney's own view – 'I let him get on with it' – underestimates his contribution to a then record partnership of 159. *Wisden* noted that 'If overshadowed by Evans, Graveney showed his class', Hazare that 'Tom knew all the shots . . . Godfrey made them up as he went along.' Between them they saw England to a first-innings lead of 302, which India exceeded by 76 in their second. Hutton and Compton made most of the required runs and England led the series two-nil.

Almost immediately Graveney played an innings of 105 for Gloucestershire against Cambridge University at Bristol. The county would finish ninth in a Championship won, for the first of seven consecutive times, by Surrey. Gloucestershire, like England, entered 1952 with the aim of 'sorting out' their captaincy, though in radically different manner. At a time when cricket was entering the twentieth century, if grudgingly, the county's reply was to appoint Sir Derrick Bailey, Bt, a Second Eleven player who would end the season with a batting average of 23 and bowling of 42. He was, says

Graveney, 'keen, almost fanatically so', which in turn communicated itself to the younger players. A number of professionals, meanwhile, expressed doubts about a man whose leadership leant strongly towards the theoretical, and the upshot was that the committee unseated Bailey in favour of Jack Crapp, a utilitarian if ever there was one. From the shadows emerged Tom Goddard, now fifty-one, who, despite having 'retired', bowled more than 400 overs and took 45 wickets. Gloucestershire thus perpetuated their image as the Peter Pan of cricket, featuring a strange amalgam of young amateurs and stalwarts from the 1930s. (The previous year Hammond, aged forty-eight, had made a one-match comeback.) Graveney insists that this added to the charm of the side, who thus regularly fielded players active before their opponents were born.

The third Test began at Old Trafford on 17 July 1952. It was a rout. Bowling with a gale veering over his shoulder, Trueman made the ball rise vilely, violently. At one point the field consisted of three slips, three gullies, a short mid-off, and two short-legs. The England catching was electric, especially from Evans, Sheppard, Lock and Graveney himself. Though originally an outfielder, he in time became a specialist slip whose reflexes rivalled Cowdrey's in the same position. At Manchester, where, according to Hutton, the Indians were 'spellbound', Graveney was outstanding. Evans remembers him as 'light on his feet, with a strong throw from the deep – over the stumps every time'; his kind of cricketer.

In early August Graveney scored 113 not out against Somerset at Bristol. The lessons learnt on the hard, arid pitches in India were practised in what *Wisden* called his 'correct but restrained batting'. The more mercurial talent of Graveney's first seasons had been tempered by the knowledge that 'in Tests, you sometimes had to grind it out'. It was an axiom particularly dear to Hutton, who, in the final Test at the Oval, ground out 86 against an indifferent attack. India collapsed and the match ended in torrential rain. In his only innings Graveney scored 13, raising his aggregate for the rubber to 191 at an average of 47. If, against India, he had failed to dominate, then the series consolidated his place as a middle-order bat. Compton (who himself scored 59 in four innings) felt that Graveney 'gave evidence of things to come . . . if still in cameo form'; Evans that 'Tom, particularly at Lord's, put the Indians to the sword.' The tourists' captain, Hazare, wrote: 'Graveney, the star of the winter tour, capitalised on his experience in England.' And experienced he was; alone of those who played in 1952, Graveney and Watkins had laboured against India on the sub-continent, and the batsman's familiarity with Phadkar, Hazare and Mankad gave him confidence; confidence, too, to hold his own in the presence of Evans, Compton and Hutton. Doubts about the Yorkshireman's captaincy were revived as, at The Oval, three up in the series, England played as though the Ashes themselves were at stake. Swanton, no advocate of cricketing levity, noted that 'England jogged along interminably'. While restating his admiration for Hutton the batsman, Graveney felt that 'for Len, cricket was life or death . . . he was eaten up by the game and beset by problems that he insisted on keeping to himself. He was either unwilling or unable to delegate.'

Graveney ended the 1952 season a changed man. In the space of twelve months he had played eight Tests, as well as matches against Pakistan and Ceylon. His batting had extended to include a range of strokes – particularly off the back foot – previously beyond him. He had scored a century for England. Personally, too, he had matured. Gone was the reticence of Graveney's youth, replaced by the conviction that, in the company of Hutton, Compton and May, he was worth his place. Graveney's development found expression in his marriage, on 30 August, to Jackie Brookman. The ceremony took place at Winchcombe, near Cheltenham; the honeymoon at the Scarborough Festival. Graveney remembers the presence in the next room of Godfrey Evans – who, he says, 'made a damn sight more noise than we did'. On 6 September he and Evans jointly represented the Players. Graveney scored 5 and 43 in a match distinguished by Hutton being run out on 99 by a nineteen-year-old named Cowdrey.

The season ended with Graveney second in the Gloucestershire averages (behind Milton) and fourth in England's. *Wisden* confirmed that he had 'maintained his reputation and position as an England player'. With England, alone of the Test-playing countries, without fixtures in 1952–53, Graveney joined a Ford distributor, Bryan Brothers, in Bristol and returned periodically to the indoor school. He celebrated the birth of his nephew, David, on 21 January. Throughout the winter, conversation centred on one subject wherever cricketers met – the anticipated arrival of the

Australians that spring. The tourists' last visit had ended in a four-nil defeat for England. Since then Bradman had been replaced as captain by Hassett, who with Morris and Harvey rendered the batting vertebrate; all three had scored heavily in the winter against South Africa and would head the averages against an England attack led by Bedser. The tourists included two wicketkeepers, Tallon and Langley, of proven genius, while in the Tests Lindwall would take 26 wickets. Miller remained capable of almost convulsive speed, chasing the ball in the follow-through as if in the slipstream of his own velocity; at Lord's, before a packed house, he scored 109. That spring Everest was conquered and the Queen crowned. As in 1981, the Tests were played in a mood of extravagant national confidence and – as then – individual talent, rather than collective merit, settled them. Talent like that of Hutton, Watson, Lock and Bedser, of Compton and Edrich. Of Bailey. When the five-act drama reached its climax at The Oval, only one England player had failed to establish himself in the public eye. For Graveney 1953 was a case of suspended animation.

It began well enough. In April he was named one of *Wisden*'s Five Cricketers of the Year. The tribute held that 'Graveney . . . delights in driving . . . When in form he enjoys himself so obviously that the spectators quickly catch his mood.' And: 'That he should be likened so frequently to [Hammond] is testimony enough of Graveney's exceptional skill. Undoubtedly no brighter star has appeared in the Gloucestershire cricket firmament since the early days of Hammond himself; some who have played with both believe that . . . Graveney in time could emulate Hammond's remarkable achievements.'

The shadow of Hammond was to fall on Graveney throughout his career. The comparison derived from nostalgia as much as an actual assessment of their skills; the journalist J. M. Kilburn wrote that, 'the two were not contemporary . . . resemblance in the eye of beholders was beauty seen and beauty remembered.' Graveney himself felt, 'I wasn't like Wally and never could be. People only compared us because of Gloucester.' To equate them was to measure genius with genius; but genius of different background, outlook and character. In 1951 Hammond played a one-match cameo for Gloucestershire against Somerset at Bristol. It was the only occasion on which he and Graveney appeared together. In fifty-three minutes Hammond scored 7 runs, batting, said Graveney, 'like an imitation of himself. And *no one* could imitate Hammond.' It is to his credit that Graveney, if not his critics, realised it.

Graveney crowned his reputation by scoring 124 against Oxford at The Parks in early May, 'excelling', said *Wisden*, 'with masterly strokes'. A fortnight later he was in action against Australia at Lord's. 'Action' in that Graveney scored 12 in an MCC first innings of 80, the leg-spinner Ring taking 5–36. The tourists went on to win six of their first eight matches by an innings. At Lord's Graveney's tactic had been to 'get behind' Lindwall, so much so that he was virtually scoreless on the off. 'Inelegant,' he says, 'but effective.' And that from the world's most elegant batsman.

The first Test began on 11 June 1953. In deepening shades of Nottingham gloom Bedser took 7–55; 'the crowd', wrote Cardus, 'emitting joyful sounds as disaster at once assailed Australia'. More subdued was the England reply, which at one stage stood at 17–3. When Graveney came to the wicket to face Hill, a back-of-the-hand spinner of medium pace, he was immediately beaten in the flight. Next over he was hit on the back by a Lindwall bouncer, and later caught by Benaud in the leg-trap. His innings belied his youth, said Compton, and Cardus, too, praised Graveney for his 'veteran tranquillity'. His 22 was third-highest in an England total of 144. Events were proceeding satisfactorily for Australia when, in the second innings, Harvey hooked a short ball from Bedser. *Hooked*: the ball flew like a thrown rock until Graveney, a dozen yards from the bat, caught it. That made it 50–3, from which the tourists collapsed to 123 all out. Graveney caught Davidson at long-on, thus, according to Cardus, 'serving his side to the value of many runs in a situation where they were at a premium'. (Evans, typically, is blunter: 'Tom was bloody marvellous.') The winning target was 229 and England ended the third day at 42–1. On the fourth and fifth it rained, the match ending at deuce with the moral advantage England's. Graveney had distinguished himself both with ball, and, in the context of the match, with the bat. Only Hutton and (eccentrically) Wardle outscored him in that innings.

Immediately before the Test, Gloucestershire had played Kent at

Gillingham, where Graveney scored 211. His innings lasted five hours, contained twenty-three fours and, according to Doug Wright, 'had everything'. Among those to suffer was Graveney's team-mate on the 1951–52 tour, Ridgway. In Evans's words, 'He kept hitting Fred through cover with a full flow of the bat. He murdered us.' The point bears repetition; to bowlers like Ridgway, Gladwin and Jackson, the 'full flow of the bat' was Graveney's trademark. Not so to Lindwall. Whatever the merits of his batting for Gloucestershire, Graveney determined from henceforth to deny his own instincts, to 'keep it tight' against Australia. The results were traumatic.

England entered the second Test in confident, almost buoyant mood. Hutton lost the toss and Australia, thanks largely to Hassett, scored 346. This was the match, played in shimmering heat before capacity crowds, that defined the mood of the series. Jack Fingleton noted a crowd of 10,000 outside the ground, Cardus an air of 'subdued expectancy' within. On the second day, 26 June, the England reply faltering at 9–1, Graveney joined Hutton. They proceeded to a stand of 168 in which, according to Cardus, 'fine strokes were plentiful'. In Kenyon's view, 'Len and Tom meshed superbly'; Cardus again: 'Technique went hand in hand with style.' Graveney scored 78, and calls it among the most depressing innings of his career.

At 5.35 that evening Hutton approached Graveney at the end of an over. 'Right,' he said. 'That's it tonight'. Graveney reeled. The Australians – Lindwall, Johnston, Ring, Benaud – had been run off their feet. A few minutes earlier Miller had raised his hands in surrender. Benaud himself had 'lost it – completely'. If ever there was a case of the initiative being seizable, this was it. Instead, just 34 runs were added in the last hour, four of them a cross-batted mow which had Graveney, if not the Australians, laughing aloud. Again Hutton loomed: 'Quiet. It's a bloody Test Match' – an observation which, says Graveney, hadn't escaped him. The day ended with England 177–1 and Graveney ordered into the nets first thing in the morning. He went shopping instead.

He was out fourth ball. Graveney's innings of 78 was his highest to date in Tests in England. During it he displayed strokeplay 'not to be estimated by the accountancy of the scoreboard' (Cardus), which 'dovetailed perfectly with Len's' (Compton). Despite which,

Graveney believes he was baulked in mid-innings, that a century had been there for the asking on the second evening. It was not to be; and in the months that followed Graveney's innings was taken as evidence of his ability to play the glittering cameo, rather than the full-blown epic; of his reputation as an under-achiever compared to Hutton. Hutton made 145.

When that afternoon the captain presented his team to the Queen, he looked at Graveney as though surprised to see him there. After a long pause the Queen shook hands and moved on. Later that year Hutton introduced Graveney to the Archbishop of York as 'Tom Goddard', with other variations following. Hutton and Graveney would never see life from the same eyes; they viewed each other as miser to spendthrift. (At Lord's Hutton's warmest greeting had been for Henry Sayen, an American industrialist who distributed substantial financial bonuses for special performances. The captain did nothing to discourage it and he, Graveney, Watson and Bailey all prospered – the last two for their second-innings rearguard stand of 163, heads down, with almost agrarian attention to the pitch.) The match, watched by 137,000 spectators, was drawn and the equilibrium of the series restored. Graveney left Lord's almost morbidly nervous of playing Australia.

Australia were the first team he faced on returning to Bristol, where he scored 52 of a home total of 137, *Wisden* noting that only he 'who drove stylishly, was really comfortable against the Australian attack on the opening day'. The tourists won by nine wickets. By now Australia had blended into a team and the sides regrouped at Old Trafford on 9 July with, in Miller's words, 'anything possible'. Again Hutton lost the toss and in bleak, dripping conditions Australia ended the first day 151–3. Harvey dominated the Thursday, the weather Friday. England replied with 276, of which Graveney made 5 'caught off a stroke', wrote the *Guardian*, 'that he would wish neither to cherish or remember'. (De Courcy took the catch at mid-off, so gently he might have held it one-handed while prone.) At this stage, and when rain obliterated play on Monday, the game lapsed beyond hope. Still Hutton harried, plotting, brooding, scowling like a man on whom fate had played a devious trick. When play ended it was like a case of euthanasia.

Hopes revived at Headingley. The ground was teeming. The pitch baked in reams of drying sun; perfect for a large score, thought Graveney; a total of 400 or more. At the close England were 142–7; Graveney top-scored with 55, implausibly caught by Benaud at slip. His innings, wrote Cardus, was 'shot through with strands of fine style and blemishes of ill-adjusted poise'. Graveney's score was more than twice that of any other batsman. Moreover, in occupying the crease for almost four hours, he demonstrated his ability to get behind Lindwall and to play in the image of Hutton, who was himself bowled second ball. ('Stay there', he instructed the incoming batsman, as though apprehensive that, with the score 0–1, Graveney might feel the need to open up.) Again Harvey was the key figure in Australia's reply, his 71 taking the tourists to a lead of 99. This became a target of 177 on a wicket now dry and turning. Impressed by his spinners on the last day at Old Trafford, Hutton took the decision to open the attack with Lock. It almost lost the Test.

When, after five overs, Australia were 27 without loss, Graveney feared the worst. Morris and Hassett were set and in the space of twenty minutes the initiative was wrested, Hutton frowning, like a man with conflicting worries. At 66–2 a posse of senior players approached him. Parallels were drawn with 1948 when, on the same ground, Australia had reached a total of 404 on the last day. (Of the five batsmen involved, four were still playing. The fifth, Bradman, was in the press box.) The upshot was that Bailey took the ball and proceeded to bowl six overs of leg-theory for 9 runs. The target receded and England achieved, rather than earned, a draw. 'The Australians had to clutch hard at the last remnants of their humour,' wrote Swanton. 'Time-wasting saved us,' says Graveney.

The fourth Test ended on 28 July. In the fortnight before the fifth Graveney could hardly hit the ball off the square, his defensiveness to Lindwall having affected other aspects of his game. He developed an obsessive fear of being out and found himself cramped and hesitant to drive. At Headingley he had struggled to deny his instincts and played as if in a coma. (That evening he gave an autograph which lapsed into a series of lateral flashes, making it seem he'd suffered a stroke in mid-signature.) His technique became confused and satisfied neither critics nor captain. ('Pity,' said Hutton, after Graveney's innings at Leeds. It was nearly a third of

England's total.) He became anxious, and his anxiety in turn affected his play.

Confirmation followed that more than one captain had taken his lead from Hutton. At Cheltenham, in early August, Gloucestershire scored 385–7 declared (Graveney 65) and forced Sussex to follow on. In the fourth innings Graveney and Crapp were batting against the clock when the visitors' captain, David Sheppard, instructed Thomson to bowl leg-theory to a packed on-side field. The match ended in a draw amidst acrimony on both sides; 'Evidence of a trend', says Graveney, 'which left me cold.' When the team for the final Test was announced, so far from 'enjoying himself so that spectators caught the mood', he thought himself lucky to be selected.

This was the match that crowned the year, and returned the Ashes for the first time since 1934. It started when, yet again, Hutton lost the toss; Australia batted and scored 275, with the recalled Trueman (4–86) raw and raucous and Evans keeping wicket like a fish flapping out of water. In reply England made 306, Graveney 4. At this stage Cardus was forced to the conclusion that 'Graveney's quality remains exasperatingly in chrysalis', while Swanton observed that 'Graveney, May, Trueman and Lock were the "babies" of the side . . . the last three, at least, rich in promise.' For the record, Graveney fell again to Lindwall (the third time that series) and ended the rubber with 169 runs at an average of 24, lower than Wardle, Bailey and Watson. To compound which, he dropped Lindwall when the Australian skied Laker to the cover boundary on his way to 62. In their second innings Australia collapsed and England were left needing 132. On the fourth day they were 24–1, 88–2; Graveney, fifth in, waited on the balcony until, the ground jammed, Compton scored the winning run. The party exploded and Hassett paid public tribute to England and privately to Lock, who, he noted, 'threw us out'. Champagne arrived and the tourists, notably Miller, proved they knew how to play as well as play. In an article entitled 'Hassett's Happy Warriors', Swanton wrote of 'a belief that dies hard of Australian grimness on the field. Nowadays this is a misconception', and, notably, after the Test the tourists played some of the most attractive cricket of the whole season. At the end of August a full-strength side engaged Kent and 'brought riches to the field' (*Wisden*) as well as to Godfrey Evans's benefit. The tourists returned with a profit of £100,000, which was to be a record for twenty years.

Gloucestershire rose to sixth in the table, capable of outstanding success yet almost wilful inconsistency. Of twenty-eight Championship fixtures, nine were won and seven lost. In a review of the county's prospects, Cardus wrote that 'A flavour of traditional amateurship has never been absent from a Gloucester innings'. In the same article he selected an All-Time XI which read: Grace, Barnett, Hammond, Emmett, Graveney, Townsend, Jessop, Sinfield, Board, Goddard, Parker. Graveney himself ended the season with 1,391 runs for his county at an average of 39, and, according to *Wisden*, 'only occasionally showed his true form'. His equally occasional bowling took twenty first-class wickets at 16.20, remarkably placing him fifth in the national averages, ahead of Statham, Bedser, Trueman and Laker.

When at season's end MCC announced the names of the touring party to the West Indies, Graveney's was among them. Suttle, the twenty-five-year-old Sussex batsman, was the only surprise, although the appointment of Charles Palmer as player-manager raised doubts as to whether he or Hutton would be responsible for discipline. (In the event, neither was.) The party left on 14 December 1953 and were promptly stranded by engine failure in Newfoundland. 'After this', remarked Compton, 'the cricket should be easy.' Little did he know.

John Woodcock, in his review of the series, referred to 'the second most controversial tour of all time'. Books on the rubber invariably allude to 'conflict' or 'cauldron' in their titles. Before leaving England the party had been briefed by Walter Monckton to expect difficulty in certain islands. It was pointed out that the political situation was delicate and that under no circumstances should players look for trouble. They found it anyway.

'As a goodwill exercise,' says Graveney, 'it was a fiasco.' MCC returned in April after a riot, intimidation, threat and counter-threat, all of which punctuated a series in which good cricket was played. Before leaving, Hutton had insisted on intensive training, and Graveney spent the months from September to December jogging, exercising and golfing at Henbury. (Trueman's comment is not recorded.) In consequence the party arriving in Bermuda was –

to anticipate a phrase – the fittest ever to leave England; Ronald Aird, secretary of MCC, also considered it the best. Indeed, fitness was a key attribute in Hamilton, where the bowlers laboured on the concrete base over which the matting wicket was stretched.

From the first ball of his tour Graveney played a shot at his ankles, and from the first ball of *his* tour Hutton was out. Much that happened in Graveney's subsequent career can be explained by his relations with his captain in the West Indies. It is clear that already lines had been drawn between soft and hard, amateur and pro, South and North. (Before the decade was out, Graveney, a professional from Northumberland, would be accused of hardness as a cricketer.) Graveney was young, inexperienced, glorying in the chance to bat for England. It was his second tour and his first in anything approaching a full team. Always believing that cricket was to be enjoyed, at this stage he was perhaps more convinced than later. Hutton, by contrast, was dour and drawn. As Cowdrey later wrote: 'He came to the England captaincy at the age of thirty-six, never having led a cricket team before. Stress was inevitable.' A cricketer who knew and played with Hutton for ten years says that no one really got close to him, and certainly human attachments held low priority for him. Four months later Hutton would write that 'Our friends in the West Indies could be numbered with one hand.'

The serious cricket began in Jamaica. The *Telegraph* noted that political prestige attached to affairs on and off the pitch, Laker that 'the atmosphere had deteriorated from the tour of 1947–48', while Hutton, with memorable understatement, wrote that 'there was tension in the islands'. Graveney's observations are twofold: the 'ordinary man in the street' had invested the series with almost imperial status, so that each match assumed the significance of a Test; while, at the other extreme, the British community pleaded with the tourists to win at all costs, adding that life would be intolerable otherwise. 'The pressure', he says, 'was, to put it mildly, trying.'

In the first colony match Graveney scored 82 as the tourists overwhelmed Jamaica by an innings. In the second, against the same opposition, Headley returned from retirement and made 53. The performance earned him a place in the first Test at Sabina Park at the age of forty-four. Controversially, for the time, Hutton chose an all-pace attack. (Lock, the left-armer, was, says Evans, as quick as anyone except Trueman. Once in that match and again later in the tour he was no-balled for throwing.) Graveney scored 16 and 34, realising that 'what Ramadhin had done at Lord's, he could do in Jamaica'. The crowd of 15,000 seethed when Stollmeyer declined to enforce the follow-on; around the perimeter, in the stands, the boughs of trees, faces flickered like a battery of faulty light-bulbs. Despite a deficit of 247 in the first innings, England began the last day on 227–2, needing another 230 to win. They were scoring them when May was given out caught; according to Graveney, at the other end, 'At no time was bat within a foot of ball.' Earlier in the Test one of the umpires, Perry Burke, had seen his wife and son attacked following a decision he gave against a local batsman, Holt. After May had gone, Evans – nursing a private grievance against Hutton – was bowled for nought. England collapsed and lost by 140 runs, Graveney's plea for 'neutral umpires' anticipating the event by forty years.

In the second Test in Barbados, England reached, in Swanton's words, rock bottom. They began by selecting Palmer instead of Suttle, who had scored 96 and 62 on the same ground. (Although Palmer's inclusion was justified by Hutton on the basis of all-round ability, he bowled exactly five overs, one fewer than Compton.) The West Indies made 383. In reply England made 181, eking out the last 128 in a full day's play. Graveney's contribution was 15 in two hours and five minutes. The brakes were applied when, early in the innings, he dispatched two half-volleys past mid-on. At the end of the over Hutton appeared with his immortal remark: 'We'll grind this one out.' Or down: so insipid was the cricket that the crowd lapsed into almost melancholy quiet. As at Lord's the previous June, Graveney was mesmerised by Hutton's caution; as then, he was out to the first straight ball he faced. At the other end the captain slumped, like a man betrayed. 'For four hours', says Graveney, 'he'd held the line for England. It never occurred to him there were other ways to do it.'

The point was taken up by the eighteen English journalists reporting the tour, the issue being whether Hutton had let the side down or vice versa. Of the former school, the *Chronicle* wrote that the captain had imposed too much caution on strokeplayers like Graveney, a policy 'which will kill rather than help to build the team'. In the *Telegraph*, Swanton observed that 'Tactics . . . must be assumed to emanate from the captain.' In his second innings Graveney scored 64 not out, his 'sensible boldness', said *Wisden*, 'emphasising the poverty of his first-innings display'. By then it was too late. England lost by 181 runs and left for Georgetown knowing they had to win the Test there to save the series. The fourth, at Trinidad, would be on a wicket from which not even the West Indies expected a result.

On Valentine's Day, 14 February, a meeting took place of the senior England players. Present were Hutton, Palmer, Compton, Bailey and Evans. According to the last, no punches were pulled in the demand that, from henceforward, strokeplayers be allowed to bat normally. Compton was adamant that Graveney and May be encouraged to attack, and even Bailey was forced to the conclusion that there was nothing to lose. Hutton yielded and the result was that, before the colony match against British Guiana, Graveney was instructed to bat naturally. He scored 231, his innings, which included a six and twenty-four fours, contributing to a stand with Watson of 402, still an English record for any wicket overseas. Hutton demonstrated the other side of his character when, out for nought, he told Graveney, 'You'll get runs here.' The result, according to Evans, was 'one of the high-points of the tour'. For British Guiana a nineteen-year-old called Gibbs took 2–126.

The third Test started on 24 February. After winning the toss for the first time in eight Tests, Hutton, according to Graveney, 'produced one of the classics' to score 169. (Graveney made nought.) In reply West Indies were bolstered by a eighth-wicket partnership of 99 between Holt and McWatt, which ended when the latter was run out – in Evans's estimation – by at least three yards. In a second bottles and other missiles dotted the ground like a tropical rash. Swanton played it down: 'They came in a shower, lasting perhaps half a minute . . . No one knew quite what caused them, perhaps a little rum, a certain amount of betting and possibly there were political origins too.' However, the threat was sufficient for the president of the British Guiana Cricket Association to suggest to Hutton that he lead his players off. (The actual words were more colourful.) Hutton declined. His statement indicating 'I want a couple of wickets tonight' was immediately answered by

Ramadhin's: 'Have mine.' England won by nine wickets, their first Test victory in the West Indies since 1934–35.

The press were ecstatic in their praise of Hutton. Aird cabled congratulations on his 'personal contribution and fine example in difficult circumstances'. Compton felt that 'Len never had a finer moment'. The mood of the team was restored, having touched rock bottom in Barbados, where Trueman and Lock (on the former's birthday) had been upbraided for 'robustness of phrase' in the team hotel. Evans, Compton and Bailey were among those who felt Hutton was too lenient with his strike bowler, who in turn resented Statham's being nursed between Tests. The team had no shortage of individuals ready to speak their minds, and Arlott noted that Hutton and Palmer faced an uphill struggle to maintain discipline. Somewhere between the polar extremes of, say, Trueman and May lay Graveney, indubitably 'one of the boys', yet not irrevocably so like Evans. An insight into Graveney's behaviour in the Caribbean is provided by Bailey, who wrote: 'We both liked hot weather and beaches, rum and Coke and impromptu parties. We were both fascinated by the calypso, though Tom sang them rather better . . . We both were keen, though far from expert bridge players and on the way home played from 9 a.m. until 2 a.m. with breaks only for refreshments.' Hutton was adamant that Graveney was no trouble, though in the middle 'his concentration seemed to desert him'. In Compton's words: 'Tom grew up during the tour.'

This was confirmed by events in England. On 11 March 1954, Jackie gave birth to their first child, a daughter, Becky. Six days later Graveney was in action in the fourth Test at Port-of-Spain, in Trinidad. On the first morning he was involved in the then most controversial event of his career. Compton was given the last over before lunch. Off the penultimate delivery Holt edged the ball direct to Graveney at slip. According to Alex Bannister in the *Mail*, 'There could be no doubt that a fair and straightforward catch had been taken.' In the bowler's view, 'It was out. No question.' Graveney pocketed the ball and made for the pavilion. After a few paces he became uneasily aware he was alone. Turning, he was confronted by Holt still at the crease and the England team, with varying degrees of tact, suggesting he leave it. Holt declined and at this stage the umpire, Ellis Achong, gave his decision – not out. Graveney saw red and hurled the ball down. 'That's the fourth —— time,' he exploded. (At Georgetown, Evans had 'caught' Holt twice early on, yet he had stayed to score 48 and 64.) The crowd seethed, Achong complained, and at a formal dinner Errol Dos Santos, president of the home Board of Control, expressed 'surprise' at England's manners, while an editorial in the Trinidad *Guardian* declared that 'Our delight in the tour is turning to dismay and embarrassment.' Graveney knew how they felt.

In the England innings Graveney made 92. Bowlers on both sides toiled on a jute matting pitch compared by Trueman to 'serving a term of hard labour', and Statham broke down and was unable to play again on tour. The match was drawn and MCC returned to Jamaica in late March. The fifth Test started in almost morbid spirits when, losing the toss again, Hutton anticipated a West Indies total in excess of 500. By tea they were all out for 139, Bailey having taken 7–34 and proving, in Graveney's words, that 'no bowler in the world was as adept at extracting help from a pitch'. Hutton insisted that the fall of each wicket be met only with polite applause and the match was played in a far happier spirit than its predecessors. The captain opened the England reply with the intention of 'making some', which he did to the tune of 205. Graveney's contribution was 11, including his thousandth Test run. England were eventually left needing 72 and made them simply enough to draw the rubber. One of the few successes had been a seventeen-year-old making his Test début, displaying, said *Wisden*, 'distinct promise'. His name was Garfield Sobers.

In the series Graveney scored 265 runs at an average of 37; on the tour as a whole, 617 at 56. Remarkably he took eight Test catches, three more than Evans behind the stumps. Hutton, no doubt recalling Barbados, later wrote that 'at times Graveney's concentration seemed to desert him'; Bannister that 'though stylish . . . he was deficient of killer instinct'. A plea of guilty can be entered to both charges. On the other hand, both Compton and Evans felt Graveney had matured as the tour progressed, and (unlike Trueman) he was paid his full bonus. On and off the field, the depths were reached at Barbados, where, on the rest day, Graveney was approached by an expatriate of military bearing who attributed England's performance to 'excessive socialising'. The reply was unprintable. Next day a cable was sent to Lord's and for a time

Graveney was under threat of being sent home. The crisis receded, but it was an example of the line trodden by all overseas teams, not least in the Caribbean. Graveney himself believes that while never imposing as a batsman (save in British Guiana) the tour saw the consolidation of his place in the team. He had played nineteen Tests, eighteen consecutively, scored 1003 runs, taken fifteen catches, and even bowled nine overs of leg-spin. As the series ended he was 'at last, in possession', though vividly aware that, under Hutton, such security could never be taken for granted. On the eve of departure the captain approached Statham, Graveney and Laker with the memorable enquiry:

'Fancy Australia, Brian?'

'Yes, skipper.'

'Tom?'

'Rather, skipper.'

'Have a drink, Jim?'

Laker shrugged and departed.

The 1954 season began on an auspicious note. In one of the wettest summers on record, Graveney opened his account by scoring 78 and 52 not out against Yorkshire at Bristol. The following week he made 177 against Glamorgan, held by *Wisden* to have been brilliant but 'inadequately supported'. The remark seemed to forecast a season in which Gloucestershire would fall to thirteenth in the Championship with an abject 96 points. The frailty of the side led by Crapp was fully exposed in Graveney's absence. During May he fell ill with what was thought to be tuberculosis. Tests proved otherwise, but the result was an enforced two-week absence from cricket. He thus missed the first Test in which Pakistan, dismissed for 87, achieved a draw in near-monsoon rain. Gloucestershire, meanwhile, lost two out of three matches in his absence.

On 16 June, his birthday, Graveney was playing at Northampton, where, two days later, he scored 125 of a total of 224. Included in the home side was a twenty-four-year-old bowler who, for that season and the next, was as fast as any in the world; faster. Evans, who kept wicket to Trueman and Statham, says positively that, on the issue of pace alone, the bowler unleashed in 1954 'was the best – bar none – I ever saw'. Graveney agrees, adding that to have been so at, of all places, Northampton, made the bowler's achievement astonishing. Frank Tyson.

Graveney returned to the England side for the second Test at Nottingham. He scored 84 of an England total of 558 for six declared, to which Compton contributed 278. The batsman felt that 'this was more like it', and Graveney noted that 'Denis played as though he were on the beach'. Compton's innings was full of improvisation; at one stage he hit four while lying on his back. So much the better, then, for *Wisden*'s assessment that 'Well as Compton batted, Graveney played even better.' The latter was, according to his captain, masterly. England won by an innings.

The captain referred to was David Sheppard. After the first Test, Hutton, on medical advice, retired from cricket for a month. The selectors – at least one of whom professed relief – appointed the sometime Sussex captain, who in 1953 had led the county from thirteenth place to runners-up. The result, says Graveney, was a holding operation, adequate against Pakistan, but which raised more questions than it solved about the winter tour of Australia. Sheppard was put under pressure to declare himself available, while Walter Robins lobbied on his behalf, and Hutton himself wrote formally to the Board expressing his willingness to tour in any capacity. The result, says Sheppard, was uncertainty, which left him feeling 'more of a caretaker than a captain'. The *Sunday Times* agreed, noting that Sheppard 'handled the side competently, but with little scope to enhance his claims of succession'.

The third Test began at Manchester on 22 July. It was drawn. On the final day the touring party to Australia was announced. Hutton was captain. Graveney, who in the Test scored 65, was included; Trueman, Laker and Lock not. The first, displaced by Tyson, was not merely disappointed – he was shocked. Next morning he took three wickets in seven balls against Derbyshire. The final surprise was the inclusion of Cowdrey, a player, says Graveney, 'who on occasion was his own worst enemy'. Cowdrey would appear each season with a different grip, different stance, different bat, while, other than experimenting with a shorter handle, Graveney's technique went unmodified for twenty years. He rates Cowdrey as the 'unfulfilled genius' of his era. After two decades their Test batting averages would be within 0.2 runs of each other.

Graveney marked his selection by a score of 222 against

Derbyshire at Chesterfield. His innings was praised by *Wisden* for its aggressive driving; by the bowler Jackson as 'responsible for losing us the Championship'. Derbyshire would finish third in a table again led by Surrey. A week later, Graveney reported for the fourth Test at The Oval, where Hutton returned. Doubts about his captaincy were revived as England contrived to lose by 24 runs in a low-scoring match, in which Graveney made 1 and 0. The critical moment came on the fourth day when, needing 168, England attempted to score them that night. Evans ('We'll murder them') was promoted ahead of Graveney and made 3. The last eight wickets fell for 34 and Pakistan levelled the series. Compton felt this to be just reward for Fazal Mahmood, who in the match took 12–99; Pelham Warner that 'it proved Hutton had no sense'. One of the few successes of the Test was Tyson, who took 5–57 on his début.

From his three-match series Graveney emerged with 150 runs at an average of 37.50, plus three catches. The batting was headed by Compton, the bowling by Wardle. The Oval, says Graveney, was proof that 'there were no more easy Tests'; England, with a view to Australia, had rested Bailey and Bedser, while the Glamorgan off-spinner McConnon replaced Laker, giving a makeshift feel to the side, which was captained accordingly. The former bowler Bill Bowes wrote that Hutton needed to 'think hard' about tactics and strategy, and the overall forecast for Australia was anything but sanguine.

Graveney scored 93 against Warwickshire in the fixture at Bristol. His season's aggregate (1,748 runs at 69) places him comfortably at the head of their averages, although it was an abject year for Gloucestershire, of whom *Wisden* noted, 'The hope of better things . . . was not fulfilled.' Graveney finished second in the national averages, behind Compton, and, in Bedser's opinion, 'had a great season for Gloucestershire, if not England'. Bedser was one of those present when, a fortnight later, the SS *Orsova* left Tilbury bound for Australia, destined to return seven months later 'after the bitterest disappointment of my career'. Graveney understood it.

Now that our perspective has altered, with the relative evenness of Test-playing countries, it is perhaps not easy to convey the significance then attached to matches between England and Australia. Evans, who toured the Antipodes four times, states that 'they were the pinnacle for every player'; Cardus, writing in 1954, that 'The proper and consistent means of assessing a Test cricketer, temperamentally and technically, is in the Ashes.' The fact is that, until the ascent of the West Indies in the 1960s, England cricketers were valued – by public, peers, press – largely on the basis of their performances against Australia. Gubby Allen, who joined the committee selecting the present side and who, from April 1955, would be its chairman, stated that 'no player was great unless great against Australia', a notion probably more critical to Graveney than most. His Test figures against Australia (22 matches, 38 innings, 1,075 runs, average 31.61) are revealing, especially when compared to those against the West Indies (19 matches, 31 innings, 1,532 runs at 58.92). Throughout his career Graveney was made aware of a belief that, as one player puts it, 'he had no stomach', – a belief at times openly shared by Allen. Of the latter's 47 Tests as chairman, Graveney would appear in less than half.

The *Orsova* docked at Perth on 7 October. A fortnight later Graveney was in action for MCC against a Combined XI. He scored nought as the visitors won by an innings; 22 not out against an Australian XI at Melbourne. As in Egypt, India and the West Indies, Graveney states he had no difficulty in adapting to the arid wickets and harsh light of Australia, but his form in the run-up to the first Test was discouraging. On 14 November, MCC were taken on a tour of Sydney; everywhere they went the team were pursued by public, pundits and the twenty-three English journalists covering the tour. Press interest was intense. ('I wonder what life would have been', ponders Graveney, 'if I'd had the same gift for PR I had for cricket?') Two days later MCC boarded the night train to Brisbane, where, in Cowdrey's words, 'We witnessed the nearest thing to a Test captain in a coma.' Hutton watched every ball bowled in the match against Queensland without saying a word. The result was an invitation to Australia to bat when the Test began two days later; the result of *that* a home victory by an innings.

Graveney sat out the Test with flu. As to whether his form had merited his inclusion, he is ambiguous. On his début Cowdrey scored 40 and 10 and did nothing to disgrace himself; he would appear in all five Tests, averaging 35. Again, from the perspective of 1992, it may seem strange that Hutton's choice of an all-pace attack was open to question, but questioned it was. Tyson, Statham,

Bedser and Bailey toiled through a home score of 601–8, in Bailey's case after publicly calling the selection madness. Graveney's view: 'Hutton had decided in advance to bowl. When conditions changed and it was a batter's paradise, he stuck to his guns. Typical of Len.'

The second Test began at Sydney on 17 December. Immediately beforehand Tyson had taken 6–68 in the first innings against Victoria; Bedser, meanwhile, had only partially recovered from a bout of shingles and the upshot was that, after fifty Tests, the Surrey bowler was dropped. (Contrary to the general view that this was a spontaneous decision, shortly before his death Hutton admitted he knew on the *Orsova* that Bedser had 'lost it'.) Wardle was included and Compton, after breaking a finger at Brisbane, replaced by Graveney. He scored 21 of an England total of 154. After the bowlers had restricted the Australian lead to 74, Hutton's mood in the dressing-room was one of grim determination. 'Come on', he told Graveney. 'Make some'.

He made nought. Attempting to drive Bill Johnston, he found the edge and was caught behind. Bowes wrote that 'Graveney's innings . . . could mean a long climb back to international cricket.' Hutton's face was ashen. The mood of Barbados was revived and it was at this stage, says Graveney, that 'I finally realised Len, to put it mildly, had mixed emotions about me.' After Sydney the captain's doubts intensified, with the result that, in five months, Graveney played a total of fifteen first-class innings. 'My sole use from that point', he says, 'was as a stand-in.'

England won the Test by 38 runs. Tyson took 10–130 in the match, 'the most important factor' in a review by Arlott which also acknowledged the roles of May and Cowdrey. Graveney's name was noticeable by its absence. He spent Christmas at the Oceanic Hotel, Sydney, and remembers Hutton 'tolerating' the players' antics once the waiters had withdrawn. In the *Telegraph*, Swanton took the opportunity to comment on the burden of captaincy and certain administrative deficiencies which meant that the professionals were paid when, and if, the manager's account had sufficient funds. (Graveney earned a basic £850 for the seven-month tour, with a spending allowance of £4 a week and the opportunity to qualify for a bonus.) The mood of the party was further unsettled when, on the morning of the third Test, 31 December, Hutton announced he was unfit. According to Compton, this was the moment 'Len's nerve began to give', and the captain relented only to plunge into further crisis by again omitting Bedser without telling him. The committee of Geoffrey Howard, Hutton, May, Edrich and Evans were unanimous in their decision to retain Tyson, and, according to Evans, 'to replace Tom with Compton, if the latter was fit'. He was. Graveney spent much of the Test playing golf while England – on a wicket which mysteriously 'sweated' on the rest day – won by 128 runs. Tyson's second-innings analysis of 7–27 had never been bettered by a fast bowler between the two countries.

Following the Melbourne Test Graveney announced his intention to return to the side. Each morning he rose at six o'clock and went for training spells, walking and running, staying until late in the nets. There were three weeks before the fourth Test and during them, in Compton's words, 'no one worked harder to force their inclusion'. In Tasmania, while the rest of the side relaxed on the beach, Graveney could be seen in the distance, waist-high in dust, arms bunched against his chest, pounding the shore. In the Tasmania match he scored 134. On 21 January a fixture began with South Australia. Graveney, opening with Edrich, made 21 and MCC won by an innings. A week later the committee met to select the side for the fourth Test at Adelaide. It was unchanged. Graveney heard the news minutes before the start and left the ground in shock. He spent much of the next week watching the nearby Australian tennis championships.

Even this had its drawbacks. Once Wardle and he were refused admission to the courts; they returned to the Test only to find themselves barred on the grounds of 'not knowing who you are'. Since both were wearing MCC blazers and white flannels, Graveney's reply was a model of restraint. (He'd learnt *something* in the West Indies.) Grudgingly they were admitted to the ground, where England won the Test by five wickets. On 2 February, chasing a total of 94, May was dubiously caught by Miller – dubiously because Graveney, from the pavilion, 'clearly saw the ball hit the ground'; Compton, at the other end, also had doubts. May departed, replaced by Bailey, who scored 15. Evans struck the winning runs and the Ashes were retained. The party returned to the Pier Hotel where they were greeted by Henry Sayen. Bonuses were distributed and most of the players prospered. Graveney finished his drink and left.

A fortnight later MCC played New South Wales at Sydney. Graveney scored 35 and 28, 'his four fine slip catches', according to *Wisden*, 'doing much to earn him a place in the final Test'. All of which was news to Graveney, who reported to the ground on 25 February unsure if he – or indeed anyone – would play. The worst rains in fifty years delayed proceedings until the fourth day. Ten minutes before the start Hutton appeared. 'Pad up,' he said. 'You're opening.' That simple. Graveney replaced Edrich and scored 111. It was his first and only hundred against Australia; he became the hundreth player to make a century between the two countries. The innings was praised by *Wisden* for its 'glorious cricket'; by May, his partner, as 'sparkling'. Bailey, who later in the match allowed his to become Lindwall's hundredth England wicket in the mistaken belief that the bowler's retirement was imminent, said 'It overshadowed everyone with exceptional style and brilliance'. Graveney, more prosaically, notes: 'It was one of those days. Each time I put my foot down the ball seemed to be there to drive.' (It is true of all batsmen, not least Graveney, that certain innings seem to 'happen' almost without effort.) When he was 85 he struck Miller for three successive fours, whereupon the bowler promptly invited a fourth. Graveney's innings was the foundation of a total of 371–7. Australia, following on, collapsed in their second innings to 118–6. Hutton kept up the pressure until two overs remained. One he gave to Graveney – mayhem – the other to himself. The match ended at 5.30 p.m. on 3 March. Four hours later the team were at Sydney Airport *en route* to New Zealand, where play was scheduled the following day. Hutton was 'quite amicable' to Graveney. He became his charge.

Even then Graveney's reputation preceded him. Praise for his innings was tempered by the belief that, at Sydney, the pressure had been off, a view shared by Bailey, who notes factually that by then the series was decided. On the other hand, Miller states baldly that 'we were trying', a notion easy to credit for anyone familiar with Australian cricket. While agreeing that the Test was a formality, Cowdrey adds that 'Tom, against a first-rate attack, was outstanding', and few of the 30,000 crowd on that day would have demurred. Compton's view that 'the Test was memorable for two reasons – the weather and Graveney' is echoed by Bedser's: 'It was the best innings of the tour.' *Wisden*, with its usual perspective, encompasses both views in its report: 'Graveney, when the tension had gone, finished in a blaze of glory.' His 44.00 led the England averages for the series.

New Zealand were diminished since their tour of England in 1949. Four days after his century at Sydney, Graveney scored 101 for MCC against Canterbury; his innings contained a six and seventeen fours. In two Tests, opening with Hutton in the first and with Simpson in the second, he did little – but in between scored 102, engaging, said Arlott, in 'exquisite driving'. So ended his third overseas tour. During it Graveney scored 855 runs at an average of 45, third behind Compton and Hutton. *Wisden*'s summary that 'it was a hard tour, with its days of triumph and days of regret' applied to him more than most. Various theories existed as to why Graveney should 'fail' in Australia – among them the higher bounce and, as in 1953, the sheer vitality of Lindwall. Darker references were made to Graveney's 'carefree' manner and indifference to team morale. Not so: Graveney cared. No one – not May, nor Cowdrey, nor Hutton – worked harder to establish himself in the side. Bailey, Evans and Compton all agree that Graveney's industry, particularly before the fourth Test, was outstanding; not even Tyson trained with the same intensity. Being omitted at Adelaide was the greatest disappointment of his career. He became, in Compton's words, 'tense and subdued', frustration vented on the Australians at Sydney. Graveney's three centuries in his last five matches were the statement of a man compensating for time lost in digression. To have been reduced, for much of the previous two months, to autograph-signing, drink-carrying and kit-packing was galling for a man who had scored 175 in his second Test, a man described by Swanton as 'the best professional batsman of his era'. Galling, too, that so long as the best professional of *his* era, Hutton, remained, Graveney would be seen as an extravagance, a luxury affordable only when other options were expended. As he returned in April, he knew that 'while Len stayed, my chances would be limited . . . and it seemed Len would stay forever'. It seemed.

South Africa were the tourists at home in 1955. In April Gubby Allen – a man known to share the 'carefree' theory of Graveney's batting – was named chairman of selectors. His first act was to reappoint Hutton, with the following proviso:

> It was decided to obtain [from Hutton] a definite undertaking that he would do his utmost to prevent 'time-wasting' and generally to speed up the team in the field in accordance with the wishes of the Board.

Whether this would have instigated a brighter, more positive approach, no one can know. On 21 May MCC began a three-day match against South Africa at Lord's. Graveney, opening with Hutton, scored one in the first-innings débâcle of 87. The captain was listed cryptically as 'ill'. Hutton had been stricken with lumbago over the weekend, and on 24 May wrote to Allen, 'I feel it would be right for me to retire from international cricket.' His successor was Peter May.

A week later Graveney scored 104 against Somerset at Taunton. As the first Test approached he felt 'as eager as ever', not least because, with Hutton's retirement, an era seemed to have ended. May was twenty-five, three years down from Cambridge; his relations with Graveney had been entirely cordial. The team selected for the Nottingham Test read: Kenyon, Graveney, May, Compton, Barrington, Bailey, Evans, Wardle, Tyson, Appleyard, Statham. Graveney scored 42 and Tyson took 6–28. England won by an innings. The Nottingham crowd became ecstatic at bowling as fast as Larwood's and Voce's; Tyson, in his ninth Test, had taken 52 wickets. As the team dispersed on 13 June, few of them, according to Compton, had serious doubts about the future.

Few of them. Two things became obvious to Graveney at Trent Bridge: first, that South Africa, witness Heine and Adcock, had a ruthless desire to win; second, that the 'new era' heralded by May bore more than passing resemblance to the old. Swanton was not alone in noting 'how similar were [May's and Hutton's] approaches . . . Both were serious, reserved, difficult to penetrate – both in turn had the added burden of carrying the England batting on their shoulders.' Or assuming it; in 1955 Graveney, Compton, Barrington, Cowdrey, Bailey and Kenyon were available and played for England; Richardson and Insole waited. May, like Hutton, took almost obsessive responsibility for England's batting and, like him, suffered something akin to a nervous breakdown.

'Peter', says Graveney, 'came alive the moment he strode on to a field, yet was strangely shy and uncommunicative away from it. It meant he was unable to give a team – particularly on tour – the leadership it needs . . . That was his failing as a captain.' Compton and Evans agree, the latter adding that May was 'found out' later in life, notably on the Australian tour of 1958–59. At Nottingham May captained with grim efficiency.

'Graveney and Kenyon', wrote the *Telegraph*, 'never quite looked the part as an opening partnership.' At Lord's they managed stands of 7 and 9. Tyson was ruled unfit and replaced by Trueman, who (*pace* Lock and Laker) competed with Statham as much as the opposition. Impatient and tense, he ran to bowl his first ball, tripped and fell; next a no-ball; a stretching catch by Evans; then another no-ball. At the other end Statham took 2–49 and 7–39 – 'an artist', says Graveney. In the first innings the batsman scored 15, c. Waite b. Heine. Barrington, in his second Test, top-scored with 34. In the second Graveney made 60, 'taking complete command' (*Wisden*) in a stand of 132. South Africa were left a target of 183 and failed by 72 runs. At 75–5 Headley Keith edged a low catch to Graveney at slip. The batsman's view was obscured and, after seeking confirmation, he left, said Swanton, 'with a smile of congratulation to the bowler'. (In 1955 such things still happened.) It was among the more agreeable moments of a match clouded by controversy, in which Cheetham, the tourists' captain, was injured by Trueman. 103,000 spectators saw the Test, which, according to the *Telegraph* 'ended with honour . . . and the promise of further good things at Old Trafford'.

First Graveney scored 101 and 75 not out against Northampton at Kettering; Gloucester won by 154 runs. The county rose one place in the Championship to twelfth. Still more than 150 points separated them from Surrey, and Gloucester's batting leant heavily on Graveney; too heavily, as his absence on Test duty proved. At season's end they were judged by *Wisden* to have 'once more disappointed their supporters'. In nineteen county matches Graveney scored 1,403 runs at an average of 43, conscious, he says, 'of the burden of expectation when I played'. The county won exactly four matches in his absence.

The third Test began on 7 July. It was the most dramatic of the series. England batted first and scored 284; Compton 158, Graveney nought. Cowdrey, on his home début, received 'the worst going-over I ever experienced' from Heine and Adcock. For the tourists McGlew, Waite and Winslow made centuries. During the first session on 9 July Tyson bowled an in-swinger to Trevor Goddard. Evans, behind the wicket, twisted his hand and turned to Graveney at slip. 'Something's wrong,' he said. It was; that night Evans's finger was set in plaster. May's request for volunteers was met by a prolonged silence as the England fielders scanned the horizon. The captain's eye met Graveney's. 'Pad up,' he said. Someone coughed. Graveney's contribution to the match thus far had been to drop three catches. Slowly he donned Evans's trademark red gloves. Tyson reached his mark. He turned. The first ball seemed to leave a vapour trail under the tip of the batsman's nose. Graveney's hands recoiled. The tourists scored 521 without further incident. In reply May made 117; Compton 71; Graveney one. The eventual target was 145 in two and a quarter hours. That South Africa reached it was due to McLean and McGlew; the latter ran byes when Graveney, crouching nearer the sightscreen than the wicket, took the ball off Tyson. Ironically he, too, was injured, as were Cowdrey, May and Compton. With nine balls left Waite drove Tyson through the covers and South Africa won by three wickets. Tyson himself turned his ankle at the close and was absent until the final Test against Australia in 1956. To add to the sense of occasion it was Bedser's last Test; he bowled 41 overs and broke down in the field. The England dressing-room resembled a field hospital at the close.

South Africa won the fourth Test by 224 runs. Graveney, as if in penance for Old Trafford, batted at six (during the series England resorted to three separate opening partnerships), making 10 and 36. Heine took four first-innings wickets, Goddard and Tayfield five each in the second – 'the most hostile attack ever,' says Graveney. At this stage in the series his average was 23. At the beginning of August Gloucester played the tourists at Cheltenham. Graveney scored nought. Next day the selectors announced the names for the final Test at The Oval, his not among them. In the second innings at Cheltenham he made 98. Meanwhile Cowdrey, after his 'going over' at Manchester, underwent a fitness test at Lord's. Allen registered almost tragic regret when the batsman failed. A message was sent to Bristol and Graveney returned to

London, uneasily aware that 'at least one of the committee would have preferred me elsewhere'. At The Oval Allen appeared not to recognise him.

England won the Test by 92 runs, though not without further controversy. May was judged not out to a roaring appeal by Tayfield (Graveney's least favourite cricketer). Silence greeted the lbw verdicts against McLean and Endean. Graveney scored 13 and 42 (batting six and three, the latter when Compton suffered stiffness in The Knee) and took the running catch which clinched the series. From it he had 219 runs at an average of 24; also nine catches, identical to Evans behind the stumps. 'At Lord's', says Compton, 'no one came close to him.' The same could be said of South Africa.

The season ended when Graveney scored 159 against the tourists at Scarborough. In the same week he made 101 of a total of 165–6 against Yorkshire and 96 for the Players. He was fifth in the national averages. The Bristol *Post* referred to him as 'the most proficient batsman of his time'. The most proficient of *his*, meanwhile, retired that winter. After appearing sporadically for Yorkshire in 1955, Hutton gave up the game in January. Among the plaudits, Graveney contributed the following:

> He was equipped with strokes as no other batsman was equipped, yet he let bowlers bowl at him. The difference between him and, say, Compton was that Denis wasn't prepared to be tied down. It irked him . . . Len was a great cricketer, but there was no joy in him. He put up with me until I failed in the Test at Sydney. After that I was history.

Hutton was on Graveney's mind as he left London on 3 March 1956 for a private tour of the West Indies. Despite objections by the manager, Swanton, the visit was widely known as an 'apology' for the ructions of 1953–54. Further controversy attended the selection of Cowdrey and Tyson, both of whom had been injured the previous summer. In the *Mirror*, Peter Wilson ('The Man They Can't Gag') wrote:

> Swanton is a cricket writer and television commentator of some note. I suggest he has struck a sour note by trying to organise a completely

> unnecessary tour . . . I should not like his responsibility to be mine, if in particular either Tyson or Cowdrey break down as a result of this out-of-season flummery.

Neither did. Both distinguished themselves at Barbados – as did Graveney, who scored 154 against an attack including the eighteen-year-old Wes Hall. 'Tom, Colin and Micky Stewart batted beautifully,' says Swanton. 'It was in Graveney's nature to show his strokes and to dictate to the bowler where he could.' He dictated again the following week against Trinidad, scoring 117. There are West Indians to this day who rate Graveney the best post-war English batsman, ahead of May and Compton, ahead even of Hutton. He returned to England, his reputation extended, the goodwill aspects of the tour confirmed by a letter to Swanton from the Governor of Trinidad: 'You and your chaps have done something which could have been done in no other way, and anyone who really thinks must be as grateful and happy as I am.'

Graveney echoed the sentiment.

'You would never have guessed how it would end . . . When I was in form I played better than at any time in my career. And I was in form most of the year.'

So wrote Graveney of the new season, his ninth, the *annus mirabilis* of Laker and England. It began with a fixture against Australia in late May. Graveney scored 30; Harvey 225. The tourists were of the type, personified by Mackay, uneasy against spin. 'Most batsmen needed time as much as runs,' said Benaud. 'We weren't given it.' In the first Test Laker took 6–87. Graveney made 8 and 10 not out in a low-scoring match – one he believes Australia could have won. Set a target of 258, they declined it; series are decided by such tactics. At Lord's Australia won by 185 runs. Graveney provided two of Miller's ten wickets in the match. 'The members as I passed through the Long Room left no doubt of their feelings.' Nor did the selectors who met at the Bath Club on 8 July. According to the minutes, it was agreed to omit Graveney and Watson, and, at the age of forty-one, Washbrook returned. He scored 98 and England won by an innings.

In his review of the series, Ian Johnson, the Australian captain, wrote:

> Figures may be produced to support the contention that Graveney lacks Test match temperament. I have heard the same thing said of many players, but rarely is it true.
>
> Graveney is a beautiful cricketer who brings to the game all the delightful strokeplay that the crowd loves. He introduces even to Tests a spirit that is a constant reminder that it is still a game . . . Some attribute his failure to establish himself so far to this attitude. All I know, as Australia's captain, is that I was always content when somebody else came to the wicket in what we thought should have been Tom's place.

During the third Test Graveney scored 90 against Surrey and 156 against Middlesex at Gloucester, his fifty-fifth first-class century. When the team was announced for Old Trafford he was reinstated in the twelve. Happily, Gloucestershire's last match beforehand was with Lancashire at Blackpool. Unhappily, during it Graveney was hit on the knuckle by Statham. At the close he reported the injury to, ironically, Washbrook, an England selector. An appointment was made to see a specialist the day prior to the Test. His verdict was decisive: 'You're in no state to play.' An emergency call was placed to Oakman, whom the police transported to Manchester. At the team dinner that night, which Graveney attended, he shook hands with both Allen and May. The significance of the gesture was lost on him until six weeks later, when his career, not for the last time, reached crisis.

While Laker rewrote history at Old Trafford Graveney recuperated for a fortnight. On 8 August he returned for Gloucester against Glamorgan at Newport. He made 200. Graveney's innings, described by *Wisden* as 'masterful', contributed to a total of 298 – the lowest ever to include a double-century. He was missing from the fifth Test, during which he scored proficiently for Gloucester; the county were to rise to third in the table, thanks to the spinners Cook and Wells, and, in *Wisden*'s words, 'Graveney . . . who often, in unhelpful conditions . . . stood alone, scoring masterfully while most of his colleagues failed.' At season's end he headed the national averages. When the MCC party to South Africa was announced he considered it 'likely, to say the least' he would be included.

He wasn't. The side which eventually left England read: May (captain), Bailey, Compton, Cowdrey, Evans, Insole, Laker, Loader, Lock, Oakman, Parks, Richardson, Statham, Taylor, Tyson,

Wardle. They drew a series which, according to Swanton, 'contained the dullest cricket – and some of the worst – ever'; even Compton admitted that 'strokeplay was at a premium'. Meanwhile the most fluent strokeplayer in England languished at home. Not untypical was Charlie Barnett's letter in the *Telegraph*:

> The worst crime against an attractive player must be this year's effort in sacking Graveney, not so much from the Test, but from the touring side to South Africa.
>
> It is little use wailing about unattractive cricket and falling gates if the hardest-hitting, highest run-making batsman in the country has his income from cricket slashed by fifty per cent because he failed in two Tests against Australia.

Shortly before he died, Ames confirmed that 'those matches, because of the nature of the opposition, were held to count against Graveney'; Allen, too, lent inordinate weight to Tests against Australia. A further version, denied by both Allen and May, is that they had shaken Graveney's hand on the eve of the Manchester Test purely to gauge the extent of his injury. When the batsman failed to flinch, the theory went, they concluded he was malingering – swinging the lead, in the army phrase. (Earlier, Allen's wrath had been incurred by the dramatic, last-minute search for Oakman, afforded full prominence in the evening press.) May's comment that 'the side was selected on merit, with local conditions in mind' is countered by at least one member of the party, who notes that 'there were certain individuals who weren't sorry Tom was dropped, largely because he was thought too easy-going . . . Hutton had drummed that in.' Whatever the cause, the effect was that Graveney, who ended 1956 nearly 400 runs ahead of any other batsman, spent the autumn and early winter at home.

On Boxing Day he flew to Calcutta, one of C. G. Howard's side celebrating the Silver Jubilee of the Bengal Cricket Association. By New Year he was struck again by dysentery. On 4 January the side moved to Bombay; next morning Graveney announced himself fit to play against the President's XI. He scored 153 and 120, dominating the match. In late February Graveney joined the Duke of Norfolk's side in Jamaica, where he scored 90 against the Next XI; 92 versus All Jamaica; 51 in the Colony match at Sabina Park.

Doug Wright, who accompanied the party, says that 'Tom was unquestionably the star' of these matches; 'a number of Jamaicans expressed surprise that he wasn't in South Africa, and, frankly, so did I.' The Hampshire batsman, Roy Marshall, went one better and wrote that 'the man of the tour, as much for style as substance, was Graveney . . . When he was good, he was the best.'

In South Africa, meanwhile, Oakman failed to appear in a single Test.

5

The End of Something

Winter passed. There was a relaxed and almost confident feel about the county, based on their results in 1956. Much as he coveted a return to the Test side, Graveney knew that his priority was Gloucester. Just as in boyhood he had admired Hammond, Emmett, Crapp, Barnett, so he now was established as the perennial man of promise. In his tenth season, Graveney was determined it would be fulfilled.

The mood was struck in early season. Against Middlesex at Lord's he scored 101 of a total of 213; 'masterly' wrote *Wisden*; 'no one could drive like Tom,' says Compton, who should know. Next week Graveney was selected for MCC against West Indies, their first appearance since 1950. Then Ramadhin had restricted him; at Lord's it was Valentine. The tourists, says Sobers, arrived in May 'with the feeling we might well repeat the success of 1950'; a strong team, the three Ws, Kanhai, Gilchrist, Hall, was again captained by John Goddard. Background interest in the series was high. Speculation arose about the make-up of the England side and whether Graveney would regain his place. After Lord's he scored 111 in two hours against Worcester.

The twelve names were announced, Graveney's among them. He drove to Edgbaston on 29 May, early in the season for a Test. He talked and practised with May; even shook his hand. Next morning Graveney was omitted. The England order read: Richardson, Close, Insole, May, Cowdrey, Bailey, Lock, Evans, Laker, Trueman, Statham. They were out for 186. Graveney stayed at Birmingham for the first day, then rejoined Gloucester against Warwickshire at Bristol. He scored 122. His innings was described by the *Post* as 'superlative', *Wisden* as 'chanceless'; he was in the best form of any batsman in the country. At Edgbaston, meanwhile, England reached 113–3 in the second innings before one of the more remarkable – and, in Sobers's view, depressing – events in Test cricket. May and Cowdrey put on 411. Their tactic was to use the pad as an adjunct to the bat. Ramadhin bowled a record 98 overs and left the field in a coma. West Indies then collapsed to 72–7 and must have lost had May declared earlier, Swanton's view being that he mistimed it by half an hour. ('Certainties', says Bailey, 'appealed to Peter more than possibilities.') None the less, said the *Telegraph*, 'it was a fabulous Test . . . [unprecedented] as one wherein the fortunes changed with such utter completeness from one side to the other.'

Ramadhin was never the same man. He took only five further wickets in the series. Even that was enough for Insole – one of the successes of South Africa – who admitted after the Test, 'I can't pick him.' Nor could the selectors Insole, who was replaced by Graveney. He heard the news on 16 June, his thirtieth birthday. At the pre-match dinner it was suggested that a 'last chance' had been offered. 'There was a sense', says Graveney, 'that my Test career hung on how many I made at Lord's.'

He made nought. Graveney's failure was as nothing compared to West Indies'; they crumpled twice and lost by an innings. *Wisden*'s assessment that 'England were vastly superior' masks the details of a match in which Bailey took 7–44 in the first innings; the tourists dropped twelve catches; 99,000 attended over three days. West Indies' morale collapsed, and, in Sobers's words, there were 'disputes' about selection; at Lord's they omitted the seamer, Atkinson, on a pitch so green that, without stumps, it would have been impossible to tell from the outfield. The result secured Graveney's place in the side, the selectors, said Swanton, 'finding that, for a change, the batsmen were more than good enough to master what on paper looked like a strong attack'. Graveney was retained for the third Test with the prospect, if he failed, of 'being banished so far . . . it would have taken a safari to rescue me'.

Within minutes of May winning the toss Graveney was at the wicket. The second ball he faced ducked, caught the edge and fell a yard short of Sobers at leg slip. Had he been caught, it is possible that Graveney's Test career would have ended; Richardson, at the other end, rolled his eyes. After that Graveney dropped anchor until lunch. He hit Valentine for four to reach his fifty. Before tea he had doubled it; May, from the balcony, bent forward and tapped his head – Stay there. Graveney stayed there the rest of that day and half the next. His 258 was his highest innings in first-class cricket; it contained thirty fours against an attack of Worrell, Gilchrist, Atkinson, Ramadhin, Valentine, Smith, Sobers. The last wrote that 'it was incredible he was left out by the selectors . . . No one approached his class'; not even Worrell, who carried his bat for 191 and secured a draw. The Test belonged to Graveney. *Wisden* saluted his 'tremendous power', the *Chronicle* his 'extraordinary timing and brilliance of drive'. Allen was conspicuous by his silence.

The fourth Test began at Leeds on 25 July. There was concern about Bailey's fitness and Dexter, twenty-two and a Cambridge undergraduate, was canvassed; his début was not yet. Graveney made 22, in *Wisden*'s view 'after a few challenging strokes, undisputably bowled by Gilchrist'. Undisputably because doubts had been raised about the action of the bowler who, in Cowdrey's words, was 'capable of producing an unplayable delivery when roused'. One such accounted for Graveney, who had the satisfaction of seeing West Indies collapse (Loader taking the hat-trick) and lose by an innings. By this time the internal divisions in the party had crystallised around the belief that, from henceforth, the captain should be worth his place in the team. (England had come to the same conclusion in 1952.) That winter Alexander was appointed to lead West Indies in Pakistan.

The week following the Test, Graveney scored 99 against Glamorgan at Bristol. His innings was recorded in the local press as 'full of glorious strokes'; next day he scored a century in three and a quarter hours against Somerset. The contrast bears repetition; patience had been a Graveney *forte* since his first tour of India. Like all stylists, the essence of his technique – with its emphasis on the front foot and drive – had been in place since his early teens; after ten years on the circuit, Graveney had added tenacity to his other virtues, and his colleague Tony Brown asserts that 'no one was more selfless in the interests of the team'. The county beat Somerset by an innings.

Gloucester had flattered the previous year to deceive. In 1957 they finished twelfth in a Championship won, for the sixth time, by Surrey. *Wisden* noted that Graveney, who finished with an average of 49, 'bore heavy responsibility'; only Milton, when available, made a matching contribution. The county won eight matches all season.

Test cricketers are sometimes pressed to motivate themselves at a lower level. Godfrey Evans, the most galvanic wicketkeeper of his era, could look ordinary for Kent; Lock was a different bowler in front of a full house at The Oval. The reverse applied to Graveney, who until 1957 (and again thereafter) was accused of under-achievement for England, a charge he answered as follows:

> I enjoyed success and put up with failure, although, as so often, the latter left a more lasting impression in some people's minds than the former. Why I should have failed, I have no idea.
>
> Everybody else seemed to know . . . I was frightened of Tests, temperamentally unsound, preferred playing for my county than my country, lacked concentration . . . all in all possessed enough faults to prevent my reaching the first eleven at school, let alone being considered for a place in an international side.
>
> The truth is . . . as I settled into an innings, my reactions, my movements, my concentration all clicked into gear automatically. I went into Tests feeling only marginally more tension than in any other match. And that itself might be the cause of my downfall. Tests don't normally contain as many bad balls as county games, and it might be that sometimes I tried to score too fast. But I always tried to play cricket on the basis that the ball was there to be hit. It might have brought some uncertainty into my play, but it gave me a great deal of pleasure, too.

Therein lies the key. Graveney's batting either 'clicked' or didn't; he made no special concession to Tests and adopted the same range of shots for England as for Gloucester. He gave preference to the drive, but, from his experience in India, learnt the virtues of back-foot play and defence. Tony Brown describes Graveney in 1957 as 'the complete player': dashing, deft, demotic, yet capable of the durable role if required. His innings against Glamorgan and Somerset showed the full range of his skills. If one of the essential features of great cricket is to offer value for money, then Graveney was undoubtedly, at the age of thirty, a great cricketer. 1957 was the first year this was established at international level, a year leading Alan Gibson to describe him as 'the most elegant post-war English batsman'; Gover as 'the best, on his day, in the world'; Sobers, simply, as 'the greatest'. When he failed he was damned for the same attributes as, when successful, he was praised. On hearing Hutton describe him as 'masterful', Graveney could be excused his wry expression. It took him back.

He reported to The Oval for the fifth Test at the top of his form. Again West Indies restricted themselves by poor selection; England batted and Graveney scored 164; the combined total of both West Indies innings was 175. Richardson and Graveney added 146 in two and a half hours, the latter driving crisply and recording his two thousandth Test run. West Indies did not so much collapse as concede to Lock and Laker and ended the series drawn and demoralised. Recriminations were vented between Walcott and Goddard. Ramadhin lost heart after Birmingham; Valentine was 'found out' and played only eight further Tests, none against England; Weekes failed. Only Sobers matched expectation, though still, as he admits, 'completing [his] education'. (Six months later Sobers scored 365 not out against Pakistan.) England won the series – from which Graveney emerged with an average of 118 – three-nil.

It is one of his endearing qualities that Graveney's batting never bears the stamp of omnipotence or infallibility; and, following the final Test, he failed in three successive innings. None the less he was at the peak of his enthusiasm (no small peak) and Tyson, appearing in the same Players side, notes there was 'as much to admire in a Graveney cameo as in three other innings'. On the basis of his performances in 1957 he was established, finally, in the public mind. People's eyes turned to him. When he walked to the wicket, upright, flowed into the drive, he relished being what he was – an England cricketer, or a professional playing for his county. The naïve being of his youth gave way to a controlled, confident, successful adult. Another Graveney characteristic: he regarded himself as an eleven-thirty to six-thirty worker with such variations as practice might demand. In that time he was happy to bat, field, even bowl to the utmost of his ability. When play ended he believed that hostilities ended too, and in later years Graveney was one of cricket's most prolific socialisers. Though an articulate speaker he was surprised, even angered, to discover that fame brought with it a matching responsibility to the press, and twice in 1957 he fell foul of their rapacity for news. Following his omission from the first Test he was said to have been 'distraught' and 'in no mood to pick up a bat'. (Next day he scored 122.) A fortnight later he was brought to another interview: 'How do you feel about Ramadhin?' Graveney indicated polite respect.

'I suppose you're fairly confident?'

'Fairly.'

BATSMAN PREDICTS TEST TON ran the morning headline. Graveney straightened the distortions by the publication next spring of his first book, *Cricket Through The Covers*. In it he appraised Hutton ('A great cricketer, not very keen on me'), May ('If anything, a stricter disciplinarian than Len'), Compton ('A law unto himself'); argued for weekend cricket; and predicted fame for Dexter. It was one of his few efforts to capitalise on his name; other than endorsing Slazenger, Graveney was wholly dependent on his income from Gloucester and England. In 1957, following the death of his father-in-law, Graveney and his family moved to Cheltenham; that winter he was employed as a salesman by Haines and Strange, a local Vauxhall distributor. (In contrast to his colleagues, Graveney wore dark jackets and sober ties. No one ever bought a car from *him* under duress.) He avoided the temptation to play cricket and concentrated on golf, a sport, according to Bailey, 'at which he would have survived as a professional'. England had no tour that winter but, had there been one, it is safe to assume Graveney would have gone. If the period to 1957 marks the first phase of his Test career, resuscitated against West Indies, it is salutary to note that the same opposition, in 1966, prompted his final comeback. Graveney's stock stands higher than most in the West Indies; justly, since he played them better than most. Why the 'clicking into gear' should occur more fruitfully than against Australia can be judged in terms other than conscious effort. As he says: 'I played almost every innings the same way' – Graveney's.

1958 was a season whose sequel changed English cricket.

The prelude was encouraging: a Test team undefeated in a series since 1950–51; record crowds, even against modest New Zealand; the Ashes to come. England, in *Wisden*'s words, stood 'at the top of the world'; in Graveney's, 'no team, for sheer ability, could compete with May, Cowdrey, Evans, Lock, Laker, Trueman, Statham' – and himself. The fall, when it came, would be traumatic.

Graveney had a neutral season. Neutral in the sense of failing to achieve the mastery of 1957. It is not the purpose of a biography to serve the interests of its subject; sufficient to note that, in what Graveney now calls a 'nothing' year, he again finished in the leading averages and played an innings whose power remains today in the minds of those who saw it. It was against Essex at Bristol in early May. Graveney scored 156. According to Bailey, 'no one, not even Hammond, could have driven with more force'; Brown adds that few of the home side had seen batting like it. With winning humanity, Graveney then failed – as usual – against Worcester and scratched 29 against Yorkshire. When the first Test side was announced he retained his place at three.

New Zealand had last appeared in England in 1949, when there had been insufficient time to complete a single Test. The reverse applied in 1958, when three of the matches were finished inside four days. At Edgbaston Graveney scored 7 and 19 and no one noticed his failure. The tourists collapsed twice and lost by 205 runs. Ten days later the sides regrouped at Lord's. On the first morning, news was received that Douglas Jardine (more than a touch of whom was in May) had died. At Lord's Graveney made 37, out, in *Wisden*'s words, 'trying to change the tempo' – or find one; the match expired on the third day when, with 25,000 present, both sides engaged in an exhibition match. (Lock had done so already, taking nine wickets.) Graveney returned to Gloucester, scored 28 against Oxford, played golf, drove to the England hotel at Leeds on 2 July. He scored 31, his Gloucestershire team-mate Milton 104 not out, and England won by an innings.

Immediately after the Test Graveney returned to the county side against Northants. The match is memorable for two points: Graveney was invited to captain and, according to Brown, did so capably, Northants winning in the final session by 16 runs; second, he scored 114 of a total of 227, described by Subba Row as 'so faultless, the only way he was going was run out', which he duly was. Graveney reported for the fourth act of the New Zealand farce feeling, justifiably, that he was approaching form.

Interest was sustained at Old Trafford (another England victory) by the announcement on the fourth morning of the touring party to Australia, Graveney included. More notable were the omissions: Dexter and, a week later, Wardle, withdrawn after being sacked by

Yorkshire. May's reaction that two spinners are enough was surprising in light of the mutinous attitude of one of them, Laker. When the dust settled, the final sixteen read: May, Bailey, Cowdrey, Evans, Graveney, Laker, Loader, Lock, Milton, Richardson, Statham, Subba Row, Swetman, Trueman, Tyson and Watson.

In a preface to the tour *Wisden* stated: 'May's achievements as captain are without parallel . . . Clearly England stand at the top of the cricket world . . . Rarely has our prestige been so high. There are some who aver that England have never possessed a better side'. Graveney, returning to the circuit, admitted to doubts that England would 'walk it'. As if in confirmation, he failed to reach double figures in two matches and made only 200 runs in the remainder of the season. (It rained incessantly.) He ended with 1,459 first-class runs, a forty per cent decline on 1957. Graveney and Milton missed nearly a third of Gloucester's fixtures, the county falling to fourteenth, their lowest since the war. 'Hopes', said *Wisden*, 'were not realised,' and in the close season the committee met to discuss the captaincy. Graveney was canvassed and found willing, declaring himself a champion of the 'bits and pieces' professional. ('Of all the top sportsmen in the world, the English county cricketer is probably the one most drastically underpaid.') Adding that 'cricket has stood still too long,' Graveney repeated his proposal for weekend fixtures and a league of two divisions, ten sides in each, with the prospect of promotion or relegation to sustain interest 'once the Championship itself' had been decided. (Surrey, in 1958, won the title for the seventh time.) He even advocated a limited-overs tournament, anticipating Gillette by five years. Graveney's radical agenda was received impassively by the Duke of Beaufort, county president, and Sir William Grant, its chairman; an eyebrow may have lifted. The fact remained that successive positions of twelfth and fourteenth undermined that of the captain, Emmett. At last Graveney was the man his supporters wished him to be: controlled, confident, a stalwart. He left the committee with his assurance of 'total commitment' if appointed.

He was named for the final Test at The Oval, only to be twelfth man. The side was experimental – with the tour ahead – and New Zealand achieved a draw. There was a month before the party set sail to Australia and Graveney spent it in Cheltenham. Anticipation was rife; everywhere he went he was accosted by those whose forecasts left no room for failure. Meanwhile, in Sydney, Benaud was writing that 'May is ill served by the pre-tour publicity which lists his team as the greatest ever to leave England . . . They have an enormous amount to live up to and sometimes that kind of adulation can be worse than criticism.'

Graveney agreed. It struck a chord.

The mood of the party was set on the SS *Iberia*. At dinner one of the players referred to the captain as 'Peter', prompting the manager, Freddie Brown, to stipulate names for the team's three officials: Brown – 'Boss'; May – 'Skip', 'Skipper'; Desmond Eagar – 'Cash'. Colin ('Kipper') Cowdrey, meanwhile, had been appointed vice-captain over Bailey, a decision both players considered a mistake. The result was that lines were drawn and, despite Cowdrey's defence of his captain – 'No one took more care to look after his team' – May remained invisible off the field. Compton's assessment that 'The round of official functions and parties wasn't Peter's scene,' is echoed by Graveney, who wrote: 'It was one of the weaknesses of the party that neither the captain nor vice-captain was socially minded. There is much to be said for both May and Cowdrey . . . but charm isn't enough to hold a touring party together. Something more tangible is needed.'

After detouring via Ceylon the party arrived in Perth, Graveney rooming with his first choice, Statham. On 17 October MCC played Western Australia. Graveney scored 177 not out, the second highest by an English tourist against the state. The run-up to the first Test was encouraging: 41 for Graveney at Adelaide, 78 versus Victoria at Melbourne. That match, and the one that followed, began the alarm that rang continually for the next half-decade. Meckiff, the Victorian fast bowler, threw. Graveney, Cowdrey, Tyson, Statham, Evans knew it; the last approached the manager. 'Don't worry,' said Brown. 'He isn't that good.' Graveney reeled. Meckiff took seventeen wickets in the series. Against New South Wales the team encountered Rorke; six feet four, bowling from eighteen yards. ('I couldn't play forward to him', says Cowdrey, 'without treading on his foot'.) Since 1955 a school, almost a generation, had grown up: Slater, Hitchcox, Tretheway; at Brisbane Lindwall introduced himself as 'the last of the straight-armers'. At Christmas in

Adelaide Graveney saw a boy bowling on the beach, no more than ten, arm bent as if hurling a javelin. 'It's easier,' he said.

MCC returned to cricket. At Sydney in late November they beat an Australian XI by 345 runs; 'still confident,' says Graveney. The first Test began at Brisbane on 5 December. It was one of the worst in Ashes history. England made 134 (Graveney 19) and allowed Australia a lead of 52. Still, they would have to bat last. In the second innings Milton and Richardson put on 28 (only two England opening partnerships exceeded that all series.) First wicket down Graveney got up, padded, eager to bat; had England accelerated, anything was possible. He was met by May.

'Hold on. Not you, Tom.'

'Who, then?'

May scanned the horizon.

'Pad up, Trevor.'

Bailey eventually made 68 in seven and a half hours. The *Telegraph*'s report of the match was headlined 'Slowest and Worst'; in it Swanton wrote: 'It would be better for the game of cricket if England were to be beaten than to succeed at the expense of the spectators on whose support the game ultimately depends.' It was that bad. Graveney, batting at four, was run out. Australia were left needing 147 and made them easily enough: one up in the series.

If Melbourne, 1951, was the dawn of an era in post-war English cricket, Melbourne, 1958, was its end. The visitors' first innings was sustained by May, who made 113 – bowled by Meckiff, 'whose jerky action', wrote *Wisden*, 'brought much criticism'. Worse was to come. In the second innings England collapsed to 87, Meckiff taking 6–38. Two down in the series, Swanton wrote:

> I was watching alone at the top of the huge Melbourne pavilion when I saw Raman Subba Row and went to join him:
>
> 'Raman, this is terrible. I can't bear to watch it.' Whereupon Sam Loxton, then one of the broadcasting team, whom I hadn't noticed on the other side of Subba Row, chipped in:
>
> 'Now then, Jim, you can't say that. The New South Welshmen thought he threw, and we had a film taken which proves he doesn't.'
>
> 'Sam, I'm not concerned with whether he threw against New South Wales. All I'm saying is he's chucking away now.'

Swanton was not alone in feeling that MCC erred by not registering their doubts privately with the Australian powers the first time they met Meckiff. Evans swears to this day that Brown and May should have protested immediately, while Graveney states bluntly that Meckiff cheated. The Australian writer, Johnnie Moyes, described the ball that dismissed May as 'coming back so suddenly, it might have bowled any batsman in the world'. 'True enough,' says Graveney, 'considering Peter was half-way through his backlift.'

The result was that, between 31 December and 5 January, watched by 230,000 spectators, Australia won by eight wickets; Graveney contributed 0 and 3. After Melbourne the balloon went up. No tour since 1946–47 (when Hammond travelled Australia by private Jaguar) knew such dissent between captain and players and, according to Graveney, 'Charming as Peter was, we hardly saw him.' Press relations were left exclusively to Brown, a man who, Swanton noted with some restraint, 'was not well cast for this particular aspect of the job'. (Benaud, himself a journalist on the Sydney *Sun*, adopted an open-door policy to the Australian media. The contrast was obvious.) Factions formed, with May and Cowdrey accused in some quarters of 'not listening' to their senior pros. Evans, a keen judge of bowlers from behind the stumps, recalls advising May, 'for God's sake, bowl Bailey,' to no avail; Graveney himself thought the captain's decision to bat at five (Cowdrey six) 'madness', and said so. The first days of the new year were spent in Melbourne, in transit, in Sydney. There was a feeling by some that May, after five series against five indifferent captains, had been 'found out' by Benaud, and Graveney can be associated with them. In his words: 'Richie outplayed us. There was a sense of impending doom, and because of expectations the team's spirits were at zero.' Benaud himself makes the point in his book *On Reflection*: 'If you have the feeling in the dressing-room you are unbeatable, because of reading about it or listening to backslappers, it comes as double the jolt when things go wrong.'

Things deteriorated further when the tour committee curbed the antics of the Saturday Night Club. This essential feature of overseas tours existed to discuss, light-heartedly, events on and off the field; toast absent friends; establish new ones – in short, build team spirit. Graveney was among those who paled visibly when May announced that, henceforth, the Club would exist in name only;

even the austere Hutton had valued its sense of unity. (Again compare Benaud: 'So long as players turned in one hundred per cent effort for me, I was satisfied.') The team arrived in Sydney in mid-January like a man, weighed down by shopping, fumbling for his door-key, hampered by the house cat; problems everywhere. More followed when no fewer than four players – Watson, Subba Row, Milton and Bailey – reported unfit, while a fifth, Laker, could hardly grip the ball, let alone spin it. Two replacements were summoned – Dexter from H. R. Spinks & Co., Paris, and, on Graveney's advice, John Mortimore from Bristol. Too late; Dexter remembers 'wandering around, not knowing how to win friends and influence people' – at least until an innings of 141 in New Zealand.

The third Test began on 9 January 1959. It was drawn. Graveney was noticed by both the Sydney *Sun* and *Wisden* for his fielding – in contrast to Dexter who, at mid-wicket, lost sight of a hook from Davidson, 'dashed to where I thought the ball would be, only to hear it land with a thump behind me, exactly on the spot where I'd been standing . . . This hardly endeared me to the senior players fighting for their lives.' The last, notably May and Cowdrey, shored up the England innings: two down, two to play.

Between the third and fourth Tests Graveney failed against New South Wales. Meanwhile the journalist Ray Robinson summarised the series thus far as having 'little to do with umpiring, bowling actions or alleged shortcomings in England's captaincy and team management', instead concentrating on three technical points: Australia's advantage in having an opening pair, McDonald and Burke, who 'invariably see the new-ball bowlers off'; the leg-spin of Benaud (31 wickets in the series); and his ability to keep more fielders in catching positions – 'notwithstanding that Graveney, Cowdrey, Trueman and Bailey make fine catches, too'. Robinson concluded by adding: 'Had the Tests been on turning English wickets, I believe Laker and Lock would again be match-winners.' They weren't; Graveney describes the pitches as the truest ever in Australia, with none of the extravagance associated with the previous two series.

It has been said that Graveney 'failed' against Australia; more particularly that he suffered a loss of nerve when the occasion demanded it. The fourth Test refutes this. Rarely can a match have been attended by such passion; sections of the Australian press became ecstatic at the prospect of regaining the Ashes, while the England hotel resembled a dressing-station as Evans and Laker struggled to regain fitness. The former played; the latter, on the morning of the Test, dropped out, claiming, 'Had I bowled I would have been letting down England.' While almost hourly bulletins issued from the Glenelg Hotel, Graveney – as he had at the same venue four years before – applied himself to the nets and, notwithstanding his fondness for golf, spent days training and running in the Adelaide bush. (On later tours Boycott would adopt a similar routine.) On 30 January May won the toss and inserted Australia, 'feeling', says Graveney, 'Trueman might do them for 250.' He did them for 476. On the second afternoon, Evans dived to take a ball off Tyson, turned to May and repeated: 'Something's wrong'; a broken finger. Again Graveney deputised and, in Robinson's view, 'showed deft work behind the stumps'. In the England reply he scored 41 and, in the follow-on, 53 not out. Evans, who batted one-handed, rated the innings among the finest of the tour. On 5 February Australia won by ten wickets and May paid public tribute to the better side.

Despite the technical views of Robinson and Swanton that 'The players are chosen on form on English wickets to play here on Australian ones . . . They have developed their play in one element, and are suddenly called upon to adjust themselves to something quite different,' one point bears repetition: the umpiring was appalling at Adelaide. The trend had been established in Brisbane; at 75–3, Cowdrey pushed forward to Meckiff and Kline gathered the ball at short-leg. While the umpires consulted, and Harvey, at cover, advised him to stay, Cowdrey walked – despite admitting later 'It was the pad'. At Sydney Graveney was lbw to a ball the batsman believes 'would have missed a second set'. That was as nothing compared to Adelaide. On the first day Evans 'caught' Burke and Mackay off deflections that he, Graveney, Cowdrey, Bailey, Statham, Lock and Dexter believed were out; not so umpire Mel McInnes. McInnes it was who, confused by the presence of a runner, gave McDonald out, realised the batsman had been behind him, then reversed his decision. Dexter's verdict – 'A great umpire when the tour began, who finished up a moderate one' – is mild compared to Graveney's: 'The umpiring was bad enough for

Right On the beach, 1930

Below Bristol Grammar School First Eleven, 1944. T.G. seated second from left

Above T.G., 1948 *(Hulton-Deutsch)*

Below Gloucestershire CCC, 1948. *Standing, left to right:* Neale, Cranfield, T.G., Scott, Lambert, Cook, Wilson, Bloodworth (scorer). *Seated:* Crapp, Goddard, Allen, Barnett, Emmett

Left
Hammond . . .

Below . . . and
Graveney

Above En route to the West Indies, December 1953. *Left row, top to bottom:* T.G., Suttle, Spooner, Watson, Bailey, Palmer, Hutton. *Right row:* Laker, Lock, May, Statham, Trueman, Wardle, Moss, Evans, Compton

Above centre c. De Courcy, b. Miller, Old Trafford, 1953 *(Hulton-Deutsch)*

Right Helpful hints from Evans, Old Trafford, 1955

Above right The Oval, 1957. T.G. scored 164 *(Hulton-Deutsch)*

Far right After scoring 258 at Trent Bridge in the same series

Left Début for Worcestershire, 1962 *(Hulton-Deutsch)*

Below Sweeping up at Lord's, 1962 *(Sport & General)*

Right Batting for MCC against Pakistan. T.G. made 110 *(Sport & General)*

Far right After the hundredth hundred, 5 August, 1964

Below right Celebrating Worcester's First Championship

Above Hitting Hall through the covers, Arundel, April 1966 *(Hulton-Deutsch)*

Below The comeback Test. In the latter stages T.G. batted virtually one-handed *(Sport & General)*

us to have protested' (as, in 1953, had Australia about Frank Chester), 'but that wasn't Peter's way. We grinned and bore it' – particularly when Meckiff took 6–38 at Melbourne with McInnes mute at square-leg.

Between the fourth and fifth Tests morale touched bottom. To have surrendered the Ashes was bad enough; to have acquiesced in cheating was even worse. As the party returned to Melbourne, Graveney consoled himself with news of his appointment as captain of Gloucester. Despite the débâcle of 1958, he pronounced himself confident of improvement. His stated ambition was to 'shake up' the county – that and develop the youngsters in the second and junior Elevens, among them a twenty-year-old named Pugh.

England lost the last Test by nine wickets. Australia played four fast bowlers (then considered eccentric) and Benaud inserted the opposition: 'There had been rain during the week, the outfield was slow and lush, batsmen were unlikely to gain full advantage and the pitch had a decided tinge of green . . . 300 would have been a good score.' England managed 205. In the second innings Graveney (54) batted for two hours with Dexter, 'A grim, miserable exercise in getting your bat in the way and hoping for the best'. Australia prevailed on the fifth morning, Graveney paying tribute to the man 'who you felt did everything for a purpose . . . He was always in command . . . Even when a batsman looked set he was thinking him out': Benaud. Commentators on both sides agreed. 'He had a hard, practical outlook under a cloak of what appeared to be extreme generosity' (Bailey); 'His opportunistic grasp of events made him the ideal captain' (Robinson); 'Infallible instincts' (Moyes). Moyes's own instincts led him to write: 'On the form he showed he was one of the poorest batsmen to appear in a Test in Australia in the past forty years'. The subject? Dexter.

In its report *Wisden* concluded that 'English enthusiasts were left wondering.' After more than thirty years, blame can be apportioned to, in no particular order: extravagant forecasts on the team's departure; Wardle; umpiring; injuries; May's shortcomings; Meckiff; Laker. Over and above which, as Benaud says, 'A number of England players, ability-wise, were on the way down rather than on the way up.' Bailey, too, notes: 'The main reason for our failure was that we never played to our potential or as a team.' Of the bowlers, Laker took 15 wickets, Statham 12; May scored 405 runs,

Cowdrey 391, Graveney 280. The party left in late February for New Zealand where, as in 1955, Graveney excelled in the diminished atmosphere of Wellington and Christchurch. In the first Test he scored 42 as England won by an innings; 91 and 108 in the provincial matches; 46 in the second Test. He returned to England in March as he left it in September. *The Times* spoke of his 'unfulfilled genius', others merely of his talent. If the difference between them is that genius requires the infinite taking of trouble, then Graveney remained, for the moment, a talented batsman.

The party returned with a profit of £16,500. It was among the few assets of a tour after which, says Cowdrey, 'There seemed to emerge a line of thought which was to have a profound effect upon English cricket for the next decade . . . It was held to be high time that certain players were brought down to size.' In the aftermath of Australia Bailey, Laker, Tyson and Watson would never play for England again, while at the end of 1959 Evans, omitted from the winter tour of the West Indies, announced his retirement. Even May would remain only two years. As he returned to Bristol, Graveney was uneasily aware that certain changes in the Test side were inevitable: 'After a four-nil loss, heads will roll.' At least for them the end was quick. In the next seven years Graveney appeared in exactly seven Tests.

If Graveney's 'shake up' had been to achieve a place in the upper half of the Championship, then his first year as Gloucester captain was seismic. It began in early May, when he scored 46 against Hampshire; in the next match 74 and 69 not out against Sussex; 'his most fluent form', said the *Post*. He was then out first ball against Worcester. Towards the end of May Graveney made 53 against a strong Warwickshire attack at Stroud; next day the team for the first Test against India was announced.

'After the heavy defeat in Australia,' wrote Swanton, 'the selectors [Allen, Wooller, Sutcliffe, Dollery] recognised that, with a tour of the West Indies coming up, some team reconstruction was called for.' Three new players – Ken Taylor, Martin Horton and Tommy Greenhough – were duly selected; two more – Barrington and Moss – returned; a fifth, Roy Marshall, being excluded on the grounds that 'it was felt undesirable to invite a cricketer to play for England who had been born abroad and had learned all his cricket in, and had played for, the country of his birth before coming to England.'

Graveney accepted the news with equanimity. ('It was time the Colonel [Barrington] had a chance.') During the series he, Pullar and Smith would establish themselves for England. India proved as undemanding as had New Zealand in 1958 and England took the series five-nil. (Between 1957 and 1960 they won fifteen out of twenty home Tests. The rest were drawn.) Gloucester, meanwhile, remained in the lower reaches. By late May, a month into the season, impressions had formed of Graveney's captaincy. According to Tony Brown: 'He was correct rather than clever . . . Orthodox on the field and occasionally rigid away from it . . . Old-fashioned in his attitudes.' The point is echoed by Cowdrey in his autobiography: 'One morning a number of Kent players appeared for breakfast in the dining-room wearing sweaters instead of jackets and ties . . . I knew that if I created a scene I would have had to live with the resentment of the players for the next two matches . . . I was perhaps weak for not interfering . . . Certainly a captain of the older school, like Tom Graveney, would not have stood for it.' On a technical note, Alan Gibson believed 'he did not have any special gift for leadership, though he was a sound tactician.' Finally, Bailey: 'Tom proved to be an adequate rather than an outstanding leader, perhaps because he tried to please everyone – nearly always a fatal policy. At the time he was – other than as a maker of runs – comparatively inexperienced and in some respects rather naïve, while the idea of a professional skipper was only reluctantly accepted by the county hierarchy.'

Graveney himself:

> I had my faults. Not that it was easy handling an attack consisting of two medium-pacers, Tony Brown and David Smith, both of whom bowled off short runs, first-class spinners Allen, Mortimore and Wells, and Cook, slow left-arm. Inevitably it took some sorting out who was to have first crack among the spinners, and I began working on the principle that the first chance went to the best bowler of the previous game. The theorist might scorn, but it was a method and worked reasonably well . . . Also, without a fast bowler, Gloucester raced through their overs to the advantage of opposing batsmen, who received more deliveries per hour than they dared expect. A standard

> performance was 85 overs completed by three-forty-five p.m. if we fielded on the first day, and there was nothing the captain could do about it. Hutton would have been driven to distraction.

The verdict must be that Graveney was not a natural captain in the sense of Worrell, Benaud, Brearley or Lloyd; that he had grasp, not genius; that, as a man who recalls carrying his captain's bags as a junior professional, he demanded respect from others. Graveney led by example. With the exception of Lord's, 1953, he was a prolific attender of nets. He believed in fitness, and at critical moments (Adelaide 1955, 1959) drilled himself beyond the meagre standards then prevalent in professional cricket. He was undoubtedly of the older school in terms of protocol, and, according to a colleague, 'not exactly a revolutionary when it came to manners'; a stickler for detail.

For instance, the matter of selection. Throughout 1959 Graveney fought constantly with his committee over the inclusion of Tom Pugh. The latter had arrived (late, after competing in a squash tournament in America) in April, endorsed by Percy Fender as 'a second Dexter'. Tony Brown, who liked Pugh, notes that 'the only similarity between him and Ted was that both were right-handed bats', and Pugh's record in 1959 is strictly in amateur tradition: 188 runs, average 23.50. His ability had been taken on trust. When Graveney first saw Pugh he registered the words 'club cricketer' and assumed a place would be found in the reserves. Not so. Throughout the early season he was confronted by those who wanted Pugh in the First Eleven: 'Baldly stated, I didn't think he was worth it . . . Not at the expense of a professional like Ron Nicholls or Derek Hawkins.' Pugh's county appearances were limited to five – even that, says Graveney, was excessive. At the time he dismissed it as a whim of the committee. Only later did his doubts develop positive identity.

Graveney's own form was intermittent. Against Derby he made 18; 48 and 60 versus Lancashire (Statham 3–13). In his absence England won five Tests; May, Cowdrey, Smith and Pullar made centuries. In early July Graveney scored 155 and 85 not out against Nottingham, not surprisingly 'dominating the match' (*Wisden*). A week later he broke a finger in the field and missed a month's cricket. In his absence Emmett, aged forty-six, returned as captain and the county won four matches. 'Coincidentally or not,' says Brown, 'we only came good when Tom was injured.'

But not idle. Graveney improvised a batting glove and appeared in the nets. He had the perfect answer to Swanton's stricture – 'Once a man has become a Test cricketer he "knows it all"' – and continued to enhance a technique described by Bailey:

> Of all the outstanding batsmen none was as predominantly front-foot as Tom . . . What one first noticed when bowling to him was the left leg thrusting firmly forward. It used to irritate me that if I managed to make a ball come back to beat his bat, his pad was invariably in the way . . . He was so expert on the front foot he was even able to hook quick bowling from there . . . The one discernible weakness in his method was that it made him slightly vulnerable to top-class off-spin . . . I always felt there was a chance of having him caught in the forward leg position. He tended to follow through even when playing defensively.

In 1959 Wells, Allen and Mortimore, three such spinners, were summoned by Graveney to the nets. He worked to control the influence of his top hand and to counter the ball that 'stopped'. His month away allowed him, he says, to modify his technique and become – as near as temperament allowed – a 'percentage player' against spin. He returned in mid-August and hit two of the best young spinners in the country, Wilson and Birkenshaw, for 67. In his absence Gloucester had contested the Championship with Yorkshire and began a fixture with Surrey on 26 August knowing the title was within grasp.

They lost it. Lock and Laker shared nineteen wickets; Gloucester collapsed twice; Graveney's new technique brought him 31 and 0. The county finished the season awaiting the outcome of Yorkshire's match at Hove. In the final session the visitors were set a target of 215 in ninety-five minutes and reached it. The pennant returned to Headingley for the first time in a decade; Gloucester were second; Surrey, after seven successive Championships, third. In its account of the season *Wisden* paid tribute to the county's 'marked improvement', noting that they fell 'at almost the last hurdle in a dramatic bid'; the *Post* referred to 'steady leadership'; the *Cricketer* to the 'well-earned position' which remains the county's highest this century. Confirming the maxim that Bowlers Win Matches, the leading players were Allen, Cook, Mortimore, Brown, Smith. The captain, in nineteen appearances, scored 1062 runs at an average of 42.

1959 was also Graveney's Benefit. When the figures were added up they totalled £5,400, nearly three years' income as a cricketer. It was, he says, enough – to pay off debts. Other than endorsements for cheese and milk (the latter, incredibly, shared by Godfrey Evans) Graveney remained dependent on his income from Gloucester and tours overseas.

That autumn he was invited to celebrate the centenary of the Transvaal Wanderers. A Commonwealth Eleven, captained by Compton, included Evans, Tyson, Close, Marshall, Sutcliffe. The visitors won three of their five fixtures and drew the remainder; 'a new trend' wrote Graveney, contrasting the relaxed atmosphere of the veldt to the 'forced labour' of Australia – 'at six months, twice as long as it need be for a player with commitments at home'. Graveney's solution: a mix of official and private tours, with Australia cut to three months by the abolition of repeat fixtures against the States. 'After all, a Caribbean tour has just ten days before the first Test. Why not Australia?'

The Caribbean was a subject on Graveney's mind that winter. He returned home in November, the week before MCC embarked on the banana boat *Camito* for Barbados. Of the batsmen selected, Dexter, Cowdrey, Barrington, Pullar and Subba Row averaged over 40; they and Smith made centuries. The series was won one-nil. In Cheltenham Graveney consoled himself with the thought that 'After the success of 1959, the new season could be our best.' It was nearly their last.

Graveney disliked playing Worcester. Not personally, but because the county's seamers – Coldwell, Flavell, Aldridge – represented the sort of parsimonious attack no strokeplayer enjoys. On 8 May he scored 90 against them at Bristol; still the visitors won. Graveney did nothing for a fortnight, then he made 76 and 62 not out against Surrey. In the final innings he set a target of 253 in three and a half hours. 'Tom knew the value of a declaration,' says Brown – even before the scripted cricket of the 1980s and 1990s, dependent on the prearranged chase on the final afternoon.

Surrey finished at 179–7; Gloucester remained in the depths; Graveney received news that a son, Tim, had been born on 27 May. He celebrated by scoring 135 against Derby at Chesterfield – ironically sharing a stand of 256 with Pugh (137) who now, ready or not, was a first-team regular. (In 1960 Pugh played 23 matches, scored 844 runs, average 22. He was nothing if not consistent.) 'Tom *could* bat,' says Graveney, 'but his main asset was enthusiasm. No one doubted that.'

On 8 June doubts about Graveney – the 'players' revolt' later dramatised by the press – took shape. The team were at nets prior to a match against Nottingham at Bristol. An hour before the start Cook approached Graveney and asked to see 'someone from the committee'.

'What about?'

'The bowlers,' said Cook. 'We're not happy at the way things are going.'

'Like to talk about it?'

'Yes. To the committee.'

Cook eventually arranged a meeting with Arthur Derrick, the county treasurer. In it he accused Graveney of failing to consult the bowlers when in the field. The captain was informed and found willing to receive advice, though without any obligation to follow it. 'After all, if things went wrong, I carried the can.' The incident ended amicably, with Graveney requesting – and receiving – Cook's appointment to the Cricket Committee. (They had comparable views on, for one, Pugh.) In mid-season the players were in uneasy truce.

Graveney missed much of July with an injured shoulder. Martin Young captained the side and was judged to have been capable, if not in resisting the decline to mid-table. 1960 saw a reversal of the previous season, when spinners had dominated: Mortimore, Allen and Cook all vanished from the national averages, replaced by Jackson, Moss, Larter, Rhodes, Shackleton. The Championship itself was altered, eight counties electing to play the others twice (thirty-two fixtures each), while the remaining nine played twenty-eight; the title was decided on the basis of average points per match. In the ensuing mêlée Sussex (fifteenth in 1959) exchanged places with Warwickshire (fourth); Surrey left the top six for the first time since 1946; Gloucester fell to eighth; chaos.

The tourists were South Africa. Dexter, Cowdrey, Barrington,

Pullar and Smith contested the England batting; Graveney listened with interest to the names for the first Test, after which he ceased holding his breath. England won the series three-nil. At Lord's Geoff Griffin was called for throwing, shortly before an ICC meeting convened to debate the issue first raised on the Australian tour of 1958–59. In the *Telegraph*'s report: 'Over the past years . . . there has sprung up an alarming crop of bowlers of whose actions it must be said, in the words of the most recently worded note to the Law, "there has been a sudden straightening of the bowling arm, whether partial or complete, immediately prior to the delivery of the ball" . . . It is nothing less than the good repute of cricket that the various eminent administrators have to safeguard this week.' Three years later Meckiff was no-balled in a Test at Brisbane and promptly announced his retirement.

'The sixties', wrote Cowdrey, 'was a decade of unrelieved turbulence . . . Controversial figures came and went . . . There were increasingly bitter exchanges' – in cricket as elsewhere. Cook's protest at Bristol seemed to forecast a decade in which throwing, South Africa, finances, Gillette would all come to prominence; in which Graveney himself would be synonymous with a major controversy. More immediately, the 'fine democratic age' noted by Swanton brought increased scrutiny of Graveney's captaincy. There were those who felt not only that he failed to consult, but that he had no desire to do so. Both Cook and Milton were known to feel excluded by Graveney. Young had reservations. In a winning side there would have been little outlet for such feelings, but Gloucester in 1960 won only nine matches. Graveney returned from injury in late July unhappily aware that, henceforth, at least part of his mind would be turned inwardly.

His form was surprisingly good. In his comeback against Sussex he scored 45, then, after a recurrence of injury, batted eleven to earn a draw. (Dexter, in his first year as captain, called the result a 'rare frustration'; he scored 2,217 runs that season.) Graveney then made 76 in two matches, both lost. More representations were received from 'the bowlers', a group which considered itself, says Brown, 'ignored or worse' by the captain. The suspicion was mutual. In August Graveney expressed the wish that the issue be resolved. 'It will be,' said Derrick. From this he drew what relief he could.

The Cheltenham Festival began on 13 August. Graveney was

eighty per cent fit, no more. He believed that personal success would revive morale – always open-handed, if not eyed. At Cheltenham Graveney made 71, 0, 142 not out, 54. The results were a win, draw, defeat. He justified himself (as if needing to) as a batsman; as captain he rang the changes and set the field. When Graveney scored a century he made no comparison with the seventy that had preceded it; he batted for the sake of batting, and to imprint his presence on the match. He remained, as one whose art existed in performance rather than management, a player of supreme consistency. 'Old Tom' he became, a man in his early thirties.

By now his colleagues had changed. Barnett, Crapp, Emmett, Goddard had been replaced by those for whom 'amateur' status was academic (it would be abolished); for whom financial rewards were paramount; above all, for whom 'the captain' lacked the near-divine status of earlier times. Not that he existed in the past, but Graveney in 1960 could be excused for comparing his position to, say, Hammond's twenty years before. (That June, members of the Oxford University side, including Burki and the Nawab of Pataudi, had been heard to mutter about Graveney's tactics against them at Bristol; his fourth-innings challenge was thought too negative. The mind reels at the thought of Hammond's response.) Slowly the feeling grew that Graveney was not a captain in the modern mould. It was his third decade as a professional.

Milton broke a finger and played no cricket after 30 June; Brown and Allen missed nine matches each; Gloucester won only two of their last fourteen. There might be thought to be relatively little news in a county falling from second to eighth in the table: indifferent pitches, injuries, Test duty (Allen) all contributed. The Championship itself defied prophecy, only one team, Yorkshire, retaining their position. None the less, news there was, *Wisden* concluding 'Gloucester sadly disappointed'; the *Post* that 'Hopes were dashed after much early promise.' The county finished in mid-table, fifty-six points behind their position in 1959, Graveney four hundred runs ahead. He did that much.

The inquest began that autumn. Aside from results (though linked) was the central issue of finance. From 1946 to 1952 the county had made an average profit of £2,800; in 1953 this converted to a loss of £416. The position then deteriorated to an extent that Derrick 'feared the worst' when the figures came to be totalled for 1960. (He was right: the Club showed a pre-tax loss of £13,000.) There was an implication that Graveney, as captain, was responsible: decline in results, decline in revenue, hence decline. His response: 'Bristol is one of the most apathetic cities in the world for cricket. It's a miracle we broke even at all.' He sat down. In the silence that followed Derrick could be seen consulting his papers. Graveney was thanked and left.

He toured Africa. The Commonwealth side to Transvaal, Natal and Rhodesia was captained by Benaud; when he broke a finger Graveney took over ahead of Illingworth, M. J. K. Smith and Bobby Simpson: 'If criticisms were made of my qualifications, they didn't reach me.' Simpson believes that Graveney 'struck the balance' between education and entertainment. 'I remember him dropping a catch when a youngster was batting – but discreetly.' Graveney scored 105 against a Combined XI and – equally discreetly – lost his wicket. The party returned home on 16 October in high spirits. 'The cricket on those tours suited me down to the ground,' says Graveney. 'I always came back feeling as if I could push a mountain over.'

A month later he tried to.

On 3 November Graveney attended a meeting with Derrick and Sir William Grant, the county chairman. The captaincy was not discussed. After reiterating the need for 'fuller' houses (the meeting overlooked the damp, dripping stands which seemed incapable of ever being full), Graveney was given permission to approach Subba Row, captain of Northamptonshire, to arrange the transfer of a fast bowler. He shook hands and departed.

On 15 November Graveney was playing squash at Cheltenham when his wife rang to say that Grant wanted to speak to him. When the call was made it had all the finesse of the Marx Brothers:

'Hello . . . Tom?'

'Sir William?'

'Why aren't you at the meeting?'

'What meeting?'

'The one here . . . now.'

'You're meeting . . .?'

'Here.'

'. . . Now?'

The story came out by degrees. Even in calmer conditions, Grant wasn't a natural communicator. Guided by instinct he went into elaborate detours. It seemed a meeting had been called at Bristol, attended by Grant, Derrick, Sir Percy Lister, Emmett and Milton. Harold Thomas, the Club secretary, was ill and failed to inform Graveney – not that that lessened the sang-froid with which Grant greeted him. In language reminiscent of his days in OCTU, Graveney was ordered to report to Lister prompt at ten next morning. Prompt at eleven Lister saw him. It was Wednesday 16 November 1960.

Lister's remarks echoed those of September. The county had recorded a loss of £13,000. Membership was falling. The new season would, in all probability, be the last. Lister paused, clasping his hands. Up to the chin he was composed. Above, all was anxiety. Graveney's attention was divided between the cut of Lister's coat and the look of business *angst* on his face.

'About the captaincy . . .'

Graveney felt the kind of shock associated with dreams involving aeroplanes or departed loved ones. He went numb. In delicate, well-rounded terms, Lister informed him that, in the interests of the side, a change had been made. The captaincy was being offered either to Barnett, fifty, or the twenty-three-year-old Pugh. Lister then suggested that it would benefit both the Club and himself if Graveney wrote to the chairman offering his resignation and pledging support to his successor. He stopped talking. There was a pause. Graveney nodded slowly. It was as simple as that: he was out and Pugh or Barnett was in.

Ten minutes later Graveney's mind resumed working. In his words:

> As I sat in the room with Lister I was in a mental vacuum. I had never before in my life been in a situation like that, and wasn't able to see my position clearly. It was too confused, too unexpected and, on the face of it, too neatly tied up for me to do anything about it. As I saw it then, the whole business had been decided, and I'd been declared the loser without even knowing I was in a contest . . . I agreed to write the letter.

Later that afternoon, after hitting golf balls further and more furiously than ever before, Graveney recanted: 'All that trouble – £13,000 down the drain and a possible end to cricket in the county

– coupled with my replacement as captain, would add up to one thing – the labelling of me as the man responsible.'

Suddenly Graveney's detachment ended. Much was later made of his change of heart – something devious and underhand being inferred, as if Graveney's plan had been to undermine the committee. The truth is that it was a point of principle. His wife's reaction lay somewhere between scorn and sympathy; she asked tacitly how long Graveney would sit, heart-wounded and full of obsolete sensibility. Next morning he rang Grant and refused to resign. Lister called and asked him to reconsider. 'I have,' said Graveney. Later still he learnt that there had been no question of appointing Barnett captain. (Barnett himself doubted whether a change was needed.) At the meeting on the 15th Milton, Graveney's Sunday golf partner, had been named senior professional. The captaincy had been offered to Pugh.

Pugh: a man, says Bailey, 'who possessed a strictly limited knowledge of the game'; 'who struggled to reach par' (Brown); who leaves no impression in the mind of Compton, Evans, Trueman, Statham, Lock. Graveney liked Pugh. He was an enthusiastic amateur for whom a place could easily have been found in the Seconds. But county captain? It seemed incredible. When Frank Rostron of the *Express* rang Graveney for his reaction to 'Tom's appointment', the phrase 'no comment' was, for once, appropriate. He was speechless. Later that day, the 18th, the Gloucestershire Cricket Council, composed of elected members throughout the county, announced the decision officially. Pugh it was. As Graveney said, 'When you get involved in a situation like that, you know how many minutes there are in a twenty-four-hour day. The phone never stops, and the worry and controversy travel with you every step you take.'

Among Graveney's steps was to arrange an interview with the Club president, the Duke of Beaufort, who had been in the chair at the Council meeting. Beaufort seemed surprised that such a motion had been tabled; he wanted to know the details and reasons for the change. Over the next week he was a regular caller, as was Ken Graveney; Grant again pressed for voluntary resignation. Letters began to arrive from Gloucester members. A newspaper offered £2,000 (two years' salary) if Graveney went public. He refused. A photographer climbed a tree outside Graveney's house but couldn't get down again. A ladder had to be sent for to free him. Graveney, his wife, daughter and infant son were under siege until 9 December, when he was invited to another meeting with Grant. It was then that he offered Graveney the following:

(1) A new contract at £1,000 p.a.
(2) Appointment as senior professional.
(3) Election to the Cricket Council.
(4) A job in industry.

Present at the meeting were Grant, Lister, the Duke of Beaufort, Graveney and his brother. The last urged him to consider. Both heard Grant repeat that Graveney 'wouldn't lose financially' (a statement held critical later on), and that a confirming letter would be sent 'within the week'. It never was.

On 15 December Graveney rang Grant to say that he would accept the offer (if confirmed), provided he, Graveney, was exonerated from blame for the Club's deficit. Grant exploded. This was the moment the chairman's guard slipped. 'Don't you know?' he bellowed. 'It was decided to appoint Pugh two *years* ago?' Graveney reeled. Two years ago he himself had been appointed. Four days later, 19 December, Grant confirmed it: 'We wanted an amateur as captain.'

The conclusion that Graveney's appointment had been nothing but a holding operation is confirmed by Swanton:

> When in the autumn of 1960 I heard of the troubles, with young Tom Pugh appointed captain instead of Graveney and the latter resigning in protest at the way the matter had been handled, my thoughts went back to the annual dinner of Gloucestershire two seasons before at which I had proposed the county's health and naturally wished Tom, the new leader, all good luck. A friend who was then in one of the seats of power told me after the dinner that if things didn't go well they had in Pugh a good man whom they were grooming for the job. When I said I didn't think a man of Graveney's reputation and character might care to be superseded by an amateur ten years his junior, the answer came: 'Oh, I don't think there would be any trouble. The pros don't like the responsibility very much . . . They're happier without it.'

In the week before Christmas Graveney received confirmation – directly from Lister, indirectly from Milton – that the committee had long decided to appoint an amateur when the chance arose. The county's decline provided it. When, on 2 January, Graveney played golf with Pugh (photographers lay crouched in bunkers and behind trees like a *Carry On* film), he heard from the horse's mouth: 'I was promised a place in the team' (Graveney nodded; those battles with the committee) '. . . and the captaincy. I thought it strange at the time.'

No more than Graveney, who on that note issued his first statement to the press:

> In view of recent events between the Club and myself, it is clear that I owe an explanation to the entire cricket public and to all my friends.
>
> At the beginning of the 1959 season I was appointed captain. The team finished second in the Championship in 1959 and eighth in 1960.
>
> On November 18 last the Club announced that one of our young amateurs, Tom Pugh, had been appointed captain. No mention of me or my position was made in the announcement and I was neither consulted nor officially advised of the action.
>
> In fact, I was told of it only two days before. Under these circumstances I informed the Club that I could not carry on.
>
> I have since had discussions with Sir William Grant and the Duke of Beaufort. It has been suggested that more money might be offered to me, but money is of no concern to me in this matter. Money is simply not the point.
>
> I am a Gloucestershire man at heart. I have served the county for thirteen seasons, always to the limit of my ability. I have never sought anything more than that right and privilege.
>
> Recently I was told for the first time that when I was appointed captain in 1959 the Club's policy even then was to have an amateur captain at some future date.
>
> This merely confirmed in my mind that the treatment I had received from the Club was irregular and a long way short of the dignity which Gloucestershire cricket and cricket in general deserves.
>
> Thus, when my contract expires at the end of the month, I shall end my association with the Club. This association has been precious to me and I hope that for my part I am ending it with some dignity.

So it went. From the moment Graveney learnt his captaincy had been only a detour on the road to appointing an amateur, his mind was made up. Both Grant and Lister asked him to stay, and Brown and Allen (the latter capped by Graveney in 1959) are adamant that 'no one wanted Tom to go' – except Graveney himself. Bailey 'ran into him in London at the time and did my best to try to persuade him to settle his differences with the county, to no avail . . . I gained the impression that the whole business might have been avoided if only a little more tact had been employed, but this has seldom been an outstanding characteristic of county committees.' Without guarantees, Graveney's position was imperfect; with Pugh's appointment, impossible. The knowledge that 'all the time I was struggling as captain, the decision had already been made' settled it. It was a point of principle.

Graveney wrote to the Club asking for his release. It was acknowledged on 9 January by a letter confirming Grant's offer of £1,000 p.a., without mention of the other three conditions. Graveney was canvassed by two former captains, Allen and Lyon, who urged him to stay – on the Club's terms; Ken Graveney and the Duke of Beaufort tried to mediate; the rest of the county 'seemed not to care'. (Of the players, only Pugh and Milton were directly involved. The rest followed events through the press.) In a month six hundred letters were delivered to Graveney from ordinary cricket lovers. Cowdrey wrote sympathetically, as did Hammond from South Africa. The first resignations were received by the Club at Bristol. Graveney repeated his request.

On 17 February the Cricket Council replied: 'It is resolved that an absolute release be granted to T. W. Graveney, and consent given to his special registration to any county . . . The Council records its appreciation of Graveney's services to the Club and expresses its unanimous good wishes for [his] future career.'

So it ended. Graveney remains adamant that, even after the revelation that his job had been to 'keep the seat warm for Pugh', he would have stayed, wanted to stay, had Grant's promises been kept. They weren't. Nor, clearly, would he be exonerated for the county's deficit. When the Council's letter arrived Graveney wrote back, thanking them for their co-operation. He concealed his real emotion, which was relief.

Immediately he was contacted by Essex, Leicester, Nottingham; by Worcester, only twenty-five miles away. While Graveney was considering his options, Harold Thomas, the Gloucester secretary, signed his application for a special registration. Not for six weeks did Graveney learn that he signed another letter, to MCC, the same day:

> The officers and my committee have made every effort to retain Graveney's services for this Club for obvious reasons. Now Graveney has both publicly and privately stated categorically that he will not play for Gloucestershire again. At the recent meeting of the Gloucestershire CCC Council, it was their desire by a resolution to grant Graveney his immediate release.
>
> For your further information, the offer we made in writing to Graveney for 1961 was a minimum salary of £1,000; this sum ensured that he would not be suffering any pecuniary loss through having relinquished the captaincy, i.e. through being deprived of the special sum which we have in the past granted as a captain's allowance.

All of which was news to Graveney as he entered negotiations with Lister and Sir George Dowty, president of Worcester. So far as he knew he was a free agent. The Club itself, after rescinding Grant's offer, had been just, even generous. The point was made in an article in the *Telegraph* headlined 'Gloucestershire Act with Becoming Grace':

> Now that Gloucester have agreed to Graveney's request for release, certain points in the story badly need underlining. In the first place, the committee's decision that a change of captaincy was desirable was influenced by the players themselves . . .
>
> This being so, Graveney was invited to resign. He agreed to do so, then later changed his mind. Hence the original publicity, the heart-searchings and so to the climax wherein the county thank him for his services and wish him well in the future.
>
> In these fine democratic days the player is always apt to be right in the popular view and the Club automatically wrong. Here Gloucestershire have surely behaved with all possible generosity . . .
>
> In the circumstances they are surely right to nominate an amateur, C. T. M. Pugh. A county can always sack a poor wretched amateur. With a professional, especially a distinguished one, the question of prestige automatically arises and it is the oldest truism in cricket that the best players are sometimes the worst captains.

Was Graveney? According to Brown, 'Tom was adequate.' Allen: 'He led by example. His main attribute was the awe in which opposing bowlers held him.' But a natural leader? No. So a case can be made, in 1960, for Gloucester's decision – notwithstanding their duplicity in promising Pugh; notwithstanding Pugh. (His status at Gloucester being comparable to, say, Peter Walker's for England.) A compromise may have been possible, but no one knew how to reach it.

Graveney signed for Worcester. Dowty was a factor; also Don Kenyon, whom Graveney had known since the Indian tour of 1951–52. Kenyon had assumed the captaincy in 1959; the county immediately dropped five places in the table. (It could happen to anyone.) Worcester also had a good wicket, on the most attractive ground in the country – nearer to Graveney than Bristol. 'It made sense,' he says.

On 4 April Graveney and his wife left for a week's holiday prior to the new season. It lasted two days. On the 6th the Registration Committee met at Lord's and 'rejected a request by Worcestershire to register Graveney specially so that he could play in Championship matches in 1961 . . . being fully satisfied that Gloucestershire made every effort to retain the player, and thus finding themselves unable to grant a special registration': Thomas's letter to a T.

The regulation by which the committee made its ruling read: 'A cricketer shall be eligible for special registration if he is not required by the county (or counties) for which he is qualified, or in which he is residing.'

The fact that 'the [Gloucester] officers . . . and committee [had] made every effort to retain Graveney's services' and that the move was not for financial gain (Graveney lost £250 p.a. by joining Worcester) meant that the county could bar him from first-class cricket – much in the way of a spouse rejecting his partner's plea for divorce with the intention of preventing re-marriage – for a year. Or more. For some time in April Graveney considered quitting cricket altogether. He was approaching thirty-four, had 48 Test caps; scored 20,000 runs for his county. Had Graveney retired in 1961 his status would be that of a gifted under-achiever, comparable, say, to that of Chris Broad thirty years later.

Later that month Thomas's letter, of which there had been no inkling, no indication, became public – and the mood changed. Graveney would fight. On that note he lodged an appeal and reported to Worcestershire for the new season. The uncertainty of the situation and of the facts surrounding his transfer were summarised by the *Cricketer*:

> Great efforts were made to induce Graveney to remain with Gloucestershire, but he felt he could no longer stay . . . The unhappy controversy was amicably settled by Gloucester raising no objection to Graveney's immediate qualification for another county . . . but a final decision was deferred.

In retrospect, there seem only two explanations for Gloucester's action: that they were opposing the onset of a transfer system whereby the best players would be monopolised by the most affluent counties, or that they were simply vindictive towards a man who had brought the Club unwelcome attention (who, moreover, had enjoyed a £5,400 Benefit two years earlier). Possibly there were elements of both, and of wilfulness on Graveney's part. As he says: 'No one gained from the whole business.' England, temporarily, lost a player of ten years' service; Worcestershire, to their credit, paid him a full season's salary; Graveney himself faced a disturbing and even demoralising crisis.

Gloucester, meanwhile, enjoyed the captaincy of Tom Pugh for two seasons until he too departed – replaced by Ken Graveney.

In early May, after playing for his new county against Australia, Graveney went to Lord's for his appeal. The case was heard by Lord Cornwallis, of the Advisory County Cricket Committee; Sir Hubert Ashton, president of MCC; Lord Portal; Tom Pearce; Charlie Palmer; Doug Insole. Graveney was represented by Ryder Richardson, QC, the Recorder of Stoke. He was asked two questions and told to wait. Minutes later Ashton announced that the appeal had been disallowed. Graveney nodded. Certain muscles in his cheeks became visible. A statement was issued and the first match he played, with exquisite timing, was for MCC against the Club Cricket Conference at Lord's. He made 100.

Graveney's main employment in 1961 was for Worcestershire's Second Eleven. The team finished fourth in a table headed by Kent. The standard was higher than expected. Graveney's sole complaint was that certain counties staged their matches away from the main grounds – understandable, in bringing cricket to a wider audience; unfortunate, in doing so on indifferent pitches. In fifteen innings he scored 552 runs, heading the county averages; Duncan Fearnley was second; for Northants a youngster called Milburn scored mightily, shaking Graveney's hand when either appeared at the wicket. Milburn seemed not to walk but sway, in the manner of a steamer ploughing through heavy seas. He listed.

At weekends Graveney was released to play for Dudley in the Birmingham League. He faced Alan Townsend, the Warwickshire bowler; Eric Hollies; even Roy Tattersall, who, despite having once taken 12–101 in a Test, was 'carted ruthlessly' by the League batsmen. Graveney scored 152 not out against Cambridge University in early June; a first-ball nought and 124 for Colonel Stevens's XI against the same opposition a fortnight later. He played seven first-class innings that season and would have headed the national averages had not the minimum qualification been eight.

England, meanwhile, were in the throes of losing to an Australian side rated by Graveney one of the weakest ever. The turning-point came at Old Trafford where the home side, chasing 256, collapsed from 150–1 to 201 all out; Benaud 6–70. John Murray, who made his Test début that summer, believes, 'We could have used Tom, even if he'd been batting on the beach . . . He would have played if I'd been selecting.' Of those who did, Graveney's nemesis, Gubby Allen, retired at season's end; Peter May, too, played his last Test.

In July Graveney went to Bermuda on a private tour under Stuart Surridge. In two representative matches he made 205 not out and 104, took 7–34, and reached the significant conclusion that 'the more I play cricket, the more I realise the value of inner confidence.' As he returned to Worcester in August he faced the future with renewed hope. He was ready.

6

ÉLITE

THE FIRST SIGHT was impressive. Tall, muscular, strong in the arms, the batsman scored 51 against a Rhodesian XI on an erratic pitch in Nkana. Later he bowled slow-medium, with a textbook sideways action: Basil D'Oliveira. That evening Graveney approached him in the bar (D'Oliveira's other habitat). 'How old are you?' The muscles in D'Oliveira's face twitched. He may have gulped. 'Twenty-seven,' he answered. Graveney nodded.

From February to April 1962 an International side under Ron Roberts toured Rhodesia, Hong Kong, East Africa, India, Pakistan and New Zealand. In all twenty-five players were recruited, nineteen of Test calibre, among them the captains of England and Australia. In the African fixtures Graveney made 112, 52 and 70; he was one of six to complete the whole tour, the first in which blacks were received – relatively – freely in Southern Africa. In D'Oliveira's words:

> We were travelling from Salisbury to Bulawayo when we stopped at a hotel in Gwelo. I was in a car with Ramadhin and Gupte while in front of us were Roberts, Weekes and Graveney. When they went into the hotel, I suggested that we wait a moment. I had a feeling . . . A few minutes later, the three of them came out. I could see they were fuming. Tom had ordered three drinks and the bartender had refused to serve them.

As a postscript, Weekes's recollection of Graveney's response to being told 'You and the other bloke [Roberts] can stay,' was to 'offer some medical advice which wasn't very practical'.

In New Zealand Graveney made 94 at Christchurch, 92 and 116 not out at Auckland. His last innings, against the Cricket Club of

India XI at Bombay, was 95; mission accomplished. He reported to Worcester in April and made a point of lodging the name D'Oliveira with Sir George Dowty. How old was he? 'About thirty,' said Graveney.

1962 was the year the Worcestershire revival took place. Had Flavell not strained an Achilles' tendon, Headley not broken his wrist, Graveney not been absent on Test duty, they must have overtaken Yorkshire as champions. The season began promisingly. Rain robbed Worcester of victory in the opening match against Glamorgan, but Graveney served notice against the Pakistani tourists in early May. He scored 10 and 117, and on the last day, 4 May, received his county cap. It was that evening that Len Coldwell made his cryptic remark: 'At Gloucester you played – with us you work,' echoed by J.M. Kilburn, who wrote: 'Graveney emerged from Gloucester a harder, grimmer player . . . Worcester's Championship contention stiffened his sense of batting responsibility, and advancing age in itself eliminated some of the frivolities.'

John Murray has another theory. One of the prime reasons for Graveney's Indian summers (all nine of them) was the Worcester wicket. It was then the best in the country; fast enough to incite bowlers, not least Flavell and Coldwell, yet allowing batsmen to play their shots. If Graveney emerged harder and more determined from the Gloucester affair, then his new surroundings encouraged him to be so. At thirty-five, an age when others were considering their futures, Graveney developed the confidence to extend the talent that had hitherto existed in embryo. The process did not happen overnight. John Price remembers bowling Graveney a bouncer as a surprise attack on his defences. 'He'd never seen a ball rise more than waist-high at Gloucester. He soon learnt.' The years 1962 and 1963 saw the consolidation of Graveney's technique until, in 1964, he graduated from being merely a fine batsman and became a great one.

Evidence of this was apparent from early season. In mid-May Graveney scored 47 and 119 against Middlesex, and, according to Eric Russell (who caught him) 'no one, not even May, hit the ball harder'. Next day Graveney made 78 against Northants. He represented MCC against Pakistan and scored 110 (the last fifty in thirty minutes), his second century against the tourists in three weeks.

1962 was also the dawn of a new era – that of Walter Robins as chairman of England selectors and Dexter as captain. The last was known to be well disposed to Graveney, whose laid-back persona was sometimes compared to his own. The other selectors were three men whom Graveney had played with and liked – Insole, Bedser and Watson. (Eight years earlier Watson and Graveney had scored 402 against British Guiana, still a record for an English team overseas.) No favours were asked and none given by the new committee, but Graveney listened to the selection of the Test team on 27 May hopeful that 'based on merit – and the retirement of May and Subba Row – I had a chance.' He had.

Graveney marked his return by scoring 97. Cowdrey and Parfitt made centuries; Statham took 4–54; England won the Test by an innings. The press were unanimous ('It was hard to see what more they could do, short of staying to sweep the pavilion') and Robins, not one to over-praise, called Graveney's innings a 'classic'. (*Wisden* used the same word.) Robins's chairmanship began an era of 'brighter cricket', and no one better expressed or translated the mood than Graveney. Two days after the Test he scored 147 not out; a year earlier he had considered giving up the game altogether.

As in 1958, interest in the home series was sustained by speculation concerning the winter tour of Australia. The stakes were raised by E.M. Wellings in the *Evening News*, who proposed David Sheppard, whose last Test had been in 1957, for the captaincy. Sheppard had since retired to concentrate on his clerical duties in the East End of London. According to Cowdrey, one of the few people who took Wellings seriously was Robins himself, who asked Sheppard to play in a limited number of first-class matches that summer with a view to his leading England in Australia. (Interestingly, it was Sheppard who had come within one vote of a similar appointment in 1954–55, when 'reservations' had been expressed about Hutton, the first professional to lead England this century. At least in 1962 the selectors had three candidates – Sheppard, Dexter and Cowdrey – who could be relied on for the niceties.)

The result was that, on 20 June, Sheppard went out to bat for Sussex watched by a contingent the size of the White House press corps. He scored 108. It was a sensational return and the media began to agitate for his appointment. Sheppard was hailed as 'a fine leader on and off the field' and photographed (in clerical garb) jumping gleefully over a brick wall. Graveney, meanwhile, returned to Worcester, scored 61, 76, and on 16 June, his thirty-fifth birthday, 164 not out against Somerset. He and Horton added 314 for the third wicket, still a county record. Graveney's innings included a six and twenty-one fours. The match ended on the third morning and Worcester rose to second in the table, undefeated, and in the eyes of many the best-balanced side in the Championship.

The second Test, at Lord's, was Graveney's fiftieth. He scored 153. By this stage he had made three centuries (and 97) against the tourists in four matches. Javed Burki, the Pakistan captain (who himself made 101 at Lord's), says that 'In that series, Tom looked like scoring every time.' Dexter's inexperience was exposed when, in his own words, 'I was persuaded to bowl Lock by elements of the crowd . . . Burki and Nasim piled on the runs and England began to look ragged in the field . . . I was so angry with myself that I failed to clap the two batsmen as they came off.' (Later in the series Dexter would order Graveney to 'get out' after reaching a century.) Although England won by nine wickets the captain was removed in favour of Cowdrey. Sheppard, meanwhile, was expressing doubts about Australia. The comeback had proved illusory.

Worcestershire's own ambitions were thwarted at Kidderminster. Graveney made 115 (caught, for the third time that season, by Andrew; the bowler was Milburn); Norman and Lightfoot scored heavily and Northants won by eight wickets; Worcester's first defeat of the season. Headley broke his wrist. Graveney reported to the third Test at Headingly uneasily aware that the tide had turned. Of Worcester's next dozen matches, five were drawn, five won, two lost. As if in illustration Graveney made only 37 at Leeds. England won by an innings.

The spotlight now reverted to Australia. As twelve years before, the Gents v. Players fixture was held critical in determining the England captaincy. (In 1950 Brown had scored 122 and promptly been offered the job.) On the first morning Sheppard scored 112. There followed a farce of Karno-like proportions when, in Cowdrey's words, 'From the windows of the press restaurant, six flights up, a number of correspondents spotted Robins walking to the pavilion. Anxious to get the tip-off that would confirm that Sheppard was the man, they attracted Robins's attention and engaged in a number of long-range signals . . . Next day almost all the headlines proclaimed 'Sheppard for Captain' and beneath them came many a story extolling the percipience of the England selectors, the dashing imagination of the whole experiment, the courage displayed throughout by Sheppard.' Later that day Dexter was named captain.

Not untypical was the reaction of the *Daily Mirror*: 'Good Lord, It's Ted.' The press had another shock when the manager was revealed as the sixteenth Duke of Norfolk, Earl Marshal of England (Bedser as assistant). The full party read: Dexter, Allen, Barrington, Coldwell, Cowdrey, Graveney, Illingworth, Knight, Larter, Murray, Parfitt, Pullar, Sheppard, Smith, Statham, Titmus, Trueman. According to the *Cricketer*, 'few were able to improve on the selectors' choice', although reservations were harboured about the bowling. Dexter himself conceded that: 'Trueman and Statham were past their best' (the latter had to be persuaded to tour); '. . . Larter was a gamble, Coldwell and Knight not likely to bother the Australian batsmen.' In the same review (which smacks of deliberate disparagement) the captain concluded, 'Graveney had been found wanting on demanding occasions' – the old chestnut.

Dexter returned as captain at Trent Bridge. Graveney scored 114, and might have doubled it had instructions not arrived, via the twelfth man, to 'hit out'. Dexter wanted to assess the other batsmen. His average that series was 100.25. During the Gents v. Players match, Worcester had met Gloucester for the first time since Graveney's transfer, Gloucester winning by five wickets; in the Test itself he missed a defeat by Warwickshire at Worcester. As Gifford says, 'We never fired on all cylinders when Tom was away' – and Worcester's success in 1964 was coincidental with Graveney's. In mid-August he scored 106 against Hampshire, after which, in near constant rain, the next four matches were drawn. (In the final Test at The Oval, Graveney, Trueman, Statham, Titmus, Lock and Pullar were rested in favour of Cowdrey, Barrington, Allen, Illingworth, Coldwell and Larter. England won by ten wickets.) The season reached its climax in the return fixture with Gloucester on 25 August. Graveney batted on the first afternoon determined, not unreasonably, to make a point. He made nought. In the second innings he scored 51 (dismissed by Cook, who, when Graveney was batting, bowled so flat his back arched like a half-open penknife).

Worcester prevailed by 154 and needed to win their final match, at home to Nottingham, to lead the table.

The game started when Coldwell had Norman Hill caught at slip by Graveney without score; in an hour Nottingham were 32–5. Opener Alan Gill survived and prospered with Carlton Forbes. They added 56, after which Millman and Corran indulged in an eighth-wicket stand of 84. Carter took the last two wickets; Nottingham all out for 193.

Worcester's nerves were betrayed by the anxiety of their batting. The atmosphere was akin to a cup-tie. Seams of flinty sunlight illuminated the crowd who, in tones of red and blue, darted like a shoal of tropical fish. Graveney departed for 19; Worcester 171–6. A flourish was added by Gifford and Coldwell (whose 37 was the highest of his fifteen-year career); 253 all out. In the second innings Nottingham made 251. Worcester had a day to win.

The rain returned overnight and on the final morning, 4 September, pocks of sawdust dotted the field like a scar. In seventy-five minutes, 91 were scored for the loss of Horton and Richardson. In sizzling rain Graveney and Kenyon then engaged in a stand of 145; Graveney's contribution was 62 not out, and, minutes before the downpour, Worcester succeeded by eight wickets. The crowd gathered in front of the pavilion. The captain led his team on to the balcony, and no one, not Coldwell, nor Horton, nor Kenyon himself, received a louder welcome than Graveney. Worcester were top of the table, and could only be denied if Yorkshire beat Glamorgan in the final match.

They did. Don Wilson took ten wickets and Yorkshire were champions; Worcester, despite losing fewer games, second. In its review of the season, *Wisden* noted that the county 'showed all-round cricket of great quality', adding: 'Kenyon seemed to enjoy [himself] more, possibly because for the first time he had Graveney, a man of equal experience and stature, in his side.' Kenyon confirms it: 'Tom was the first person I turned to,' underlining the belief that Graveney was one of cricket's NCO's, not a field marshal.

There was less than a month before MCC flew to Aden, where they boarded the *Canberra* to Fremantle. As on the previous tour of 1958–59, the mood of the party was established on the outward voyage. On the second morning, 30 September, Dexter learnt that the Olympic athlete, Gordon Pirie, was on board *en route* to New Zealand. Pirie was sounded and organised a series of morning training sessions. The idea was to circumnavigate the deck for the equivalent of a three-mile run. Pirie was soon in splendid isolation. Graveney and Statham would complete a lap and disappear down one of the central hatchways, emerging later to complete the course in high spirits. (Trueman's approach was less subtle. Graveney swears he heard him ask Pirie 'Canst tha' swim?' with 'definite menace' in his voice.) Suitably impressed, *The Times* reported that 'There will never be a fitter English cricket side than that arriving in Fremantle tomorrow.' Trueman's reply is not recorded.

Robins made his presence felt in Australia. (He it was who, in April 1960, arrived at a Test in Trinidad to demand that Cowdrey declare in order to 'give the others a chance'. Cowdrey's reply was unprintable.) Graveney believes that Dexter 'was stifled by the promise of attacking cricket . . . and by the presence of the Duke as manager. The latter was a superb ambassador, with little or no experience at this level . . . A lot of work fell on Bedser accordingly.' Among Bedser's work were cars, hotels, expenses, chaperoning Dexter's father – everything, in short, except cricket. Nor were Cowdrey and Sheppard, rival candidates for captain, much help. The former was invisible off the field, while Sheppard rapidly converted the tour into a personal crusade whose highlights were the Sunday sermons, not the cricket in between.

The result was that Dexter felt free, even obliged, to indulge his many theories: on David Allen – 'I was worried about the line Allen bowled . . . I felt it too defensive in character and told him so . . . The result was I lost his confidence and deprived the side of a great bowler'; Bill Lawry – 'he kept the bat close to his body and it was almost impossible to pierce his defence . . . I decided that if we kept Lawry pinned down, especially at Brisbane, he would get frustrated and the other batsmen would suffer' (Lawry scored 98); The Ashes –'a bane and a nuisance . . . they should be abolished and each man paid £1,000 for a result'; even breakfast – 'all my men will eat it.' (Statham, who had last eaten breakfast in the 1940s, was said to have smiled and lit a cigarette.) Matters were compounded when, as in 1958–59, the Captain's Wife became an issue. Susan Dexter arrived in Melbourne on a modelling assignment, prompting Miller to ask 'what the crowds would be like . . .

if her name was Jones or Smith.' Later in the tour Dexter also quarrelled with Neil Harvey.

Against this backdrop, good cricket was played by both sides. MCC beat Western Australia by ten wickets, lost to a Combined XI by the same margin, then faced South Australia at Adelaide. Graveney scored 99, engaging in a stand of 168 with Barrington. (John Murray, who was watching, considers them the two greatest of his time, not excluding Dexter and Cowdrey.) He then scored 52 against Queensland, took two wickets and pronounced himself confident of selection for the first Test at Brisbane. Almost inevitably he was omitted.

The batsmen chosen were Pullar, Sheppard, Dexter, Cowdrey, Barrington, Parfitt. The captain made 70 and 99 and the Test was drawn. During it word arrived from Lord's that amateur or 'gentleman' status was being abolished. Although certain critics demurred ('The evolution of the game has been stimulated from its beginnings by the fusion of the two strains . . . England has been at its best when there has been an even balance' – the *Telegraph*), most were relieved that cricket had entered the twentieth century; none more so than Graveney, who formed a bridge between the Duke, Dexter, Cowdrey, Sheppard and A.C. Smith ('Them') and the remaining thirteen ('Us') – a distinction that, as late as the New Zealand tour in March 1963, involved the use of two separate dressing-rooms. Murray again: 'Tom had the respect of both camps. He put our views to them and theirs to us.' When, following the Brisbane Test, MCC flew 1700 miles to an up-country match in Bendigo, a separate table had been laid for the four amateurs.

Graveney scored 118 against a Queensland Country XI; 59 at Bendigo; 40 against Victoria at Melbourne, where Meckiff took 3–53; then, on 24 December, 122 not out against South Australia. At the other end Cowdrey hit 307, his highest first-class score; it was his birthday. The stand was worth 344 and Sobers, appearing for the opposition, says that 'In quality, Tom conceded nothing to Colin . . . If anything he was the more natural player.' Graveney's driving that day was reminiscent of Hutton, even Hammond; his style, like theirs, was a fusion of body, blade and ball. That night Dexter, with a view to the second Test, approached Graveney at dinner. 'Merry Christmas,' he said. 'You're playing.'

MCC arrived in Melbourne on 27 December. Two days later

nearly 70,000 spectators saw the home side dismissed for 316 (Titmus 4–43; Graveney himself bowled three overs for 10). England replied with 331, of which Cowdrey made 113, Dexter 93, Graveney 41, including his 3,000th Test run. Overnight Australia were 105–4, at which point, in his own words, Dexter 'rang the changes . . . keeping Trueman, who I reckoned to be our one real weapon, up my sleeve. I resisted all temptation to bring him on . . . I held back and prayed that when the new ball came he would do the damage . . . The moment came and Fred took three wickets. My gamble had paid off.' England won by seven wickets. The *Telegraph* heralded 'one of the most complete and thoroughly merited victories in the history of these Tests', adding, 'The onus is now on Australia to upset the tremendous confidence England have acquired.'

Too much, perhaps. MCC played only one first-class game, in Tasmania, before flying to Sydney. Graveney fell ill with a virus on the eve of the Test. His replacement, Parfitt, confirms that 'England, if anything, were too keyed-up . . . That sort of confidence can be more dangerous than the reverse.' Dexter himself thought there was insufficient evidence to break up a winning side and picked one spinner on a spinner's pitch. England lost by eight wickets.

Between the third and fourth Tests Graveney was contacted by his brother, Ken. Pugh had left Gloucester at the end of 1962 and the committee asked if the elder Graveney, thirty-eight, would return as captain. No one detected the presence of irony in their voices. The result was that Graveney captained the side for two years, in which they finished eighth and seventeenth in the table. 'I tried,' he says.

The younger Graveney played in the fourth Test at Adelaide. This was the match when Sheppard arrested forever the cause of cricketing clerics by dropping four catches. Australia batted first and scored 393, Harvey 154, after being missed on 8, 9, 12 and 26. ('Put your hands together, Rev,' said Trueman, 'and pray like the rest of us.') England replied with 331. The outfielding reverted to type in the Australian second innings, and the eventual target was 356 at a rate of six an over. Benaud:

> I was without the injured Davidson and had Mackay opening the bowling with McKenzie. After we had knocked over Pullar and

> Sheppard there was a partnership between Barrington and Cowdrey of 94 in only 86 minutes, but, although we dismissed Cowdrey, there was never any real chance of a result on what was still a good batting pitch.
>
> However . . . Barrington and Graveney suddenly realised there was an opportunity looming for Australia if McKenzie were to pick up wickets with the second new ball, and declined to take any singles off three overs from Simpson and myself . . . I put Lawry on with instructions to bowl so wide the ball would run away to the fine leg boundary and the 200 (and new ball) be brought up. There was criticism of my tactics but the batsmen gave me no choice.

Benaud was not the only one criticised. Dexter remembers looking at the wicket and finding it 'green, so green that I refused to believe it would last . . . Nothing would change my mind and I played the two spinners we should have included at Sydney.' It was after this that Graveney, having originally thought Dexter the best available, changed his mind: 'At the beginning of the tour he was tremendous . . . But Ted lacked staying-power . . . I think his mind wandered after the second Test. Captaining a team for six months was too much for him.' England left Adelaide one-all in the series, with one to play.

MCC returned to Melbourne where, against a strong Victorian XI, Graveney scored 185. His innings, which included twenty-three fours, was hailed by *Wisden* as a 'delightful display of elegant driving, glancing and hooking,' all in dangerous light. Allen calls it the innings of the tour. From there the side travelled to Canberra where, on 6 February, they played a Prime Minister's XI including, aged fifty-four, Bradman. He faced five balls. Off the second, from Graveney, he scored four. Next over Statham bowled outside off stump. The ball clipped Bradman, clipped the pad and brushed the stumps. A bail fell. It was the worst moment of Statham's professional life.

Before the final Test Graveney scored 106 against a New South Wales Country XI. (Regardless of his 'failure' in Tests, there are Australians who to this day rate him more highly than Dexter and Cowdrey.) Background interest in the series was intense as the teams regrouped at Sydney. Immediately the Test started England knew it would be drawn. Not only was the pitch dead, so too was the outfield; even Dexter had difficulty piercing it. The *Telegraph* felt that 'England should have been the aggressors, but started slowly on the inaccurate assumption that the pitch would not last . . . Thereafter they strove to make up time, but were prisoners of circumstance.' The point is echoed by Graveney, who notes there was 'heated debate' in the visitors' dressing-room 'as to whether we should throw everything away trying to win . . . or play the game as it came.' The latter school, including Graveney, prevailed and match and series were drawn. The Ashes remained Australia's.

Dexter has 'many happy memories of the tour . . . though I doubt anyone will believe it.' Swanton says that, 'Taking the series as a whole there was some good cricket . . . Barrington had a great tour, and the England batting with Dexter, Cowdrey, Sheppard and Graveney in support was mostly set in an attractive key.' Cowdrey, after paying tribute to the Duke, adds that 'Dexter was supremely confident in every situation.' (Confidence was never one of Dexter's shortcomings.) *Wisden*, on the other hand, noted that 'in general his leadership lacked inspiration' and the *Express* went one better by stating that 'Australia . . . is seething with savage, indignant reaction to the ghastly flop of the Test series . . . If Dexter survives the latest broadsides to captain England again he will be a very lucky man.'

Graveney himself wrote:

> The selectors made a mistake by omitting Lock. I thought then, and still do, that he should have gone . . . As the tour unfolded, some of the players came unstuck, notably Smith and Larter . . . Expectations were high because of the recent West Indies' tour of Australia and the promise of 'brighter cricket' . . . It was disappointing, simply because both teams wanted to win and neither gave the other a chance.
>
> Benaud gave a lot of trouble at the start but became a very ordinary bowler later and presented no problems. He seemed to lose some of his flair . . . Dexter was a magnificent bat who should never have captained England. He completely misread conditions at Sydney and Adelaide and seemed to drift in and out of the game. He almost destroyed David Allen as a bowler.

Graveney played three Tests, scored 116 runs, average 29; on the tour as a whole 737 at 53. For the third time he had failed to do himself justice in Australia. The psychology of Graveney as a Test batsman is complex. In 1962–63, as 1958–59 and 1954–55, he proved capable of the full-blooded innings only when the pressure, relatively speaking, was off. His 185 was one of the vivid memories of the tour (Murray remembers 'even Dexter' being impressed); a week later he batted like a novice on an admittedly dead pitch in Sydney. If, as he says, Graveney went into Tests feeling only marginally more tension than any other match, then the cause of his failure may lie in the belief, upheld by the facts, that he batted more fluently in a winning team than a losing one. (Of Graveney's eleven Test centuries, five each came in matches England won or drew. The sole exception was Trent Bridge, 1966.) If, as some claim, this leads to the assumption that Graveney lacked heart, then it was a grievous fault and grievously he answered it. Nor was it a conscious omission. As he says: 'I played almost every innings the same way', lacking the extra application of a Barrington or Boycott. If Graveney's charm was that he played cricket for cricket's sake, it was also his failing.

Graveney, like Statham, Allen and Pullar, was excused the tour of New Zealand (where England won three-nil). He returned to Cheltenham facing the county Championship with renewed confidence. It was misplaced. From runners-up, four points behind the champions, Worcester fell to fourteenth. Yet even in this there was promise.

Cricket was being reviewed. There were changes. As forecast in Australia, the gentleman-player distinction was abolished. The no-ball law was amended and the Championship again decided on points without recourse to averages or percentages. Finally, Robins's plea for 'brighter cricket' found expression in the first one-day knockout competition, sponsored by Gillette.

When, in 1920, Warner wrote that 'Though a democratic form of government is, no doubt, the most suitable for the time we live in . . . I should be very sorry to see the government of cricket in the hands of [those who] would order out any batsman who was guilty of playing a maiden over, or who failed to score fifty runs an hour,' he eerily foretold conditions forty years later. (Warner died in January 1963. His comments on the Gillette Cup are not recorded.) Even a player as bold as Graveney had doubts about one-day cricket, fearing it would 'only reflect the established order of the Championship'. He was mistaken.

The first Gillette Cup, restricted to the seventeen first-class counties, was played over 65 overs. (In *Wisden* it is referred to almost coyly as 'The Knock-out Competition'.) The first tie was played on

1 May at Old Trafford, where Lancashire beat Leicestershire by 101 runs.

Worcester's début came three weeks later, at New Road, against Surrey. The home side began badly before Graveney and Headley added 145 in two hours. The eventual total was 229–9. In reply Surrey, having been 82 without loss, were 115 all out. The hero was Standen, medium-pacer and sometime goalkeeper for Arsenal and West Ham, for whom he won an FA Cup-Winner's medal. (Not surprisingly Standen was an outstanding catcher.) Graveney left New Road that night convinced of one thing: the 'bits and pieces' player, like Standen, capable of accurate bowling and sudden runs would be invaluable in this form of cricket (at what cost, no one had then calculated). A crowd of 9,000, twice that for the final day of the 1962 season, saw the dawn of an era.

Worcester, meanwhile, went until mid-July without a win in the Championship. Graveney's scores (49, 8, 21, 29, 24, 42, 4) are those of a man batting simply because there was no legal way to avoid it. When the first Test team was announced against West Indies, Close (whose England career is more fitful than Graveney's) was included; at various times Sharpe, Stewart, Bolus, even Peter Richardson played. Not Graveney. He watched from the sidelines a series, won by the visitors three-one, in which the sole draw, at Lord's, was among the most dramatic in Test history. This was the year in which Worrell, each time the England side was announced, asked, 'Is Tom playing?' and, on hearing no, was seen by Sobers to smile – but ruefully.

The first Test had been lost when, on 12 June, Worcester beat Glamorgan in the Gillette Cup at Neath. Graveney scored 93. In deference to the occasion Kenyon decided beforehand that, regardless of conditions, he would bat if given the choice. (His logic was that Worcester were a better side scoring under pressure than chasing runs.) Even this grasp of the basics of one-day cricket baffled certain bowlers who saw only a pitch of enticing Welsh greenness. The tactic worked: Worcester made 238–8, Glamorgan 192. Graveney was Man of the Match.

Two weeks later England drew with West Indies at Lord's, though 'draw' barely conveys the drama of a match wherein any one of four results was possible as the last ball was bowled. In his autobiography Dexter, reviewing the England team, refers to the middle order (himself, Barrington and Cowdrey) as 'hardy stalwarts'; to Close as 'not having the best technique . . . but knowing how to defend wicket and body against fast bowling'. In the event Dexter, Cowdrey and Close failed once; the openers, Stewart and Edrich, twice. Next day the *Telegraph* published a letter deploring the long gap between the West Indies' tours (1950, 1957, 1963; the next not scheduled until 1971) and MCC promptly offered an invitation for 1966. Graveney noted the date.

The Gillette Cup resumed on 10 July. In ashen light and teeming rain Flavell took six Lancashire wickets for fourteen. Worcester were left a target of 60 and achieved it easily enough; suddenly, to their own surprise, they were finalists. Not for the first time, the focus of the team's attention altered and Graveney admits that 'from then, we were hardly functioning in the Championship.' Worcester, with the zeal of converts, invested heavily in the new competition and the final at Lord's was over-subscribed. The reverse was true of their remaining county matches, whose apogee was the visit of Derby in mid-July. Graveney scored 100 of a total of 210, the second fifty in an hour; Worcester registered their first win of the season. A fortnight later they hosted the champions, Yorkshire, in Flavell's benefit match. Graveney scored 89, 70 in boundaries, described by *Wisden* as exhilarating and by Kenyon as one of the two best innings by a Worcester player that season. (The other was also Graveney's.)

August saw Worcester in mid-table. Resigned to failure in the Championship (Kenyon 'knew it was over' when Coldwell broke down after six matches and his deputy, Carter, never came to terms with the front-foot rule), Graveney settled into life with his adopted county. He was an orderly man. For a quarter-century he followed an essentially unchanged routine, timed to:

> . . . arrive at the ground by 9.30 for at least fifteen minutes' serious batting in the nets . . . I always believed there was only one way to use nets, and that was for batsman and bowler to put in as much effort as if they were in the middle . . . I sometimes looked askance at the casualness of England players in that respect.

On away matches Graveney '. . . went for an early breakfast and a gentle loosener, usually a stroll around town . . . The modern fetish for exercises and gymnastics terrified me. Playing cricket was the only exercise I needed.'

If this has the ring of the banal, of a cricketer almost morbidly devoted to his cricket, then it is salutary to note that Murray, on tour with England in 1962–63, describes Graveney as having been 'the last to bed every night . . . and the first to be up next morning'. Statham, too, confirms that 'Tom could hold his own socially . . . no matter how late the party, he was always first in to breakfast.' (Statham was last.) A Worcester colleague, with more than a trace of envy, recalls that no amount of drink seemed to affect him. D'Oliveira's abiding memory is of Graveney 'not losing control' at a players' party at which D'Oliveira himself lost consciousness. If little about Graveney, including his batting, was extrovert, it is the extroverts who most admire him.

On 14 August Worcester played Gloucester, captained by Ken Graveney, at Cheltenham. The two brothers drove to the ground together, posed for pictures, changed in separate rooms. It was a turning wicket and the home side made 104. In reply Worcester scored 217, Graveney 58, before rain intervened on the third day. The festival crowd welcomed Graveney 'reasonably', no more, when he appeared to bat. Of his former fans none remained but a few observers. There was ironic applause when he was caught.

A week later Graveney scored 62 against Somerset, following that 66 versus Middlesex. In late season he was running into form. Hopes revived for the first Gillette Cup Final at Lord's on 7 September. The atmosphere that day was charged, the fans in a riot of expectation. For the first time hooters and drums attended the fall of each wicket.

Dexter won the toss and Sussex batted. Their innings was built on a foundation by Langridge and Oakman, supported by Parks's 57. The captain considered the final 168 'relatively poor' and feared the worst from the Worcester top order – Kenyon, Horton, Headley, Graveney, Richardson. At 103–4 it looked all over. Then Dexter, in his own words, 'threw the ball in desperation' to Oakman; the man who seven years earlier had taken Graveney's place on tour in South Africa. He proceeded to bowl thirteen overs for seventeen, including a vital wicket – Graveney's. The momentum of the batting side halted and they lost their last six wickets for 51. In Dexter's words: 'The match showed me once and for all the advantage of batting first in such a competition: if you get a big score on the board you are invincible; if you get a medium or even a small one, the other side will always adjust their scoring rate to yours – and you have a good chance of putting on the pressure and getting them out.'

The interesting thing about the above is that it was rare, in 1963, for a captain to have given much thought to the demands of one-day cricket (Cowdrey admits that, for a season, it baffled him); it says much for Dexter, whose temperament may have suited it more than most. Swanton agrees that Dexter's captaincy was 'imaginative'; Graveney that he 'handled the bowling cleverly, maintained the pressure and set a field that kept us under control . . . On the day, Ted deserved to win.' On the balcony the MCC president, Lord Nugent, presented the Cup and medals; Frank Woolley beamed; 'young Norman Gifford' (4–33) was Man of the Match. He won £50.

Few who played in the Gillette Cup had débuted as early as 1948. Graveney, in his thirty-seventh year, admits to difficulty in adapting. He still had moments: but they were moments. Had he retired that September, his reputation might have been that of an Amiss or Fletcher; he had played 55 Tests over twelve years without ever imposing as an England batsman. That season the averages were led by players, like Edrich and Boycott, who had been schoolboys in Graveney's pomp. In October he considered his prospects; there was talk of one more year at Worcester; of 'the certainty' that his Test career was over.

In November Alf Gover took a Commonwealth side, captained by Peter Richardson, to Pakistan. The tour was notable for two facts: in Gover's words, it 'restored Tom's confidence'; in Graveney's, it brought a great cricketer to Worcester: D'Oliveira. After four years qualifying for Middleton in the Lancashire League, D'Oliveira was anxious to advance. At dinner at the Metropole Hotel, Karachi, he asked Graveney for a 'frank assessment' of his chances.

'Chances? You're about the best bloody player here.'

The upshot was that, in early 1964, Graveney, after consulting Kenyon, arranged an interview for D'Oliveira with Sir George Dowty. The two agreed terms after the Club had volunteered to find D'Oliveira a house (he lives there today). The negotiations were conducted in the knowledge that Worcester urgently needed both a batsman and seam bowler, and that another county had solicited D'Oliveira's services: Gloucestershire.

On tour Graveney scored 500 runs. Griffith remembers the wickets in Pakistan as being like mud, which they frequently were. For the Commonwealth Kanhai, Ibadulla and Nurse scored freely; in two unofficial Tests Graveney made 164, 107, 97, 55. He returned home, says Gover, 'the hero of the tour', confirming his manager's view of him as the equal of the best post-war English batsmen (Hutton, Compton, May). He reached Cheltenham on 14 December. On the 21st Jack Hobbs, who had delighted in Graveney's batting, died; a memorial service filled Southwark Cathedral. Graveney spent Christmas with his wife and children. He spoke to Kenyon about D'Oliveira and his own hopes for the season. Kenyon's reply 'We're all behind you,' must have revived his ambitions. The man who toured Jamaica in January 1964 was, says his county captain, 'frighteningly good'. Compton himself showed touches of the old magic and in a week he, Dexter and Graveney made centuries. The last's 108 against Jamaica was the innings of the tour. Graveney returned in February a changed man. He had survived and even prospered from his crisis. If September had seen him depressed at a time when, dropped by England, he had his leanest season with the bat, by April he was determined to prolong his career by another year, if not two. Bets began to accumulate on his reaching a hundred first-class centuries.

A foretaste of Worcester's season came in the nets. Graveney had taken guard, touched his cap, smiled and was half-way through his backlift when a ball from Coldwell burnt past his nose. The next knocked out his off stump. Later Graveney asked the bowler if anything was wrong. 'Wrong?' said Coldwell. 'What could be wrong?' That season he and Flavell took 205 first-class wickets.

Worcester went out of the Gillette Cup on 25 April, beaten by Glamorgan, before the season had begun. After a dressing-room inquest, it was Kenyon who crystallised the team's ambitions: win the Championship. Dowty, at his shoulder, nodded. 'We're behind you, good, bad or indifferent,' he said. 'We'd prefer the former.'

Worcester won seven of their first nine matches; the remainder were ruined by rain. Against Leicester Graveney scored 78 (four sixes and seven fours); against Yorkshire 68; Kent, 63. At the end of May the county had 52 points from six matches, the same as Warwickshire with whom they were level at the head of the table.

On 30 May Sussex appeared at New Road. For forty minutes Coldwell and the rejuvenated Flavell bowled electrically at Dexter; when the first Test side was announced next day, both were included. (Dexter later admitted that Flavell's selection, at the age of thirty-five, was optimistic.) The batting places went to Barrington, Boycott, Dexter, Sharpe and – incredibly – Titmus, who opened in Edrich's absence.

Compton:

> The only challenger was Graveney, a player of proved class who was having a wonderful summer . . . It is hard for me or anyone to preach aggression to modern players when they can say: 'Tom Graveney plays strokes better than anybody, and he can't get in.' Sometimes I despair of the way the people running our game scream themselves hoarse for something they call brighter cricket and then ignore the people who provide it.

Rex Alston:

> Anyone who has seen Graveney gracing our cricket grounds this summer must wonder why the selectors continually ignore him . . . Our opponents are always delighted when he isn't there and spectators are deprived of the pleasure of watching him in action.

It is salutary to note that Graveney in 1964 thought it 'certain' his Test career was over. In a book published the following year he wrote, 'I doubt if I shall tour for England again.' The belief was based on the fact that he had been tried – and tried – and found wanting; the tour of 1962–63 provided the last straw. There is evidence that, to this day, the selectors prefer the yeoman to the man who fails in three innings and flourishes in the fourth, particularly if the failure can be attributed to the player's own shortcomings. (David Gower confirms it.) Only mediocrity is always at its best. While Graveney appreciated the support of Compton and others, it did nothing to alter his belief that, in 1964, his energies might best be concentrated on Worcester; and concentrate he did.

While England drew the first Test, Graveney scored 60 to help beat Derby at Chesterfield. The winning target was 174 in even time; Graveney's innings, in watery light, altered the complexion of the match. Worcester won by one wicket. When, in mid-June,

Warwickshire arrived at New Road there were 13,000 present on the first morning – more than at any match since the visit of Bradman's Australians in 1948. The fixture ended in a draw after Kenyon, affected by the tension of the occasion, had delayed his declaration. (During the match Graveney, in eerie portent of an event five years later, played in a Benefit game at Leamington on the rest day. He was hit by a throw-in and cracked a bone in his hand. Only Bill Powell, the Worcester masseur, was ever told.) Two weeks later, against Oxford, D'Oliveira played his third match for Worcester. He scored 101.

By now the Championship had developed into a duopoly. The return match with Warwickshire was played in mid-July in the knowledge that one or other would emerge with a lead. The Birmingham wicket was, in *Wisden*'s word, 'uncertain'; on the first day the totals were 119 and 72. On the second Graveney played 'the most disciplined knock of the season' (Kenyon): 95 in five hours. If ever there was an argument against his being wayward, this was it. 'Tom was the most difficult to bowl to,' says Cartwright, who should know. The result was that Warwickshire were left needing 306 in five hours. They failed by 220 and Worcester took a nine-point lead at the head of the table.

Lest confidence overcome them, the county promptly lost three of their next four matches. Graveney's scores – 51, 19, 37 – were solid, not spectacular. That came against Yorkshire at Scarborough where, on 22 July, Graveney scored 122. (Powell had recently told him not to exert himself.) Ten days later he added a century against Leicester, his ninety-ninth in first-class cricket.

Only fourteen players had preceded him. It says much for Graveney, a batsman sometimes thought frail or fitful, that he should enter the society of Grace, of Bradman, Hutton, Hobbs and Sutcliffe; one celebrating not fleeting genius but sustained effort over a decade or more; one excluding, moreover, May, Harvey, Washbrook, Sobers, Gavaskar. On the morning of 5 August Graveney stood on the threshold of batting's highest order. His emotions at the time are those of the professional, the common man, of Old Tom, a player in his thirties:

> The day was warm and, on a turning wicket, Northampton bowled their two left-handers, Steele and Scott . . . I kept my head down and

> remember creeping on to 99 . . . I had to face Larter for a full over. The first five balls were very fast and straight. The sixth was a head-high bouncer which I managed to hook down in front of square for a single . . . There was cheering and Larter led the players who congratulated me . . . It was a sweet feeling, because I'd wondered whether I would ever score a century again.

Characteristically, Gifford recalls congratulating Graveney at the interval, only be told, 'Now let's win.' The next morning's papers were effusive, even if Graveney's reputation preceded him.

> It is only a pity that someone of such infinite gifts should not have given more to England . . . He expresses as well as anyone the beauty in batting. (*The Times*)

> Few have been as exquisite in their range of strokes . . . Yet there is a suspicion, even now, that he could have done more. (The *News*)

The *Cricketer*, on the other hand, felt that 'Never in his career [had] Graveney been more reliable when reliability was needed.' As if to prove which, he scored a century in the next match against Essex. If, as has been said, Graveney approached every innings the same way, then the knowledge that his side depended on him, that they associated him with success and other values, seems not to have hurt. Compton's view that 'England never appreciated Tom until it was too late,' is echoed by Bailey: 'He succeeded at Worcester because he was recognised as a great batsman.' Graveney's own belief that 'The more I played cricket, the more I realised the value of confidence,' found expression in a glorious six-week period from July to September: he hit five centuries, a thousand runs and, according to Kenyon, was 'the best batsman – bar none – in the country'. England, meanwhile, lost to Australia.

Graveney returned to Cheltenham in mid-August. Again his reception was ambiguous: resentment tinged with envy. Gloucester were set a target of 282. With thirty-five minutes left Ken Graveney, number eleven, came to the crease. He defended for ten overs, fenced in the eleventh. Gloucester lost by 107; that season they were seventeenth in the Championship.

A week later the sides met at Worcester. In balmy weather, before capacity crowds, the home side scored 398. Kenyon and Headley made centuries, Graveney 57; the crowd stood to him. He was a stylist as Kenyon and Headley were not. Like all stylists he could force bowlers to adapt to him. Allen remembers Graveney hitting him inside out, against the spin – for four. After rain fell overnight the visitors were 28–4, 86–7; thanks to Mortimore, 192 all out. They followed on. Gloucester's second innings proceeded in similar key. Ken Graveney came to the wicket at 179–9. Again he endured; the close fielders, including his brother, crouched and coiled for thirty minutes. At last, at 3.10 p.m. on Tuesday 25 August, Gifford turned a ball past the edge, past Graveney, and Booth completed the stumping. Worcester had won by an innings. As in 1962 the team awaited news of their rivals, though the delay was shorter and the result more agreeable. Two hours later it was confirmed that Warwickshire had lost. Worcester, for the first time in their history, were champions.

In a life not untouched by irony, it was the most ironic of Graveney's achievements to succeed at the expense of Gloucester. If, that night, he nursed feelings against Young, Brown, Allen, then none were apparent. The last remembers Graveney as 'unassuming' in victory and taking no pleasure in its manner. Others confirm that he was 'contained' at the celebration. There were two further victories in the next fortnight and in them Graveney scored 164, 70 and 50. He finished the season with an average of 54. Of Worcester's twenty-eight Championship matches, eighteen were won, only three lost; their margin of 41 points was greater than had seemed possible.

Only then did Graveney's mood change. For years critics had told him of his faults while he stood, believing and resenting all. They seemed to believe he had it in him to be a different player, while the key lay in external factors. For a decade he was misused, at least misunderstood, a luxury discarded when times were hard. Had Allen, Hutton and May realised it, he had it in him to be the most consistent batsman in England – had he been consistently encouraged. Kenyon's first words to Graveney on his joining Worcester were to 'play naturally'; he promptly hit over 2,200 runs. If some react to praise, others to passion, it is possible that Kenyon was the first to establish the balance. 'Tom', as he says, 'was unique.'

WORCESTERSHIRE V. GLOUCESTERSHIRE

Played at New Road, Worcester on 22, 24 and 25 August 1964

WORCESTERSHIRE WON BY AN INNINGS AND 2 RUNS

WORCESTERSHIRE	FIRST INNINGS	
*D. Kenyon	b Mortimore	114
M. J. Horton	c Meyer b Windows	96
R.G.A. Headley	not out	103
T. W. Graveney	c Windows b Mortimore	57
D.W. Richardson	not out	18
J.A. Ormrod		
†R. Booth		
N. Gifford		
B.M. Brain		
L.J. Coldwell		
J.A. Flavell		
Extras	b 6, lb 3, nb 1	10
Total	(for 3 wkts dec)	398

Fall: 1–187, 2–223, 3–349

BOWLING	O	M	R	W
A.S. Brown	29	3	121	0
Windows	15	2	58	1
Mortimore	39	10	89	2
Graveney	12	2	29	0
Allen	24	5	91	0

GLOUCESTERSHIRE	FIRST INNINGS		SECOND INNINGS	
R.B. Nicholls	c Ormrod b Coldwell	7	lbw b Flavell	22
†B.J. Meyer	c Headley b Brain	25	(10) c Booth b Flavell	5
D.M. Young	c Kenyon b Flavell	2	(2) c Booth b Gifford	10
D. Brown	c Headley b Flavell	0	(3) b Brain	0
J.M. Bevan	lbw b Flavell	0	(9) not out	8
A.S. Brown	c Horton b Gifford	21	(5) c Booth b Flavell	18
D.A. Allen	c Graveney b Gifford	22	lbw b Gifford	68
R.C. White	b Gifford	12	run out	21
J.B. Mortimore	c Graveney b Flavell	47	(6) b Gifford	9
A.R. Windows	b Brain	28	(4) c Richardson b Brain	1
*J.K. Graveney	not out	19	st Booth b Gifford	19
Extras	b 3, lb 5, nb 1	9	b 13, lb 7, nb 3	23
Total		192		204

1st inns: 1–22, 2–28, 3–28, 4–28, 5–50, 6–64, 7–86, 8–95, 9–148
2nd inns: 1–22, 2–23, 3–31, 4–56, 5–71, 6–77, 7–171, 8–172, 9–179

BOWLING	O	M	R	W	O	M	R	W
Flavell	20.3	5	44	4	26	3	69	3
Coldwell	20	11	14	1	6	4	9	0
Brain	17	4	52	2	12	0	32	2
Gifford	24	8	61	3	32.2	15	50	4
Horton	7	4	12	0	10	2	21	0

Umpires: W.E. Phillipson and F. Jakeman
*Captain; †Wicket-keeper

The feeling was mutual. In its review of the season *Wisden* noted that 'Graveney was quick to voice the opinion that Kenyon played a leading part by his quiet efficiency'; the *Cricketer* praised him 'as much for his steadying influence as his strategic insight'. The same article added that 'Graveney's batsmanship turned many matches'; that the pennant would 'fly . . . in one of cricket's most attractive settings, before some of the game's most devoted followers'; and that the side would be strengthened in 1965 by 'D'Oliveira, the coloured South African'.

In 1964 D'Oliveira scored 825 runs and took 71 wickets for the Seconds. (That year the reserves were runners-up in their own championship. Among those with whom D'Oliveira played were Knott, Amiss and the England footballer Geoff Hurst, appearing for Essex.) The prospects were certainly encouraging. Membership increased; in Kenyon Worcestershire had arguably the most able captain in the country; Graveney himself, said the *Mail*, 'can seldom have been more masterful in his long career'. That winter the county went on a world tour and, after starting quietly, Graveney played a cameo of 136 against Rhodesia. After that he opened up; his next eight innings were 104, 161, 92, 58, 44, 116, 132, 85; he returned with an average of 86. The tour, said *Wisden*, gained much prestige, not least for Graveney, for whom the arid pitches of Salisbury and Singapore might have been made.

> It was a dream to play on a fast wicket . . . The difference was marvellous because I learned most of my cricket at Bristol, where they used to hold an inquest if the ball ever got as high as the bails . . . The result was that I was constantly in trouble when I played on pitches where the ball flew. If somebody bowled a bouncer at me I used to have a fit – not through fear but because I simply didn't know how to handle it.
>
> Batting at New Road strengthened my play . . . I was never a hooker, but I could cope with the bouncer. The first years at Worcester, and the overseas tours, made me a better player.

In conclusion:

> For three years or so, from 1962, I had a feeling at the back of my mind that I was the best batsman in England.

In April Graveney returned to Cheltenham; opened a sports shop in Redditch; noted the averages of Barrington, Barber, Boycott on tour in South Africa. In early spring his second book, *Tom Graveney On Cricket*, was published. In it he addressed the Gloucester Affair ('In the five months this tawdry saga dragged on the executive made no effort to suggest a formula which would have eased my position and enabled me to carry on'); Dexter ('His grasp of tactics was bad . . . a man who made up his mind and stuck to it'); and his own prospects ('I feel I have a few more years'). His immediate ambition was not a return to Test cricket ('unlikely'), but the retention of the Championship. It was Worcester's centenary.

A month later Graveney must have wished he could recall the book from the printer. His forecast for 1965 ('The committee's only problem will be to leave out deserving players') found expression in only one win, over Lancashire, being recorded in May. Kenyon, co-opted as a Test selector, missed a number of matches and Graveney, promoted over Horton, led the side in his absence. Again the old favourite: was Graveney, as Wellings suggested, 'more ideally equipped to be first mate than captain'? Was 'Old Tom' too austere or too amiable? (Both were suggested.) Was Graveney, a strong character, insensitive to the needs of the weak?

Perhaps; to know Graveney is to know consent. His speech is shot with affirmatives: Right, Of course, Don't worry. At times his face, grooved with veins and scowling, reverts to Old Tom, the county pro; the suspicion of impending doom confirmed three, four, a dozen times in his career. Graveney (like Hammond) could be testy. He could be touchy. As noted, he functioned better in a winning team than a losing one. A colleague calls his captaincy of Worcester after 1968 'patchy', with a bias towards demonstration, not explanation. ('I can do it; why can't you so-and-sos?') Others, including D'Oliveira, maintain that Graveney 'led from the front'. His success was leadership. Leadership was not his success.

Against touring New Zealand Graveney scored 84; next match 104 v. Essex (D'Oliveira 106). Despite the form of these two, and Flavell, nothing went right for Worcester. 10,000 saw them lose to Sussex in the Gillette Cup. At the end of May they were fourteenth in the Championship, despite a crushing win (Graveney captaining) over Lancashire.

Things deteriorated. On 4 June Worcester lost to Kent after 'two indifferent batting performances . . . on a fast but by no means hostile pitch' (*Wisden*). Meanwhile the first Test team was announced: M.J.K. Smith (captain), Cowdrey, Barber, Barrington; England won the series three-nil. For the third summer running Graveney listened to the BBC announcement and, for the third summer running, declined to hold his breath thereafter. 'Once dropped,' he says, 'your fate hinges on others' – for instance Barrington, who scored 137 at Birmingham, 163 at Leeds. Smith, ironically, was known to be a fan; Kenyon, too, may have pressed the claims of his county colleague. But once the momentum of the side was established, it would have taken a crisis – or the need to experiment before the winter tour of Australia – to reverse it. Graveney, it was agreed, had made his last tour of Australia.

On 10 June Worcester played a one-day match with MCC to celebrate the county's centenary. (The actual foundation was 11 March 1865.) Graveney scored 44 and, according to Compton (who, appearing for MCC, aged forty-seven, made 75), 'batted beautifully' on a fast pitch. Next week Worcester beat Compton's former county in a match played in convulsive winds. Graveney batted with the detached swagger of a man in his garden. At month's end the county drew with Gloucester, captained by Mortimore, and Graveney, desperate for a century, made three. As July began they were twelfth in the Championship.

On 2 July Hammond died. In an essay published two years later, Kilburn wrote:

> There was no conceit in him, no boastfulness. He could not escape awareness of his own superiority but he never emphasised it by comparison. He accepted his talent for what it was and the talents of other cricketers for what they were. Circumstances and his nature induced him to look after his own interests and he assumed the same capacity in others. In captaincy, in play, he conceded individual rights of self-expression, maintaining that cricketers selected to play should be good enough to know how to play and to discern the policy required by situations.
>
> Hammond was not a selfish or a thoughtless cricketer. He was a self-centred cricketer because his talent made him so and the course of his career compelled him to isolation . . . His stature was simply not comparable with that of his companions and they, with public opinion, looked up with awe rather than understanding.

Again the echo. Graveney led the side against Glamorgan in the second week of July. In a low-scoring match Worcester needed 143 to win. Graveney went out to bat, according to a colleague, 'amazed at the failure all around him . . . His expression said, "If you can't, I will."' He made 79. Worcester won by six wickets and promptly drew against Middlesex, Warwickshire, Northants. On 24 July the county were ninth in the table, the season apparently over. Graveney admits: 'Like the rest, I was resigned to losing the Championship . . . There are years when, for reasons other than talent, things don't go right. This was one of them.'

That day Graveney scored 66 and D'Oliveira 107 in a run-a-minute stand against Kent. 'He [D'Oliveira] gave you an hour, then all hell broke loose,' says Underwood. The two batted in sharp relief: to the end of his days Graveney employed a high backlift and the full swinging drive that was his trademark. D'Oliveira, who learnt his cricket on the gravel hills of Cape Town, raised his bat like a golfer in mid-putt; the power was in his forearms. Unlike Graveney, he loved to hook: '[As a boy] I was bowled at by a lad standing on the stairs of one of the tenement blocks which led into the street. He stood at the top and aimed to bounce the ball off the bottom step . . . When he did this, the ball would scream at me in a rising trajectory.'

The result was a thirty-three-year-old who batted and bowled as if compensating for lost time; Graveney agrees that 'Basil, in his first year, was outstanding.' Amidst press agitation that D'Oliveira play for England he recalls 'some good advice from Tom about keeping my head down'. He did, scoring over 1,500 runs, cuffing the ball while Graveney collared it. Once, when D'Oliveira was batting, there were three men at the sightscreen to stop him. He straight drove, piercing them, to reach his fifty.

Worcester beat Kent by nine wickets; Sussex, in the next match, by eight. On the last morning, in pale, lemon light, Graveney scored an unbeaten 63. The county were sixth in the Championship and it was at this stage, early August, that hopes revived. Derbyshire were beaten by an innings at Chesterfield and in the next match Graveney ' . . . piloted his side through testing conditions . . . while scoring 80 and for this was applauded all the way back to the pavilion, not only by the spectators but by the Hampshire players' (*Wisden*). In the last innings Hampshire, chasing 157, slumped to 62–8, but dropped catches allowed them a draw. D'Oliveira remembers

Graveney being particularly keen on practice next morning. Suddenly he had cause to be.

They were the two most prolific batsmen in England. Next match Graveney scored 126, D'Oliveira 103 not out. Flavell and Coldwell then bowled unchanged as Leicester were dismissed for 52 in sixteen overs; another innings victory. On 11 August Graveney drove – he could have walked – to Cheltenham, where, in Mortimore's Benefit match, he made 47 and 59. (In the nine years after he left, Graveney never scored a century against Gloucester. He tried.) D'Oliveira took 4–52, scored 81 and 55; the visitors won by seven wickets. More significantly, Northampton were beaten at Worcester, where Slade returned figures of 14.4–7–16–5 in the second innings. The *Mail* again compared Graveney to 'the great Hammond', while at Nottingham a twenty-one-year-old South African scored 125 against England in an innings 'which in point of style and power, of ease and beauty of execution [was] fit to rank with anything in the annals of the game' (Swanton), prompting comparison with another incomparable, Woolley: Graeme Pollock.

Worcester's last home match was against Surrey. The outcome was settled on the first morning when Coldwell, thirty-two, returned the best figures of his career: 8–38, two catches dropped. In reply Headley made 86, D'Oliveira 69, Graveney 35; Worcester won by an innings. Northampton led the table by sixteen points. Worcester, two matches in hand, needed to win both to pass them.

The first was at Bournemouth. In the first innings Graveney scored 104; Ingleby-Mackenzie, the Hampshire captain, declared it miraculous. Kenyon declared at 363–9. The clouds lowered. Next day there were three hours play; Hampshire batted until the last morning, when, the follow-on averted, they declared. Ingleby-Mackenzie then opened the bowling; after one ball Kenyon, too, declared. (At the time it was forbidden to forfeit an innings.) The eventual target was 147 in 160 minutes. As soon as the openers took guard, shafts of drying sunlight broke through the cloud. Steam was seen rising from the pitch. The close-catching was electric. No Hampshire batsman reached double figures, and in sixty-five minutes they were all out for 31. Coldwell and Flavell took five wickets apiece.

Next day, 28 August, the same two dismissed Sussex for 72 at Hove. Worcester were then 33–3, 68–4; Graveney's 49 was a third of the total. In the second innings Pataudi scored 60 and Worcester needed 132 to win the match and Championship. Graveney was convinced that 'with players like Kenyon, Headley, Ormrod, D'Oliveira and myself, we'd walk it'. An hour later all five were in the pavilion. It was two utility players, Booth and Richardson, who endured to 121–6, when Booth was caught. Slade and Richardson scored the last 11 to retain the Championship.

The title was won by four points, with seven minutes of the season remaining. In five weeks Worcester had won ten of their last eleven matches. *Wisden* believed that 'Seldom can a county have won with such devastating conclusion'; Kenyon that 'team spirit saved us'. Both paid tribute to Graveney, who in *Wisden*'s words 'was his immaculate self, giving the batting class as well as stability, [also leading] the side well on the occasions that Kenyon was absent.' For the record Graveney scored 1768 first-class runs, average 49, fourth in the national averages behind Cowdrey, Edrich and Parfitt; D'Oliveira was sixth.

At thirty-eight, Graveney was playing the best cricket of his life. Kenyon, D'Oliveira, Murray, Graveney himself, agree that batting at Worcester made him. This by Brian Johnston:

> From the moment [Graveney] glided out to the wicket, tugging at the protruding peak of his cap, he looked all that a cricketer should be. Immaculately turned out, he had a certain quality which attracted attention. Once at the crease, every movement was of graceful elegance, not just with his attacking strokes but also in defence . . . He was a batsman who compelled you to watch and enjoy the manner of his batting.

Elegance was only half Graveney's genius. D'Oliveira confirms he could be stubborn (a quality noted in Graveney personally), and in 1965 he rescued Worcester more than once by the grit, not glamour of his play. He was a reliable catcher, tireless practiser and, says D'Oliveira, 'bought his round' at the close of play. He could be moody, but once the momentum of the side was established, magnificent. 'Quite simply,' says Kenyon, 'he was the best.' That autumn Kenyon helped select the England touring party to Australia, Graveney not among it.

Few would have blamed him his moment of introspection. All the gifted, the highly talented, see themselves put on for ever by mediocrities, bled dry by the media. Graveney was an exception. He liked the press and, with few exceptions, the press liked him. There was unusual interest in the tour of Australia, in which there were similarities to Dexter's three years earlier. Whereas Dexter (and, for that matter, May) had been criticised for being joined by his wife, Smith was seen by Johnston 'coming down the steps of an aircraft to meet the waiting press, carrying a baby, sometimes two, in his arms'. Smith was an adequate batsman who finished the tour with an average of 17. As a captain he was considered negative and it was announced on tour that the manager, Billy Griffith, would be responsible for overall tactics. The result was a drawn series in which England, according to Swanton, 'more often than not held the initiative' while lacking the ability to bowl Australia out. While there was satisfaction that Barrington, Titmus, Cowdrey, Parks, Edrich, Boycott and Barber all averaged over 40, the team, says Ian Wooldridge, 'would in no way have been weakened' by the presence of Graveney.

On balance the selectors improved Graveney's chances. They discredited themselves. That winter Worcester toured the West Indies. Graveney, whose last appearance in the Caribbean had included a century against Jamaica, withdrew at the last moment when his wife developed jaundice. In wintry Cheltenham he was visited by the critic John Thicknesse, who wrote an article aptly titled 'Out In The Cold'. Graveney was said to be 'pessimistic' about his chances of playing for England, though, as Thicknesse noted, 'He must have a chance . . . A couple of months ago he made Kenyon a partner in his sports shop.' Other journalists began – some had never ceased – to speculate on his chances of making a comeback. Johnston remembers 'terrific support' for Graveney among those covering the winter tour. The visitors in 1966 were the West Indies, against whom in 1957 he averaged 118.

Critics found him polite but restrained. Certain visitors left bemused. Graveney's eyes, unlike theirs, never widened; his deeper opinions never reached them. When journalists flattered him Graveney shrugged and thanked them. He had no illusions. If he had 'not been good enough' in 1964, when he had scored more runs than any other batsman, why should he now? It was three years since he had played for England, during which a generation – Boycott, Edrich, Barber – had grown up. Three tours had been undertaken and none lost. That Christmas Graveney received a gift, one of the first Polyarmoured bats. He hoped to 'score some' with it, for his county.

Worcester was among the first stops for the West Indian tourists. Graveney scored 41, and, according to Sobers (who caught him), 'still had it'. May was dank and dripping; Graveney's scores – 30, 11, 26 – were respectable, no more. Against Sussex he made 77; ten others totalled 74. After the long winter he was playing by rote, improvising until his form returned. Nottingham, the weakest side in England, appeared at New Road in the Gillette Cup. They lost narrowly, by 19 runs. There was a feeling that the wave had broken; that certain players (Kenyon was forty-two, Flavell thirty-seven, Graveney himself rising thirty-nine) were drowning, not waving. Batsmen were not helped by the rule limiting each side's first innings to 65 overs in the opening matches. Of all the steps taken to promote 'brighter cricket' this was probably the most mistaken – no small accolade.

Meanwhile the West Indies fast bowler, Griffith, was no-balled nine times against Lancashire – the last for throwing. (When Barrington met the tourists at a party that May he refused to shake hands with Griffith. Eighteen months earlier he had refused to play against him.) Graveney's view: 'While I sympathised, I thought it a tactical mistake as it had the effect of drawing attention to [Barrington's] aversion to the bumper,' is tempered by the 'certainty' that Griffith, on occasion, threw. 'Top batsmen pick up the line and to some extent the pace from the bowler's arm as it rotates from three to twelve o'clock, the moment the ball is released . . . Griffith's action often made that impossible. Added to which he was accurate.' Having said which, Graveney endeared himself to the establishment by writing: 'I thought it prudent to maintain a discreet silence, though I never had any doubt that the blame should be laid squarely at the door of the authorities . . . The various Boards were pitifully weak in passing the buck on to the umpires, some of whom argued, in turn, that bowlers would not have been chosen in the first place if they were throwers.'

The morning after the Gillette Cup, 22 May, it was learnt that Tom Goddard had died. In 1939 Goddard took seventeen wickets in a day; nearly a decade later, aged forty-seven, 238 in a season. 'A ripe character, full of chaff . . . what one might call a genial grumbler,' wrote Swanton; a central influence on Graveney's life. The Australians' destruction of Goddard in 1948 was the saddest sight of his career.

Graveney continued in mid-form: 16, 33, 36. On 1 June Worcester travelled to Northampton. Graveney, leading the side, scored an unblemished 82 and earnt praise for his captaincy. The visitors won by 180 runs. Meanwhile, at Old Trafford, England lost the first Test by an innings. Mike Smith, whose sole error had been to lose the toss, was sacked; even Cowdrey, who replaced him, thought this tough. (Twenty-five years later, one of the selectors responsible admitted that Smith's 'blindness' to the bouncer hadn't helped. There was genuine concern that the captain had come close to being hit.) There was a call for further changes and Cowdrey admits that 'something radical' was needed. The press directed his attention to Graveney.

Graveney was in his worst form since 1963. Early June saw him weak and wavering. He participated in a Worcester total of 87 against Warwickshire. On 8, 9, 10 June the press continued its campaign for his recall. Next day he went out to bat against Middlesex: 'It was the first time I used a Polyarmoured bat. The ball went off it like a rocket . . . Suddenly everything clicked . . . I got eighty-odd [88] and, for the first time, felt that I had a chance of being named.'

The selectors that season were Insole, Bedser, May and Kenyon. All had played with or against Graveney. Insole, the chairman, had made way for his return in 1957; May seen him score 258 as a result; Bedser and Graveney had appeared in thirteen Tests together, including the 1954–55 tour of Australia (the bowler's last); Kenyon needed no persuasion of his talents. Cowdrey himself wrote: 'While Graveney was a very fine strokeplayer as a Gloucester man, he became a much more complete player with Worcestershire . . . [I could not] help feeling a mistake was made when he slipped out of the side.'

On 12 June Graveney was selected.

There was no hint, no aside. The news informed him that he was in, just as it had that he was out. He was quoted as being 'surprised', 'pleased', even 'flattered', photographed with his son, Tim. In the four days before the Test there was a conscious effort to motivate and involve; Insole and May assured him he was 'the best' (according to Bailey, 'nearly everyone in the game, other than the selectors' knew this already); Kenyon expressed delight, Cowdrey congratulations. Graveney received a hundred letters. He replied to each, though few revealed his real emotions:

> It was a hell of a risk.
>
> The selectors had got themselves in a mess, and in a way, I was forced on them . . . I'm certain that, when I came back from Australia in 1963, they were determined never to pick me again. There were times, in 1964 and '65, when I was batting better than at any other stage. They ignored me.
>
> I never expected to play for England again. It seemed there was nothing left I could do – except, as it turned out, wait for other people's failures.

In an article entitled 'My Seven Year Stretch' (1962), Gubby Allen wrote obscurely: 'I have often been asked whether selection committees are sometimes guided by intuition. I think the answer is that an occasional choice looks strange because all the facts have not been known or the motive behind it has not been fully understood.'

He refrained from specifically mentioning Graveney. In his book *Sins of Omission*, Allen Synge considered 'the psychology of Graveney as a Test match batsman'; in addition to incurring the wrath of Allen and Hutton, the player's cardinal error had been to fail against Australia at a time when, in Cardus's words, 'that was the proper and consistent means of assessing a Test cricketer'. Brian Johnston is blunter: the selectors 'misused' Graveney, failing to appreciate his 'special skill' until it was too late. Compton, Cowdrey, Bailey and Evans agree that 'someone, somewhere' erred. To this day Sobers is convinced Graveney was the 'great stylist' of his generation. When touring sides learnt of his omission they suspected a trick, as if something devious were intended at their expense. Not so; the truth, as Swanton says, is that, 'For years there were dark insinuations about [Graveney's] lack of temperament.' He was considered too offhand, profligate, carefree. Too separate. (Hendren had the same reputation. He scored 57,000 runs in a thirty-year career.) When events forced the selectors to reconsider,

Graveney was in his nineteenth season. Of the current side only Cowdrey (five years his junior) had known Hutton, faced Miller and Lindwall, seen Tyson bowl in Australia.

Nervous as never before, Graveney awaited the start on 16 June. It was his birthday.

7

Fulfilment

Lord's applauded him to the wicket. Graveney touched his cap and took guard; in the far distance Seymour Nurse conferred with Hall. The first ball Graveney faced was a screaming bouncer. He hooked it. The fielders looked at each other and strolled back a pace – several paces. Sobers shrugged.

Graveney's innings proved, says Boycott, that he could still play. 'And how,' adds Sobers. Graveney eventually batted four and a half hours, over two days, for 96; he was caught trying to cut Hall for four. The ground rose and for the first time in his career, Graveney had the feeling that 'Everyone wanted me to succeed . . . That was obvious. Even the West Indies looked disappointed I was out.'

Actually Sobers's face was blank as a mirror. (Ten years earlier, Miller had been 'uncertain whether to laugh or cry' when Compton returned for one Test. He made 94.) Graveney's innings, and Parks's 91, allowed England a lead. Forty minutes before lunch on Monday, the tourists were 95–5, 9 runs ahead. Sobers and Holford, the latter without known form, then dropped anchor. They put on 274, engendering criticism that, yet again, an England captain had misjudged the opposition. In Cowdrey's words

> Upheavals like that traditionally demand a scapegoat and I was the victim . . . Much of the criticism implied that I had not worked hard enough at finding the right tactics . . . The reason that I did not encircle Sobers with close fielders the moment he arrived at the wicket was that I knew him . . . Had a ring of fielders surrounded him he could not conceivably have played [naturally], and the last thing I wanted was for him to steel himself into getting his head down.

Holford himself believes that 'Garry, in the space of an hour, realised we could save it.' Sobers declared at 369–5, leaving England to score 284. Only a century by Milburn saved them.

Milburn was one of four players to début that season. Of the others, Amiss, Underwood and D'Oliveira, the last scored 27 and twice dismissed Nurse at Lord's. 'A natural,' says Graveney. The rest he hardly knew. The format of the team had changed in his absence.

'In the fifties there were only five batsmen. Bailey went in at six, Evans seven. Then the bowlers. The first five had to score or it was all over. By 1966 the pattern was different. There were batsmen all down the line. Basil went in seventh, and he was among the best in England. There was a trend towards the player who could "do a bit".'

What Graveney was witnessing was the dawn of an era, typified by one-day cricket, in which the player 'doing a bit' would dominate; in which even the wicketkeeper would be obliged to score or be replaced. Of those, other than Graveney, who played that year, only Cowdrey and Barrington – and later Boycott, Snow and Underwood – are recognisably 'great' cricketers. There was nothing great about Russell, Allen, Higgs or Jones. In all, twenty-three players represented England that season. No one can disrupt the pattern of a team like the West Indies.

The press hailed Graveney's return. 'He made cruelly clear what Test cricket has missed' (the *Telegraph*). The *News*, too, rued 'what might have been'. His wife's reaction was disbelief ('At *your* age?'). A West Indian spectator asked if there 'weren't a pension scheme' in this country.

Graveney himself: 'Against Sobers's team I saw myself as the number one batsman. Whether I was or not is of no account – it was the way I felt and the thought spurred me. In the 1950s I was the schoolboy among adults and considered myself a nonentity . . . Occasionally I played like one.'

He was no nonentity. In 1966 the minor details of his past were overwhelmed by the present. He was the stalwart, the star – particularly when, before the next Test, Barrington dropped out with nervous exhaustion. Graveney himself played no cricket for a week. At Lord's he injured his thumb and, under other circumstances, might have considered withdrawing. Under other circumstances. In 1956 he had missed arguably the most dramatic Test in history, not to mention the boat to South Africa. A decade later he would have played in plaster cast. On 29 June Graveney arrived at Trent Bridge, where his last Test score, four years earlier, had been 114. Next evening Cowdrey joined him at the crease. They batted out the session in ashen light. In the morning Cowdrey scored 96, Graveney 109. This was the innings that made the comeback. That night Insole, a reserved man, had tears in his eyes. It was that good. Again the press descended and Graveney became in late career what he had never been before: heroic, masterly, even 'determined' (*The Times*). As at Lord's West Indies recovered from a first-innings deficit, setting England a target of 393. They failed to reach it. With the match won, Griffith unleashed a bumper at Underwood, number eleven, singeing his lip. Sobers spoke to batsman, umpire, bowler; Griffith went off. 'Charlie liked to bounce you the last ball of the over,' says Underwood. 'It left you wondering what to do next.'

Graveney's own priority was accepting his status: 'Nottingham marked the end of the first phase of the comeback. With two scores it was clearly going to be permanent. But perhaps the most surprising aspect of it was the reaction of others . . . The size and strength of support doesn't occur to you when you are simply going through the routine of playing . . . It isn't until something happens that you realise how many people are involved through you.'

Vicariously. In the next week Graveney received a hundred letters, then another. He had become a focus of nostalgia, a landmark, appreciated not just for the present but his association with the past. (Graveney knew Hammond; Hammond knew Hobbs, whose début match included Grace.) His comeback had been a romantic as well as real success. The thousands who watched him at Lord's and Trent Bridge marvelled not only at the supreme batsman he was but the huge attainments he brought with him. When Graveney drove, he expressed not merely the stroke but the memory of other matches. It took you back.

The day after Nottingham Graveney was in action against Northants. He scored 48 (caught, for the umpteenth time, by Andrew) and, not surprisingly, looked tired in the field. His totals that season for Worcester are uniform; for once his average, 47, is an accurate reflection of his scores, not the median between them. Against Gloucester, captaining, he made 7; a week later 'playing delightful cricket' (*Wisden*), 109. Graveney reported to

Leeds for the next Test, his fifty-eighth. It was the most unpleasant of his life.

England were 18–2 when Graveney faced his first ball from Griffith. The bowler (whose action was compared, on occasion, to a dart player's) accelerated like a lorry approaching a light. According to those who saw it, the ball was among the most vicious ever bowled. Graveney never saw it. As he straightened he saw umpire Elliott walk from square-leg to his colleague, Buller. One man the mind, the other the muscle. The ground silent. Sobers describes what followed:

> At the end of the over Elliott said to Charlie: 'You can bowl, but any more like that and I'll call you. That ball to Graveney looked funny.'
>
> Griffith was upset. He came to me and said, 'The umpire is being influenced by the England players. I saw Graveney turn to him as if to say, "What about that one?"'
>
> I went to Elliott and asked: 'Was that your decision or the batsman's?' Elliott replied: 'It was mine, and mine alone. I just didn't like the way he bowled to Graveney.'

Despite Sobers's claim that 'Charlie then bowled even faster' most observers, including *Wisden*, agree that the fire was extinguished. Griffith took only one more wicket in the match. Much was later made of Graveney's trying, by expression and deed, to 'influence' the umpire. (About as likely, in Elliott's case, as influencing a High Court judge.) There was a feeling that certain England batsmen (Graveney, Cowdrey, Barrington and Dexter *in absentia*) were anxious to remove Griffith. Basil Butcher believes 'a lot of talk' went on, not least from those who reacted volubly when D'Oliveira was given not out after a disputed catch. According to Graveney the ensuing dialogue was 'brisk'. Sobers and D'Oliveira, two of the game's most genial characters, had to be physically separated. When the latter was out he left in silence.

West Indies won the Test by an innings, Graveney scoring 8 and 19. When at the close of play Cowdrey went into the visitors' dressing-room Griffith refused to acknowledge him. Outside, his car had been vandalised. Cowdrey left the ground on 8 August beaten, bewildered, relieved of the captaincy. In the inquest that followed England (not for the last time) were said to be in crisis, and wholesale changes were demanded. The atmosphere deteriorated and proved contagious. The headlines ('Pitiful', 'Shame', 'England touch bottom') left Insole little choice. Six changes were made for The Oval, with Close – a player whose fitfulness rivals Graveney's –recalled as captain.

Graveney played twice in the next week, scoring negligibly against Hampshire and Derby. The fifth Test began on 18 August. Despite being three down in the series, Graveney maintains 'the only thing dividing us was confidence'; that and Sobers. Sobers scored 81 at The Oval and the tourists were dismissed for 268. (Kanhai's century was his first in England.) In reply Barber, Boycott, Edrich, Amiss, D'Oliveira and Close had a top score of 36 between them. When Murray joined Graveney at the wicket England were 166–7.

What happened next has been explained in terms of West Indies' indifference. The tourists, the theory goes, 'weren't trying' – a charge refuted by both Close and Sobers. Charity was the last thing on Griffith's mind as he rapped Murray's pads first ball. Murray survived (Buller again) and went on to score 112. Graveney, meanwhile, played the innings of his life. In six hours, attended by hooters and drums, in piercing reams of sun, he made 165. Murray to this day calls it 'the greatest'. As had Sobers at Lord's, Graveney protected his partner until protection was not needed. The total approached the tourists' and overtook it. The batsmen added 217 by brilliant opportunism. They ran singles with breathtaking nerve. Between overs Graveney was calm, composed, collected. 'We can bat all day,' he said. They nearly did. 'Nothing that happened suggested there was any reason why either of us should get out. Hall, Griffith, Sobers, Gibbs, Holford and even Hunte came and went . . . The end, when it came, had to be self-inflicted. It was; I ran myself out.'

After Snow and Higgs had added a last-wicket flourish West Indies collapsed and lost by an innings. The sheer shock of the result crystallised the press. Some became ecstatic; others insisted it had been, in the *Mirror*'s phrase, 'a glorious fluke'. (The pressure was off.) Members of the second school noted that, as at Sydney, 1955, Graveney had deferred his genius until the series was over. Sobers himself is adamant that 'we played to win', attributing the result to 'technically superior England batting' (read Graveney and Murray) and the 'imminent demise of some of my players'. (Hunte, Nurse, Hall and Griffith would play fewer than thirty more Tests between them.) *Wisden* believed that Graveney 'showed his determination'; Murray that 'he batted as though there were no chance – literally none – of being out'; Close, more prosaically, that he was 'bloody brilliant'. Still the memory of Sydney revived.

A more telling analogy might be The Oval, 1953. As then, the match was played in a mood of extravagant national confidence. (Then it had been the Coronation; now the World Cup.) As then, the victory heralded a half-decade in which England would be unbeaten in a series. Of those who played in 1953, only Graveney remained. Hutton, Compton, Evans, Bedser, May, Edrich and Laker had retired; Bailey and Trueman were in limbo; Lock in Australia. Whatever the merits of Graveney's innings – and Sobers to this day praises it – it was not the least of his achievements to serve as a memorial to other times. 'The old maestro', *Wisden* called him. He was thirty-nine.

Graveney ended the series with an average of 76. He returned to Worcester and went one better, literally, than at The Oval, scoring 166. Next week the county lost to Sussex and were beaten by Yorkshire to the title. On 3 September they appeared in the Gillette Cup Final. In hard light and drying sun Worcester scored 155–8 (Graveney 18); even this might have sufficed had Graveney caught Alan Smith before scoring. (As a slip Bailey rates him 'outstanding without ever quite attaining true greatness'. That season Graveney took twenty first-class catches.) Warwickshire won by five wickets. That evening Worcester could reflect that two days earlier they had had hopes of a double, yet achieved neither. Still there was much to commend the season and Graveney, once more, dominated. He led the national averages.

That winter MCC sent a questionnaire to England's 150 capped cricketers. The first question asked if they 'enjoyed playing county cricket'. Yes, said Graveney, resisting the temptation to add:

> The game is complicated enough. The last thing it needs is more regulations.
>
> At the time some extraordinarily inept ideas, notably bonus points and the restriction of first innings, lowered standards and the credibility of the Championship . . . At one time even the follow-on

was forbidden . . . All of which widens the gap between Championship and Test cricket. The answer should be a programme of sixteen four-day matches.

The cry for 'brighter cricket', personified by Robins and Billy Griffith, reverberated in 1967. In the first Test against India Boycott scored 246. He was dropped. At some stage in his nine and a half hours at the crease Boycott was joined by Graveney, who scored an almost dissolute 59. Speculation arose as to whether Close, as captain, had 'ordered' Boycott to accelerate, the latter denying it. (Close's own recollection is that 'At the tea interval . . . I said: "See if you can open up and play your shots."' In the next two hours Boycott scored 43.) Engineer, the Indian wicketkeeper, says, 'Tom batted like a master, Geoff the pupil.' England were left needing 125 and made them simply enough. In damp, December conditions the match was played to belted crowds, elements of whom (at *Headingley*) jeered loudly. 'If the critics weren't pleased, neither were the Indians,' says Boycott.

Before the Test Graveney scored 113 against Warwickshire; at Lord's the side was remodelled to include Barrington (ironically dropped in 1965 in similar circumstances) in place of Boycott. The distinction of the match was again Graveney's and Murray's. The latter took six catches in the tourists' first innings of 152. Graveney alone made 151. In Close's words: 'A storm had left the wicket wet . . . Chandrasekhar made the ball bite and lift . . . Tom mastered both the conditions and the bowlers. He was as valuable as he was stylish.'

Graveney was forty. A year after his comeback he was an England regular, the first person to whom Close looked for advice. Alone of those who played against India he was ingrained in the public mind; of Graveney's colleagues Amiss was sixteen years younger; Brown fifteen; Snow and Milburn fourteen. Among fans and fellow players he enjoyed uncourted popularity. Graveney leavened his normal reticence with an unexpected vein of humour, and, as noted, was the life if not soul of the party. In his twentieth season he gave flesh to the newspaper reports of his fame. For his runs and the style with which he made them Graveney attracted a second generation of followers. Fan mail increased. He was aware, he says, of the pressure this exerted; of the thought that as Graveney failed, so did England. When Close or Edrich or Amiss were out they disappointed themselves and the side; when Graveney was out he spoilt the day for thousands. Others, like Hutton, had let this restrict them. Graveney's achievement is not only that he carried England's batting, but that he did it Graveney's way.

Following the Test he scored 108 in three hours against Sussex. Worcester were in transition. Coldwell and Flavell were injured for much of the season and the latter retired in September. Kenyon, too, announced his departure. Graveney, who had captained sporadically for two seasons, was approached by the committee. If doubts remained in the wake of 1960 they were concealed from the new captain, who received 'total support' and the personal endorsement of Kenyon. 'He was the obvious choice,' says D'Oliveira. Too obvious, perhaps; at Gloucester Graveney had proved that natural leadership was not in him. A more imaginative choice might have been Gifford or even (in amateur tradition) Fearnley. Graveney it was; he led by example.

The third Test, at Birmingham, was a rout. Graveney scored 10 and 17 and England hardly missed him. In the series he averaged 50; Boycott, restored at Edgbaston, 138. Boycott was missing from the first Test against Pakistan a fortnight later. Milburn and Russell opened, departed and were replaced by Graveney and Barrington. These two, of disparate style, the willowy genius of one complementing the oaken talent of the other, 'emphasised the value of class' (*Wisden*); they developed a stand of 201, of which Graveney's 81 was full of darting improvisation. After rain fell overnight England lost eight wickets for 86. In reply Pakistan were 25–2, 76–4, 99–6; only Hanif survived. He alone stood between England and the virtual certainty of victory. 'His attacking strokes', wrote Swanton, 'were without flamboyance' – or frequency. Hanif batted nine hours for 187. England collapsed to 95–4 ('over-eagerness', says Close), recovered and secured the draw.

Graveney secured his second century against Warwickshire. Worcester were sixth in the table. The cricket press, a body rapidly assuming its present characteristics, demanded changes for the second Test and hailed the result ('INSOLE'S SIX HIT') with typical restraint. At Nottingham Knott and Arnold débuted; Cowdrey, Boycott, Underwood and Titmus returned. It was the ninth Test of Graveney's comeback, Graveney ascendant, and he did nothing. By contrast Barrington made 109 in almost seven hours, prompting public debate between Swanton ('He can be tedious in a way not justified by the bowling or the state of the pitch') and Fender ('Writers who have never played in a Test . . . should not be allowed to pontificate on a matter of which they know so little'), concluding, in the former's words, that 'the crisis in English cricket lies in the example at the top'. At the top an example was made.

On 18 August Yorkshire, captained by Close, bowled twenty-four overs in nearly two hours against Warwickshire. The *Sun* reported this as 'the most cynical time-wasting' in fifteen years of cricket reporting; the *Mail* as 'flagrant cheating'. There was a further report that Close had been 'involved' with a Warwickshire supporter, and that 'Trueman . . . had to restrain one spectator beside himself with rage'. On the 23rd Close was summoned to Lord's and a statement issued:

> We came to the unanimous decision that the Yorkshire team had used delaying tactics . . . and that these constituted unfair play and were against the best interests of the game. The committee held the captain entirely responsible for these tactics . . . They have severely censured him and their decision will be conveyed to the Yorkshire club.

The final Test ended on 28 August. England won by eight wickets, Graveney scoring his four thousandth Test run. At the celebration Close was taken aside by Insole. After seven matches, six of which had been won, he was informed he was being dropped. Cowdrey, a man who, by his own admission, had 'given up' after the Leeds Test the previous year, was named captain in the West Indies. His reaction – shock – was nothing compared to Close's ('I saw a glass on a nearby table . . . I reached over and swallowed the lot. To this day I've no idea what was in it'); or, for that matter, the media's:

> Close is by record the best captain since the war . . . He wants to win and occasionally takes actions that every captain has taken at some time or another.
>
> The *Mail*

> England make me laugh . . . [They] boot Close out because he delayed a game. Cricketers have been doing that since they pitched stumps.
>
> Keith Miller

> I was not there . . . but certain respected colleagues who had seen it all were still spitting with anger days later.
>
> E. W. Swanton

To counter this, Graveney adds that Close's 'real sin' was not the original offence but the refusal to apologise later. For years nothing happens; then everything happens. The call for 'brighter cricket' had already cost Barrington and Boycott their places, Swanton noting darkly that 'the crisis lies at the top'. Close failed to take the hint. His tactics against Warwickshire played into the hands of his not inconsiderable enemies. Even then, says Graveney, Close could probably have survived by public contrition. Instead he flashed his '*Me? Apologise?*' look, his blunt razor mouth. 'Anyone would have done it,' he says.

Graveney:

> He was an odd captain . . . In the field you eventually found yourself covering every blade of grass. Close gave the impression he was shifting his field for the benefit of the press box and to make certain the spectators had no doubt he was in charge . . . By sheer force of personality he made himself felt, but, tactically, wasn't as good as his reputation.

Graveney's final comment – 'Lord's loves a captain who speaks his mind, until he does so to them' – would be echoed by, among others, Illingworth, Gatting, Botham. Close was a man who, in his own words, 'played cricket to the limit'. He was brought up in the Yorkshire dressing-room of Hutton, Sellers, Mitchell. Of Trueman. Close played to win – or, failing that, not to lose. At a time when the England captaincy was the preserve of men like Smith, Dexter, Cowdrey, Close's leadership was rough, raw – abrasive. His priority in 1967 was to 'win the Championship'. He did so – at a price.

Worcester were fifth. Their batting, to *Wisden*, looked 'thin' in the absence of Graveney and D'Oliveira. On 1 September Kenyon led the county for the last time. He scored 67 not out. (Glamorgan forced a draw.) Kenyon left Worcester after twenty-two years, 34,490 runs, 70 centuries; he played with Howorth and Wyatt. Graveney, proposing his predecessor's health, knew Kenyon's would be a hard act to follow. Flavell, Standen and Richardson also retired. The

Championship-winning side had all but gone. There was concern that youngsters like Hemsley, Bayliss, Griffith would need time to settle. Graveney asked for patience.

Late in November MCC called a two-day meeting of the England tourists at Crystal Palace, ostensibly for net practice. The real purpose was for Cowdrey to state the following:

> Apart from one or two bolts from the blue our playing record is not as good as it should have been . . . In the last year there have been difficulties and embarrassments . . . I want you to know I only accepted the captaincy because of circumstances beyond my control . . . My idea is to steal an idea from soccer and establish a squad of players, to establish continuity in the game . . . Apart from whether we win or lose in the Caribbean, cricket has much to gain from this approach.

Cowdrey stopped talking. He sat down. Someone coughed. In the previous eighteen months, twenty-seven players had appeared for England under three captains. The idea of continuity, a squad system, was unknown. It was reiterated at dinner that night at the Carlton Club. 'We can break the mould of English cricket,' said Cowdrey. 'Interesting,' said Graveney.

The party left London on Boxing Day. Given the prelude to the tour, and its outcome, the full side is worth recording: Cowdrey (capt), Titmus (vice-capt), Barrington, Boycott, Brown, D'Oliveira, Edrich, Graveney, Higgs, Hobbs, Jones, Knott, Milburn, Parks, Pocock, Snow. The manager was Ames, who had known and played with Cowdrey for twenty years. There grew up between them an understanding responsible for much of what happened later. This was one tour, says Graveney, when 'everything clicked'.

Not at first. The team came close to losing to Barbados Colts; the bowling disparate, the batting desperate. New Year was spent in contemplation of the series and celebration of Graveney's award of the OBE, rare for a current player. (Trueman, for one, waited twenty years.) In the next match Cowdrey scored 139, Boycott 135, Graveney 9 against a President's XI. There was a fortnight before the first Test. MCC drew against Trinidad and the committee – Ames, Cowdrey, Titmus, Graveney, Barrington – met in the knowledge that the late arrival, MCC having promised the players

Christmas at home, limited their options. After Snow fell ill, the main choice centred between Milburn and Edrich as opener. The committee ('playing safe', says Graveney) chose Edrich. He shared in a stand of 80 with Boycott; Cowdrey and Barrington consolidated until the second morning, 20 January. Graveney appeared and scored 118 in three hours. His innings, including twenty fours, 'a glorious exhibition of cultured batting' (*Wisden*), won the Lawrence Trophy for the fastest Test century of 1968. It was, says Sobers, 'genius', yet included a scene of unbridled hostility:

> I'd reached 60 when Griffith gave me a bouncer which I hit to the fence. The next one was a beamer. It hit me on the right thumb as I shoved the handle in front of my throat and flew off somewhere – I still don't know where.
>
> I never stopped to look. I went off down the wicket waving my bat at him like a club . . . It must have looked funny from a distance, but Griffith was close enough to know better. I got four or five yards down when he waved his hand. Immediately the lights went out and everything started to calm. 'Sorry', he said. 'It slipped.'

Deliberately? Yes, says Graveney; Griffith was always deliberate. After that England were all out for 568. West Indies followed on and seemed certain to survive until, on the last day, Brown took three wickets in an over. He then vectored a ball between Hall's bat and pad only to miss the stumps. Hall played, missed, missed again, while England, says Graveney, 'could smell the champagne'. Cowdrey was less sanguine: 'Brown and Jones were exhausted and I had no Snow to throw the ball to . . . It slipped away.' West Indies escaped. The tourists were crushed; none more than Barrington, who tapped his watch, flat as a wafer: 'We had them, we had them.' Sombre Snow appeared at the hotel. The only consolation was that, not for the last time, an England touring team in the West Indies had exceeded expectation. Unfortunately so had Hall.

Snow returned for the colony match against Jamaica. He took 5–36. From there the balance of the series altered. (A month earlier manager and captain had watched Snow from the balcony at Bridgetown. 'He's going to be a waste of time,' said Cowdrey.) The tourists beat Jamaica and were blending into a team. The second Test began on 8 February. Ames, Cowdrey, Graveney and Titmus

Above Catching Hunte at Trent Bridge, 1966 *(Hulton-Deutsch)*

Below Before the storm: at home between the Third and Fourth Tests, 1966 *(Hulton-Deutsch)*

Above left Bowled by Hall at Headingley – 'The most unpleasant Test ever.' *(Sport & General)*
Above right Hooking the same bowler off the front foot at The Oval
Below About to be run out by Gibbs *(left)* in The Oval Test *(Hulton-Deutsch)*

Above Returning with Murray after their stand of 217. Note Sobers's reaction *(Hulton-Deutsch)*

Left Meeting a fellow Lord's Taverner, June 1967 *(Sport & General)*

Above left Jackie, Tim, Becky and Tom Graveney, OBE, at the Palace, 1968 *(Hulton-Deutsch)*
Above right Home from the West Indies, April 1968 *(Hulton-Deutsch)*
Below The England batting trio of the sixties – Cowdrey, T.G., Barrington – with the Queen at Lord's, June 1968 *(Sport & General)*

Above left Hitting out at Edgbaston, Third Test, 1968 *(Hulton-Deutsch)*

Above right Last shot in Test Cricket: T.G. bowled Holder 75, Old Trafford, 1969 *(Hulton-Deutsch)*

Left 'A man out of jail': T.G. in 1970

Above left Doing what comes naturally with Peter West

Centre left With Evans and Laker, 1985

Below left Four England captains – T.G., Tony Lewis, Mike Denness, Sir Leonard Hutton – at Laker's Funeral, 1986

Right Ken, David and Tom Graveney

Below Still swinging – with Peter Alliss and Henry Cooper

Above Tom, Dorothy, Maurice, Margaret and Ken Graveney, 1988

Below Tom and Jackie Graveney, 1991. 'I looked around and thought, "Hold on. We're the only two still together."'

inspected the wicket. The pitch was brown and parched, the outfield grooved like the hills that rose, deeply separated, in the distance. England made 376 (Graveney 30). The reply was 143 in forty-eight overs; Snow 7–49. Lloyd top-scored and had he been caught by D'Oliveira the West Indies must have lost. By now the pitch had deteriorated into a series of lateral cracks. Batsmen came, feeling their way over the gaps, staring blankly into the sun. 'Happy?' the groundsman asked Sobers. He looked the captain over. Not much happiness there. Sobers rated the pitch 'abysmal'. In the follow-on he scored 113. Before then Butcher was taken down the leg side by Parks. An obvious catch; Butcher walked. A bottle, beaming in the sun, came dipping over the fence. Then another. Graveney could be forgiven his moment of nostalgia. He alone had played at Georgetown fourteen years before.

In the inquest that followed various causes were suggested for the riot: 'local politics'; a Communist plot; as Swanton had written in 1954, a product of 'rum and a certain amount of betting'. (West Indies were 204–5 at the time.) Graveney approached the crowd under the scoreboard – he was an inveterate talker in the outfield – and asked, 'What's it about?'

'Butcher.'

'He was out.'

'Not if he'd been English.'

The reference was to the Edgbaston Test, 1957, when Cowdrey and May had established a stand of 411, using the pad as adjunct to the bat. (No one remembers these things like a West Indian). Graveney shrugged. Cowdrey, meanwhile, attempted to calm the crowd. (Another analogy: in 1954 Hutton had refused to leave the field, adding: 'I want a couple of wickets tonight.') There was an eight-foot fence surrounding the field, and while the bottles flickered and flew Cowdrey found them 'easier to dodge than a slashed top-edge catch'. Less straightforward was reasoning with the crowd. By this time Ames had appeared with the chief of police who ordered, rather than invited, the players into the pavilion. He flicked his tongue against his lip and held it there, like the spring of a trap. 'We're using gas.'

This was confirmed as thick, acrid smoke filled the pavilion, stands, dressing-room – everywhere but the source of the trouble. Several players were affected and sat, steaming in towels, as in a sauna. While the glare of fires lit the stands, the snagging sparks drifting in the eddies of an easterly wind, a Jamaican official approached Cowdrey and asked how soon 'normal' cricket might be resumed.

> Our hosts were distraught, repeatedly apologising . . . They saw our point of view and the chairman, Cecil Marley, said: 'We've proved such poor hosts that it is hard for us to have any further say in the matter. If the England team insist on no further play today, we must agree.' He then added: 'As you see this will create difficulties . . . I fully understand your position and all I will say is that if you *could* start again it would be enormously appreciated.'

Cowdrey adds that he found this 'extremely moving'. The result was that England agreed to return to the field, with the proviso that an extra seventy-five minutes be added 'in the unlikely event it be needed'. Everyone, Cowdrey, Graveney, Ames, even Sobers, expected England to win; eventually. Doubts were raised about the wisdom of returning to a pitch still dotted with glass. Graveney, for one, thought it 'madness' – and said so. For the remaining ninety minutes that evening the Test was forgotten. England failed to take a wicket and left uneasily aware that their momentum had been halted.

That night nobody talked cricket. The players either 'discussed theories about what would happen . . . or exchanged war stories'. Tactics were ignored. Ominously, the West Indian batsmen were Sobers and Holford, a partnership previously demonstrated to England's cost. When play resumed West Indies took the score to 391. (When Sobers was 7 he was dropped by D'Oliveira substituting at slip. Graveney caught birds in flight in that position.) Sobers declared, setting England a target of 159. The pitch was brown and broken. Suddenly, as Cowdrey says, 'There was no way we could win.' England were left to play out time on the fifth day. After forty minutes they were 19–4. Graveney was caught after the ball deflected eighty degrees off short leg into the hands of mid-wicket. He hurled his bat thirty yards in disgust. It was then that Sobers appeared in the England dressing-room. 'We're claiming the extra seventy-five minutes', he said. Cowdrey went white. From a position of being certain to win, England on the last morning looked likely to lose. In the end they survived. While the Jamaica *Gleaner* found 'much to commend' in the West Indies' performance, few of the tourists had any doubts. The riot changed the complexion of the match. 'Had it been a normal Test,' says Graveney, 'we would have won.' Sobers agrees.

From Kingston the party flew to Antigua where Boycott scored 165, Barrington 100, Graveney 23. He had 'no form' on that tour, except in Trinidad. No form – but influence. D'Oliveira remembers him 'enthusiastic' and 'invaluable' in interpreting local conditions. (It was his sixth tour, of varying sorts, to the Caribbean.) Graveney's influence was paramount when, before the next match, against Barbados, the vice-captain lost four toes of his left foot in a boating accident. While Titmus was being operated on in Speightstown Cowdrey was 'as close to personal panic' as ever. Graveney took over. He captained the side at Bridgetown – superbly. Boycott remembers that Graveney 'was anxious to take a psychological advantage into the Test . . . He practically ordered me to make a score.' He made 243. It was the greatest of Graveney's virtues, and not the least of his failings, that he was direct to the point of bluntness. With some it worked. D'Oliveira notes that 'with Tom, you knew where you were'; Knott that 'he made himself clear'. Graveney asked only for what he thought reasonable. Boycott he considered a player of talent, even genius, 'who developed a fetish about not getting out'. He craved assurance, approval. Graveney provided it. Boycott admits he found this exhilarating and, in an England career encompassing 108 Tests, unique. Boycott admired Graveney. He respected him. Graveney respected those who fulfilled their potential – or his judgement of it. The West Indies tour gives no occasion to retract the verdict of him as captain. Tactically Graveney was correct, not clever. Psychologically he was no Brearley, or even a Benaud. He could be moody, morose. But it is not the least of his achievements that he related to 'difficult' players – Laker, Trueman, Boycott – and encouraged them to be natural. He knew how they felt.

The Barbados Test that followed was the most ordinary of the series. England were distracted by Jamaica, by Titmus's injury. Their merely limited attention lowered expectations. Still, Edrich scored 146, Boycott 90, Graveney himself 55. In the second innings Lloyd, on 11, deflected a bouncer to Parks. The England players were already congratulating themselves when, not for the first time, the home umpire hung his head. Lloyd survived. The tourists exchanged glances. 'You had to be twice as good as West Indies to beat them,' says Graveney. England weren't; the match ended in a draw, the series level with two to play.

The party flew to Trinidad. Graveney enjoyed aspects of the West Indies. He played golf. He drank rum. After his feats in 1957 and 1966 he enjoyed celebrity status in the Caribbean; Sobers says 'no one, except possibly Milburn' was more popular. Other features of the tour were less agreeable. The umpiring was errant, the pitches erratic. Elements of the press seemed bent on undermining the tourists' morale. Then there was Griffith, with whom Graveney exchanged a dozen words during the tour, half of them unprintable. On the positive side Cowdrey and Ames managed the side superbly. Great players may be weak, they may be wilful, but their greatness is in itself estimable. So it was with Cowdrey. For once in his long career the captain exerted, even asserted himself. Discipline was strict. D'Oliveira, not averse to the good life ('the tempting mixture of rum and sun', in Johnston's phrase) was gently upbraided. Milburn was spoken to. As Graveney says, 'When Colin held the captaincy without looking over his shoulder, precious little could be said against him.' Cowdrey led from the front. Reciprocally he acknowledges the support of Graveney and Barrington, the former of whom was 'never – not once – flustered'. The mood of the party on the eve of the fourth Test was of quiet confidence.

To understand what happened next is to understand Sobers; a man, says Swanton, 'whose attitude to the game, sense of adventure and willingness to take a risk . . . and inborn sportsmanship . . . marked him out'. Sobers was a gambler. He studied, and studies, form – and nothing in England's form to then indicated a desire to chase runs. Sobers also gambled by bowling Rodriguez and Butcher, whose occasional leg-spin took 5–34 in the England first innings. This pleased Sobers. It persuaded him. Spin was the way he had seen the match being played and Butcher confirmed it. West Indies took a first-innings lead of 122. The game was receding to a draw when, at 92–2, Sobers declared. The target was 215 in 165 minutes. Sobers, says Graveney, made two basic assumptions: that spin, provided by Rodriguez, Gibbs, Butcher and himself, would prevail; that England, in any case, would never attempt to win. Both wrong. It has been written that there was dissent in the England dressing-room over tactics. There was none. Both Graveney and Cowdrey agree that the policy was to consolidate until tea, when England were 73–1. At this stage, according to Boycott, 'Cowdrey was still inclined to bat for a draw . . . Graveney agreed with him but Edrich, Barrington and I thought we should go for the runs – and said so in no uncertain terms. The conversation was a little heated.'

Graveney's version is different. Immediately before tea Rodriguez had bowled a half-dozen overs from the pavilion end where, in Cowdrey's words, 'at the critical moment, his hand was completely invisible against the grey background . . . making it impossible to read'. (Graveney himself says that 'at no time, either against Trinidad or West Indies, could I read Rodriguez'.) Graveney, Barrington and Ames were all none the less convinced England could win. (In 1986 Ames admitted that, frustrated by three successive draws, he urged Cowdrey to accelerate. 'Tom', he said, 'agreed'.) The result was that Boycott made 80, Cowdrey 71, Graveney 2. England won by seven wickets with three minutes to spare. At the close the West Indies' over rate was nineteen an hour. 'It never occurred to me to slow down,' says Sobers. 'That wasn't my style. I was trying to win the match, not draw it.'

In the inquest that followed it emerged that Weekes, the West Indies manager, had been a party to the declaration. In Cowdrey's words: 'He knew the England players were weary, and apprehensive of Rodriguez . . . It was worth a chance. Moreover, he assumed that we would not go for runs . . . If he had got an early wicket or two Rodriguez could have won it.'

Cowdrey's account ends by stating that Sobers 'accepted the criticism without once hinting that Weekes had been involved'. Criticism there was; later that evening the tourists found Sobers in a bar – alone. For days afterwards his motives, character, even his right to continue playing, were debated. Spring was heavy and close. At night the ceiling in Graveney's room seemed a foot above his face. He liked Sobers. He sympathised. 'Garry', he says simply, 'miscalculated. He declared because he thought he could win, largely because of the way we had batted in the first innings against Butcher. To impute any other motive is to do him an injustice.'

The fourth Test ended on 19 March. Two days later Graveney captained MCC in a colony match against Guyana. The tourists won by ten wickets. (Lloyd, who made his home Test début that series, felt Graveney did a 'solid' job and that his presence itself commanded respect.) The fifth Test was played on the slowest pitch in the Caribbean. When Sobers won the toss a local journalist, Brunell Jones, leapt up in his fedora. 'Win,' he screamed. 'We'll win!' His confidence was based around Gibbs, appearing on his home ground. It was well founded. On the final day England plunged to 41–5; Graveney and Barrington both out for nought. Knott joined Cowdrey. The sky was cloudless but colourless, the crowd tense and teasing, Gibbs (6–60) reeling maidens. As Cowdrey said:

> It was the longest day of my life . . . We couldn't win, so runs were of little value. All that mattered was the minute-hand creeping round the clock. I recall Knott at one stage leaning back to cut a four off the top of his off-stump. I went down the pitch to him and said: 'Thank God there is still one batsman in the world who intends to hit every bowler out of sight' . . . Knott grinned and acknowledged the point. It was the last risk he took.

Cowdrey was out after tea; Snow, Lock (recalled after four years) and Pocock followed; England 206–9. In the dressing-room Graveney sat staring at the wall. Cowdrey watched the last overs through cracks in doors and windows. For seven minutes Jones and Knott survived – in England radio relayed the drama in which each ball, each shuffling lunge, brought the Test nearer to climax. Jones played the last over without making contact with a single ball. Knott came down the pitch and claims his partner looked straight through him. The last ball turned and touched the pad. There was an appeal. Impassive, the umpire declined. England survived. The series was won. Sobers made a gracious speech and agreed privately with Graveney that England were the better side. 'If play had been analysed, on a daily basis, it would have been no contest.'

Wisden agreed, adding that from the English viewpoint, the tour was a conspicuous success; this despite the 'difficult attitude' of the home Board, who took travel and hotel arrangements entirely out of the hands of MCC – a point echoed by Graveney who, as in 1953–54, felt that there had been a conscious effort to undermine the tourists' morale. That it failed was due to Cowdrey and Ames;

Barrington; to Graveney himself, who, if disappointing with the bat (389 runs on tour, average 25.93; 261 in the series at 32.62) was variously thought by Cowdrey, Edrich, Knott and D'Oliveira 'solid', 'dependable', 'controlled' and 'confident' – particularly when, following Titmus's injury, he was appointed vice-captain and led the side against Barbados and Guyana. Graveney proved himself a popular and perceptive leader, wholly without intuitive style; as Wellings said, 'more ideally equipped to be first mate than captain'. A member of the team notes that 'Tom was a very different proposition when things were going badly . . . He tended to withdraw.' On the other hand, things went sufficiently well under Graveney's captaincy for MCC to enforce the follow-on against Barbados and beat Guyana. Ames felt that he did everything that was asked of him.

Graveney returned immediately to Worcester. His first act as captain was to sign the Barbadian Vanburn Holder. Later the county was strengthened by the arrival of Glenn Turner, who at that stage was widely regarded as 'strokeless'. (In fifteen years Turner would score 22,298 runs for Worcester, average 52.) Both men, says Graveney, were 'made' by their experience at Worcester, this being the era when English cricket was a finishing-school for overseas players. Despite which, the patience requested by the new captain was sorely tested in early season. The opening partnership of Headley and Fearnley failed; Holder struggled; Graveney himself was out of form. In early May Australia arrived. Their match at Worcester was abandoned without a ball bowled. At noon it was nearly dark. As the silhouette of the cathedral turned black, the hollow interior filled with hundreds of lights, like champagne bubbles. Rain destroyed the build-up to the first Test – until early June, when Graveney scored 107 against Leicester. Next morning he reported to Old Trafford, where England played for a draw and duly lost. According to *Wisden*, 'Few, except the Australians themselves, believed this possible.' Graveney agrees, adding that 'choosing a team of batsmen and all-rounders was a mistake . . . Colin had an unholy fear of losing.' (Cowdrey's reputation after the West Indies tour lasted exactly two months, after which there was renewed criticism of his captaincy. In mid-May Titmus, restored after injury, led MCC at Lord's.) At Manchester Graveney scored 2 and 33; 52,037 spectators paid an average of 50p (in the new coinage being introduced) to see the tourists win by 159 runs; never had England held the Ashes after being beaten in the opening match at home. It was the youngest Australian side in history and even Benaud, from the press box, conceded that England were better. *Wisden*'s view was more explicit: 'Of the twenty-five Australian teams that have visited the United Kingdom the latest combination under Lawry was perhaps one of the most disappointing.' After the Test Graveney stated publicly: 'My own taste is for the game to be played more freely . . . At Old Trafford we were knocked unconscious before we got out of our corner.'

A week later Worcester were beaten in the Gillette Cup by Nottingham; Graveney and Sobers, two of the pre-eminent bats in the world, scored 74 and 95 respectively. A commentary on the summer is provided by the fact that the match had been three times postponed by rain; and rain it was that characterised the season. Graveney, at forty-one, travelled the country like a Yukon miner: Derby, Birmingham, Taunton, Abergavenny, Leeds; first in to breakfast, first in the nets, determined, as he puts it, to prove his captaincy. Worcester, meanwhile, languished in mid-table: in some matches they failed to bowl the opposition out, in others rain cut play to the bone. At Lord's Australia escaped after being dismissed for 78. It was at this stage that Graveney began to wonder if it would be much of a season. Next day he was out for nought against Nottingham. Yorkshire and Kent led the table. D'Oliveira says that Graveney 'under the circumstances, handled the team well'; his first sustained captaincy since 1960 was generally successful. It was extended when, in the third Test at Edgbaston, Cowdrey pulled a muscle in his leg and left the field. Graveney scored 96 and captained on the last two days. He defied tradition by relying on his two spinners, Illingworth and Underwood, who took 3–37 and 3–48 respectively. Australia narrowly avoided the follow-on. As Graveney says, few would choose to captain by default: 'There is a responsibility not to lose, and no time to put personal theories to the test . . . A holding action is expected.' In which case his leadership was widely considered adequate, even adventurous. *Wisden* noted that many were surprised by England's positive approach. Among them was Lawry, who admits that 'Graveney was always at us'. Underwood, too, was gratified by his captain's confidence. The match ended when, on the fifth day, rain halted the Australian response. They retained a one-nil advantage, though, as in the Caribbean, observers agreed that England were unlucky. Even Benaud described the tourists as only 'potentially' brilliant.

There were nine days before the fourth Test. On the second it was announced that Graveney would retain the captaincy. On the third he cut his left index finger to the bone and rang Donald Carr at Lord's. Had Graveney not played it is probable that Illingworth, or even Dexter (recalled after thirty-one Tests) would have captained – a prospect sufficient for Carr to reply, 'For God's sake be there.' Graveney's hand was strapped until the eve of the Test, when coagulants were applied to stop it bleeding. On the first morning, 25 July, he announced himself fit. It was his seventy-fourth Test and the nineteenth since his comeback – the longest uninterrupted sequence of his career.

By coincidence Lawry had also been injured at Edgbaston and Australia, too, were led by a surrogate, Jarman. Graveney lost the toss and England fielded – badly. Within an hour Fletcher had dropped three catches, to the derision of the Yorkshire crowd. (In later years Fletcher anticipated visits to Headingley with the relish of a repeat offender at the Old Bailey.) Australia, who in *Wisden*'s words 'concentrated solely on avoiding defeat', scored 315. In reply England batted – and batted – through the third day: Prideaux 64, Edrich 62, Underwood, incredibly, 45; Graveney, virtually one-handed, 37. The match was played under leaden skies, the pitch dank and dripping, unhelpful conditions in which to defeat any side intent on avoiding it. Australia applied the brakes in the second innings while Graveney persisted with Illingworth (6–87); he baffled Jarman by his tactics and willingness to experiment. Jarman said so. The eventual winning target was 326. England finished at 230–4 and there was general criticism of a Test which, plainly, only one side had wanted to win. As Graveney left the ground on 30 July he was stopped by Freddie Brown. 'Well done,' he said. 'The players enjoyed it.' Underwood confirms this. 'Given that he was on trial,' he says, 'Tom did well.' Still the verdict was out.

August brought a reversal of Worcester's fortunes. Graveney (who played in only half the county's fixtures) continued in mid-form; D'Oliveira excelled more with ball than bat. Turner and

Holder gave evidence of their potential; Booth proved a capable leader in Graveney's absence. By mid-August the county had risen to seventh, a position they held at season's end. Graveney remembers it as a transitional year, in which the last elements of the Championship team were disbanded, the way paved for future success. (Worcestershire were to win the title again in 1974.) Others recall Graveney as steady, unhurried, his sinews stiffened by the realisation that it would be five or more years before the team could be compared to Kenyon's. (Compared it was.) Cricketers, after all, can be baked gently, not microwaved. D'Oliveira insists that Graveney spent time encouraging and appraising the junior players, and was certain that Turner, for one, would succeed. It was Graveney's twenty-first season, his twentieth in Championship cricket, yet he professed himself as eager as ever. Out of low clouds like a row of torn cushions rain fell as the captain played, practised and coached. 'No one', says D'Oliveira, 'took more trouble. He always had a word of advice.' Graveney had mellowed.

D'Oliveira was a central figure before, during and after the last Test. On 20 August Prideaux reported unfit and Cowdrey – restored as captain – rang New Road to invite D'Oliveira to The Oval. The player heard the news from, of all sources, Trueman:

> I reached Worcester . . . and stopped at some traffic lights by a pub . . . I parked the car round the corner, started to walk towards the entrance and bumped into him. We were playing Yorkshire over the next three days.
>
> We chatted idly, then started leg-pulling. I said I'd give him some stick next day.
>
> 'What do you mean?' said Fred. 'Well,' I joked, 'you've slowed down, mate, and I'll give you a bit of stick.' Fred's face puzzled me. 'But you won't be here, cock . . . '

The dreamlike events that followed began dreamily. D'Oliveira, dropped after the first Test, rejoined the team on the eve of the fifth. That night Insole asked the players to confirm their availability for the winter tour of South Africa. 'Of course,' said D'Oliveira. Next morning Cowdrey won the toss, batted and Graveney and Edrich enjoyed a stand of 125. England were 238–4 when D'Oliveira came to the crease. ('I was so eager to bat that, when Redpath held the catch to dismiss Graveney, I was on my way before Tom left the middle'.) Next day he scored 158. D'Oliveira returned to a standing ovation. Public opinion, Cowdrey admits, maintained he was 'certain' for South Africa.

Graveney agreed. In the two days before the Test he spoke to Cowdrey twice. When Prideaux, then Cartwright and Knight stood down, Graveney lobbied for his county colleague. It was due to his influence that D'Oliveira played at The Oval. On the rest day, referring to South Africa, he assured the all-rounder, 'You're in', a confidence the extraordinary climax to the Test did nothing to deter. D'Oliveira it was who, on the last evening, made the breakthrough by bowling Jarman. Underwood returned figures of 31.3–19–50–7 and England won, with six minutes to spare, by 226 runs. From the drawn series Graveney had 337 runs at 42 and left the Test knowing it would be his last against Australia. Even with the run debt, the trauma, the tours, he would have liked one more series; one.

Next day Worcester played Sussex. Graveney scored nought, D'Oliveira 128. At 6.00 p.m. the players gathered in the home dressing-room to listen to the news from Lord's. D'Oliveira remembers 'everyone standing, as if waiting for an announcement of national importance' as the names were read – his not among them.

> I felt my arms unfold and fall to my sides . . . The next thing I remember was that Graveney was swearing furiously. I had never heard him do so before or since . . . I had absolutely no control . . . Tom gave me permission to miss the last half-hour of play. I woke up on the bed at home.

Graveney:

> I could hardly believe my ears . . . I was so flabbergasted that I was convinced a mistake had been made. I saw the pain of disappointment in Dolly's eyes, and all he said was: 'The stomach has been kicked out of me.' For a moment he was lost, and he would have been less than human if he had not suspected that he was once again the victim of politics. As the selectors were honourable men, Basil accepted fully – as I did – the later statement that the omission was entirely on cricketing grounds, but equally I found it incomprehensible that

Dolly was not considered among the first sixteen cricketers in the country.

On what 'cricketing grounds' was D'Oliveira excluded? Were there any? (Graveney himself had been omitted from the 1956–57 tour of the same country because of 'local conditions'.) First, foremost, the player's form between the first and final Tests (D'Oliveira admits, 'my performances at county level fell miserably'); that and Cowdrey's conviction that South Africa would be a 'seamer's paradise', in which case Cartwright and Knight took precedence. Finally, D'Oliveira's performance on and off the field in the West Indies, where he scored 137 runs, took three wickets, and was 'quietly spoken to' by both Cowdrey and Ames.

Little of which conveyed itself to the public, elements of whom divined a conspiracy in D'Oliveira's exclusion. The events that followed can be easily recalled: the correspondence in the press; the raised voices of MPs; the first resignations from MCC; the formation of a protest group under David Sheppard; the sending of flowers by Cowdrey's wife to Naomi D'Oliveira; the subsequent announcement that, because of Cartwright's injury, D'Oliveira would tour after all; the State President's refusal 'to accept a team thrust upon us'; the melodramatic journey to London by members of the South African Association; finally, a month after the original selection, MCC's announcement that since their side was not acceptable the tour would not take place.

Throughout which it became uneasily apparent that certain groups were using, and continue to use, cricket as a channel for political dogma.

Graveney:

> The issues have become so fudged with prejudice, malice and distortion that had a solution not been found the fabric of the game could have been ruined. Only a mischievous idiot would want to see cricket divided into two implacably hostile camps . . . But that was exactly what might have happened.

If anyone has a right to be heard it is D'Oliveira, raised in ruins, ghettos in which sprouts of foliage and weed obtruded at angles, where only refuse or the occasional overturned car gave evidence of life. D'Oliveira loves South Africa. He admits to 'improvement' since he left in 1959, while noting that part of the change has been cosmetic: 'A black or brown is equal to a white on the field, but off it still subject to the law.' Had D'Oliveira toured South Africa in 1968 he would, in his own words, have been 'conscious of how important it would be to comply . . . to know where I could go and not go . . . I presumed that, if I was in the team, I would be there with them. I would remain strictly within the limits of the itinerary and at no time allow myself to be spotlighted as an individual outside the context of the tour.'

Even that was too much.

In October it was announced that England would visit Ceylon, India and Pakistan. It was the last overseas Test tour administered by MCC; that summer the Cricket Council, with three component parts – the Test and County Cricket Board, National Cricket Association and MCC itself – came into being. It was also announced that from 1969 a 40-over competition would be played on Sundays. In Cheltenham Graveney spent the autumn and early winter absorbing the fact that cricket, as he knew it, had changed. His mood was sombre. A return to the sub-continent had not been among his plans. In the event finance caused the Indian half of the tour to be cancelled. Resigned, Graveney gave an interview looking forward to resuming 'normal' cricket. Except nothing that winter would be normal.

In the week before Christmas Graveney was awarded the Lawrence Trophy for the fastest century of 1968. It commemorated his 118 at Trinidad, described by Swanton as 'the best I ever saw him play . . . not only enthusing the Trinidadians and all who listened, but impressing the West Indies generally'. The award was made by D'Oliveira. The two names had become linked for Worcester, for England. Graveney's reaction to D'Oliveira's exclusion had been profound. He seriously considered withdrawing from the tour in protest; that profound. By year's end Graveney was reconciled to the new itinerary. With no tour scheduled in 1969–70, he knew the three Tests in Pakistan would be his last overseas. Younger players – Fletcher, Amiss, Luckhurst – were pressing for recognition. Graveney was forty-one and on occasion felt it. Despite captaining England, 1968 had not been a happy year. He finished with 712 Championship runs at an average of 33.90. Despite his repeated pleas for calm, a number of Worcester supporters were not; there was even a motion that Kenyon, forty-four, be brought out of retirement.

(Kenyon scotched it.) As he prepared for his seventh official tour Graveney, not for the first time, considered retirement. He was not a wealthy man. Other than his sports equipment shop he had few or no commercial interests. Prospects of employment were no more engaging than in 1944. It was his, and others', misfortune to play professional cricket at a time when that paid barely a living wage. Still, twenty years' familiarity had bred habits he would miss. As he left his wife in January 1969 his parting words were 'We'll discuss it.' The decision was deferred.

Ceylon was a revelation. As Graveney says, 'If you had to pick a place to spend two weeks in January, it would probably be in the first three'. He played golf, tennis; even cricket. Against a Board XI Graveney scored 30; against Ceylon 106 in 'an innings of lovely strokeplay' (*Wisden*). The hosts, wrote Wellings, were 'considerate' and 'showed excellent organisation'. Everywhere the tourists went presents and plaudits attended them. At night they gathered in the manager's room where, crackling and incongruous, the radio broadcast: riots, even revolution, in Pakistan. Graveney consulted Cowdrey who in turn approached Ames. A day went by. Then another. Word came back. The tour was on. Responsibility for this lay with Lord's who, pressed by the Foreign Office, insisted that aspects of normal life be maintained. That meant cricket.

The first Test at Lahore was constantly disrupted. There was scarcely a session without invasion by rioting students. Even this was an achievement in view of the fact that, on arrival in Pakistan, the tourists had no idea of their itinerary. The situation, says Graveney, was 'chaotic, ludicrous and frightening'. Having got nowhere with the home Board, Graveney, Ames and Cowdrey flew to Rawalpindi to meet Fida Hassan, its president; eventually Tests were arranged at Lahore, Dacca and Karachi. The first was merely a farce. The second had the making of a tragedy. Dacca was in a state of siege. The army had withdrawn. There was not a policeman in sight. After the West Indies tour certain players had said 'never again'. That was nothing compared to Pakistan. Graveney felt like a phoenix chasing arsonists.

> Immediately we went into session with the High Commission. The debate was heated. It was of little interest to us that we were supposed to be safer without the police and army, as the sight of them only

> provoked the students . . . We were told in Rawalpindi we would have protection, yet the only people in uniform were a handful of traffic policemen. Nor could we turn round and go . . . God knows what would have happened had we done that.

Graveney, Cowdrey and Ames also met the student leaders. The oldest was nineteen. It was they who promised 'security' for the England team and whom Ames in his wisdom chose to believe. ('Les', says his biographer, 'wanted to keep the flag flying.') It was the only time Graveney publicly fell out with his manager. The word 'lunacy' was expressed. Cowdrey acted as mediator. He seemed lost, distracted, diminished from his role in the West Indies. The ship was rudderless.

Mutiny became possible. In Ceylon (as initially in the Caribbean) Snow had done nothing to inspire confidence. He was omitted from the first Test. Prior to the second Graveney organised nets. When he himself went to bat Snow could be seen limbering up in the mid-distance. Graveney tensed.

> I looked up and saw him on the horizon using, I imagine, his full run for the first time that tour. A warning bell rang and, sure enough, the first ball was a bouncer which struck me on my top hand. Whether or not it was bowled in a fit of pique . . . or he felt he had a personal point to make . . . is not for me to say. It was a stupid thing to do. We had only six batsmen in the team.
>
> I took eighteen or nineteen balls from Snow, of which seventeen were bouncers. At the end of the net I said 'Thank you' and walked away . . . Ames joined me and was beside himself. He talked about sending Snow home on the spot . . . I convinced him this might be counter-productive.

Meanwhile Prideaux, captain of Northants, could be seen giving a trial to a twenty-year-old named Sarfraz Nawaz.

In the Test itself D'Oliveira scored 114. The pitch was hardened mud. The players went through the motions against a backdrop of blinding flares, students with swords and knives, the loud grief of sirens. The city in bedlam. Cowdrey's pocket was picked in the width of a pavement from the team bus to the hotel. At night the glare of rockets and guns was followed by intervals of silence. At breakfast Cowdrey was like an elementary reader poring over a book. His lips moved but speech failed to occur. He gave Graveney a look of abject and withering doom.

The Test was drawn. The party flew to Karachi. There conditions deteriorated. A number of players – Fletcher, Underwood, D'Oliveira – approached Graveney and expressed concern. He shared it.

> There was no doubt they were terrified of taking the field and being exposed to the whims of agitators seeking a platform for demonstrations denied them in the streets . . . I firmly believed – and events bore me out – that the players were not over-reacting, and had every right to fear for their safety. Even their lives were at risk . . . it only needed one maniac in an uncontrolled crowd. Because I shared the alarm and was a senior player, I became the team's spokesman. It cost me dear.

So Graveney became an agitator, a shop steward. Someone had to. Cowdrey by this stage had a pained, distant look, like a man with conflicting worries. Ames (who won plaudits from *Wisden* for remaining calm throughout) appeared in a different dimension. Graveney took charge. On the eve of the third Test, 5 March, the tour management – he, Ames, Cowdrey, Edrich – sought assurance from the home Board of Control, the very title of which was ironic. At one point Cowdrey delivered a speech about the need for 'normal relations'. Ames, at his side, nodded.

Graveney exploded.

> I lost my temper . . . I regret I swore and finally retired to a corner with the words: 'You make your own arrangements. I know what I think and what the England team thinks.' What the team thought is unprintable. But, apart from the ambition to return home in one piece, there was a general feeling that they had been kicked around long enough by authority in one guise or another for ends other than cricket.

Ames, in 1989, admitted that Graveney made his point, adding 'he expressed the players' feelings succinctly.' Graveney in turn felt Ames (whose management he admired in the West Indies) to be 'one of the old school who clearly thought it bad form to complain . . . Another case of politics-before-players.' (A decade earlier, in Australia, Brown had refused to complain about Ian Meckiff. The bowler took 6–38 at Melbourne and virtually clinched the series in an afternoon.)

Thus the Test started as scheduled on 6 March. Milburn, recently arrived from Perth, scored 139. He was engulfed in a crowd of three or four hundred invading the pitch. Graveney flailed at them with his bat. Cowdrey later called this 'excessive' and 'not entirely in the interests of the tour'. (Was it Pope who was unable to drink a cup of tea without a strategy? Cowdrey, too, believed all threats, risk, insults, abuse were excusable in the interests of the tour.) Next day Graveney himself scored a century. His 105 was his eleventh three-figure score in Tests. Like his first it was a monument of patience. When he left the field on the second day he was found to have lost nearly a stone. D'Oliveira remembers him 'hardly able to speak' in the dressing-room. (It is not the least enigmatic aspect of his character that, for a man thought mercurial, Graveney was capable of tenacity of which Bailey would be proud.) Outside, in the stands, in the streets, the riot continued.

Next morning the dam burst. A crowd of three thousand charged the main gate. It burst with a noise like rolling thunder. Immediately the mob stormed the VIP enclosure, one of whose tenants, Fida Hassan, arrived, ragged and breathless, in the England dressing-room. 'The match is over,' he announced.

'And the tour?' said Graveney.

'And the tour.'

By this time he was technically captain of England. Cowdrey's father-in-law, Stuart Chiesman, had died. According to one of the team, 'Colin reacted in typical fashion . . . first he was flying home, then staying, then flying again'; in the end he left hours ahead of the main party. Even then Graveney was able to imprint himself on the tour. Murray describes him as 'clearer' than Cowdrey; more first mate than captain.

The tour itself was a débâcle. In *Wisden*'s view: 'With one exception nothing went right with England's plans . . . Cricket was unhappily caught between two bigoted groups exploiting an opportunity to further their political aims, and the proposed tour of South Africa had to be abandoned . . . It was then planned to visit India and Pakistan . . . a fiasco . . . The one exception was a twelve-day visit to Ceylon, which opened up new prospects for touring there.' The same review concluded that: 'Graveney, who otherwise did little, followed a sparkling century by Milburn with one of his own.' Little was unkind: Graveney's average on tour was 53, in Tests 44. According to Underwood 'he looked as good as anyone, under the circumstances'. The circumstances included anaemic management, erratic pitches, capricious umpires; all to a backdrop of latent anarchy. Excuses were elaborate. Even at the airport Hassan was in a feverish state of apology. Graveney shook his hand and boarded the plane. Several of the players applauded as it left the ground.

On 25 May Kent played Glamorgan in the newly-devised Sunday League. Cowdrey scored 39 before, shaping to drive, he slipped on the wet surface. The crack as his Achilles tendon snapped could be heard on television. Once the extent of the injury was known speculation arose concerning the new England captain. Graveney was favourite.

The alternative candidate was Illingworth. (More imaginative minds suggested Close.) Graveney's immediate reaction was confidence of his own appointment. On two previous tours he had been vice-captain. In 1968 he deputised for Cowdrey at Leeds. 'In experience', he says, 'I was ahead of anyone else . . . On my record over the previous three years I was also entitled to think that I was one of the few regular members of the team.'

The selectors demurred. A week passed after Cowdrey's injury. Then another. Graveney grew less sanguine. 'If they were going to name me,' he reasoned, 'they would have done so . . . They knew my batting. They knew my captaincy. My claims were the best known and the least complicated.'

That month also saw the injury to Milburn. In late May and early June a number of cricketers visited him in hospital where it was they, not he, who became depressed. Among them was Illingworth. He remembers arriving with McKenzie *en route* to a match at Hove. After leaving Milburn they reached the Imperial Hotel, where Illingworth found a riot of reporters on the doorstep. That evening the selectors had appointed him England captain for the first Test. At the very moment Illingworth was with Milburn, Bedser had announced the news to the press.

Graveney sagged. As he says: 'You can work things out until the situation is plain, but there is still that flicker of hope . . . You feel it when it finally goes out.' Graveney admits he wanted the captaincy – badly. At the time he had played seventy-eight Tests, Illingworth thirty. The latter's appointment surprised him, largely because Illingworth was not considered a regular member of the side. Pocock, if anyone, was the more promising spinner. (Cowdrey himself describes Illingworth's Test career to then as 'patchy', while noting that his impact at Leicester was 'tremendous'.) The new captain considered the news 'more a relief than a surprise'. Of the rival candidates, Illingworth felt Graveney had the best chance because of his experience. 'On the other hand, I knew that Tom might not be an entirely unanimous choice of certain selectors.' When was he?

Immediately the story circulated that Graveney's 'outspokenness' and 'readiness to voice complaints' in Pakistan had been held against him. In April Ames had filed his tour report, which Graveney considers unlikely to have been flattering. More pertinently, his record as captain was ambiguous. Nothing in his terms at Gloucester or Worcester indicated high strategic awareness. He was solid, not spectacular. Illingworth in this respect had the advantage. In his first month at Leicester he was hailed as a genius. Great things were predicted, if not fulfilled. (At season's end the county were fourteenth in the Championship.) Faced with a choice between sombre Graveney and sparkling Illingworth the selectors opted for the latter. No deeper explanation is required. Graveney's own view – 'The reason I was passed over is a mystery . . . There were no complaints about anything I had done when I stood in for Cowdrey' – is disingenuous; as is that that events in Pakistan decided the issue. Bedser's statement that 'all the factors were taken into account . . . the decision was unanimous' needs no amplification. The man of promise won over the man of performance.

Ironically on 3 June, the very day of Illingworth's appointment, Graveney had himself spoken to Bedser. The conversation brought him to the last great crisis of his career.

In July 1968 Graveney spent an evening at the Cricketers Club in London. He stepped over the thick carpets of the bar where bottles shone, and obscure figures nodded in the amber light. One was Colin McDonald, the former Australian opener. McDonald in turn introduced 'my boss', director of Legal & General, also chairman of

Luton Football Club, Tony Hunt. Hunt admired Graveney. He liked him. Cricketers are used to being cornered in bars and clubs, talking about series, matches, innings, being reminded of their own achievements. As Hunt was going to dinner he asked Graveney 'how they were treating' him at Worcester.

'I'm due for a Benefit next year.'

'Oh?'

'Interested?'

'Come to dinner,' said Hunt.

The result was that, in return for 'playing at Luton one Sunday', Graveney was offered £1000; that simple. He took all of a second to agree. (At the time the fee for playing in a Test was £120.) Numbers were exchanged and Hunt ordered a bottle of wine. Graveney sipped it. Promises made at a bar, he knew, were rarely carved in stone. Only later, when McDonald uttered the cryptic aside, 'He means it,' did Graveney consult his diary. 'I'll come back to you,' he promised.

In the following weeks Graveney captained England, endured the D'Oliveira débâcle, heard the promise of an alternative tour. (Little did he know.) Hunt, meanwhile, wrote requesting dates. It became apparent that, with the introduction of the Sunday League and his own Benefit, there was only one day available in the new season: 15 June. It was the rest day in the first Test.

> It wasn't easy . . . People have since accused me of putting my bank balance before my country, but at the time there was no guarantee that my country would need me the following year. The tour to South Africa was still pending.
>
> At forty-one I was in a vulnerable position. Clearly the mint of runs was not going to last forever. I was due to face what I thought was the best side in the world on pitches that were the fastest in the world.
>
> After that there were two series in 1969 against a faded West Indies and New Zealand – with no winter tour to follow. I could see that if I had a thin time in South Africa I could well be dropped and a younger player blooded.
>
> I decided to make up my mind. If I waited until I came back from South Africa it would probably be too late to arrange a fixture at all.

Graveney agreed to play on 15 June.

In October, the South Africa tour off, Graveney attended a meeting of the umpires' sub-committee at Lord's. By then he had already confirmed dates with Hunt.

That evening he met Billy Griffith, secretary of MCC. Griffith in turn referred him to Bedser. (Bedser, with whom Graveney had played and toured, whom he had sought out in February 1955, the two most distraught men on Hutton's team.) Bedser's reply was blunt: 'I can't worry about next season. I don't even know if I'll be a selector.' It was left at that.

Graveney returned from Pakistan. One of the hundred letters awaiting him was confirmation from Hunt: Graveney's XI v Bobby Simpson's XI, Luton, Sunday 15 June. On the 3rd he rang Bedser. The first Test team was announced that weekend and he, Graveney, wanted 'no misunderstanding' about his position.

The conversation ran as follows:

TG: You remember that I mentioned this Luton match? I'm playing. Is that all right with you?
AB: I'm not sure. Ring me tomorrow.

(Bedser, says Graveney, had a 'faintly distracted' tone – not surprisingly, since at that very moment he was trying to reach Illingworth to appoint him captain of England. The two discussed the matter – briefly – when the conversation resumed next morning.)

TG: I need to know, officially, whether I can play.
AB: I don't know.
TG: I'm committed . . . If that's your position, don't pick me for the Test.
AB: Don't say that. I'll talk to Hunt.
TG: Do what you like. I'm playing at Luton unless you come to another arrangement.

On 8 June the first Test team was announced. Graveney was included. He was surprised – and relieved. Nothing more had been said by Bedser, Illingworth, or any member of the England team. This, he assumed, meant that Bedser, having consulted the selectors, had relented. He drove to Old Trafford.

On 12 June the Test, Graveney's seventy-ninth, began. He scored 75 before being bowled by Holder, the man whose cricket he had encouraged at Worcester. (Sobers says, 'Tom batted beautifully.') That evening in the dressing-room he was approached by Bedser.

'You can't play at Luton.'

'It's too late. I'm going.'

'I'll contact Hunt.'

Bedser never did. Hunt was in hospital and reappeared only on the day of the match. That morning Graveney left the England hotel and drove to Luton. He changed, greeted Simpson and Benaud, batted against the slowest bowling either could muster and fielded at third man. ('I couldn't have been injured if I tried.') Hunt approached him, a cheque changed hands and Graveney returned to Manchester at midnight.

As usual he was first up in the morning, 16 June, his forty-second birthday. At breakfast Bedser informed him he was being reported to the disciplinary committee. 'Fair enough,' said Graveney. That afternoon he heard over the Old Trafford tannoy that he was due at Lord's on the 19th. A few spectators jeered.

England won the Test by ten wickets – their first victory at Old Trafford since 1958. The West Indies, as had been evident in the Caribbean, were in a state of transition; and would not win another series until 1973. Graveney left the ground (venue of his first Test, eighteen years before) and returned to Cheltenham. On 18 June he told his wife to 'prepare for the worst' and drove to London. Suddenly his detachment ended and he found himself in a state; the man of talent saddled with committees and hearings.

Immediately at Lord's there was evidence of tension. It centred on Bedser, a slow, sober figure who claimed: 'Tom never made it clear he was unavailable for the Test if permission to play at Luton was withheld.' Bedser stopped speaking. He sat down. Ashen, Graveney replied that his phone call on 4 June had stated just that. For what other reason had he made it? The chairman, Edmund King, asked Graveney a question and then he was invited to wait.

He braced himself by sitting on a pavilion bench. Outside Middlesex were playing Lancashire. Resigned, Graveney realised the committee would never support him against Bedser. Who, after all, was he? A filmy, transient figure, eccentric and fractious. They disliked his style. They distrusted it. For twenty years, rich in promise, he had enchanted and exasperated, like all the highly gifted forever put on by those lacking his ability. Suddenly Graveney saw himself from the committee's perspective. He was pleased. He was illuminated. At that moment Donald Carr put his hand on Graveney's shoulder and invited him in.

Earlier he had been asked if permission to play at Luton had been refused before the Test started? No. (Bedser's only statement on 4 June had been to promise to contact Hunt.) Now King began to strafe him in earnest. 'The chairman of selectors says he told you after practice on Wednesday that permission had been denied.'

Graveney looked at Bedser.

'I'm sorry,' he said. 'I don't recall that.'

Ten minutes later the committee issued its verdict.

> The disciplinary sub-committee of the TCCB have considered the facts relating to the apearance of T. W. Graveney in the match at Luton on Sunday June 15, while a Test match in which he was taking part was in progress. They have ruled that Graveney be severely reprimanded and the selectors have been informed that he must not be considered for selection for England in the next three Test matches.

Graveney's response – 'I'm very disappointed' – concealed the certainty that, at forty-two, his Test career was over. The committee's rider that 'In coming to their decision they gave full consideration to Graveney's long and outstanding contribution to English cricket and the various pressures on him in connection with the match at Luton' only underlined the fact that '. . . before he accepted an invitation to play in the Test match, Graveney had been made aware that permission to play at Luton would not be granted.'

Or had he? Bedser, interviewed in 1989, says only that 'Tom was fully aware', a view shared by an England contemporary who adds: 'For years Tom felt he was misused by the selectors. Even after his comeback he knew he was there under sufferance . . . When he was offered the money I think he thought, "To hell with them. I'll take it." He knew what he was doing.'

None of which answers the question: did Bedser explicitly refuse permission for Graveney to play at Luton before the Test? The committee evidently thought so. The press, with few exceptions, agreed. (In an ingenuous twist, *The Times* claimed that Graveney had appeared at Luton 'out of pique' at being passed over for the captaincy. Unfortunately the match was arranged nearly eight months before the captaincy issue arose.) The consensus, in 1969, was that Graveney had indeed 'known what he was doing'. So it might have seemed had he not heard, years later, that of Bedser's co-selectors (A. C. Smith, Sutcliffe, Kenyon), not one had known of the Luton match before the start of the Test. Graveney's assumption: that Bedser (distracted by the captaincy issue), having failed to consult his colleagues, 'covered himself' by subsequently inventing a conversation of which Graveney had, and has, no memory.

Whatever the cause, the effect was to end his Test career. When the ban was lifted England had beaten the West Indies and led New Zealand one-nil – 'Not a time', says Graveney, 'for forty-two-year-olds rounding off their careers.' From Lord's he returned to Cheltenham, where sympathy was rife. He was always well received in his home town. Elsewhere opinion was divided. Having played for England, been dropped and recalled, Graveney's career ended, perhaps suitably, on a note of dissent. He enjoyed briefly the prestige of significant controversy.

Worcester held little comfort. Holder and Turner were both absent on tour; Booth departed and Cass struggled to fill his place; in mid-season Coldwell also retired. On 5 July Worcester played Gloucester in Graveney's Benefit match. He scored 24 and 59 (retiring hurt, with a pulled hamstring), misjudged his declaration and saw Gloucester win by three wickets. More ominously, despite constantly fine weather the crowds stayed away. Only £437 was collected at the match, contributing to a total Benefit of £7886 (putting, if nothing else, his £1000 fee from Hunt into perspective).

In Graveney's place Hampshire played for England in the second Test and scored 107 – yet by mid-season he, too, was discarded. In the space of a year England had lost Graveney, Barrington, Milburn and, at least temporarily, Cowdrey. The team entering the 1970s would be unrecognisable from that of five years before.

Equally novel was the Sunday League which, in Graveney's words, 'to a man of my age was nothing less than an act of cruelty'. His sole contribution with the bat was to score 48 against Leicester (significantly, being run out); in the field he floundered. At season's end Worcester finished twelfth, the captain convinced that 'There are pressures in the game not there when I started . . . Then you just tended to drift through a day waiting for something to happen . . . The League has changed all that. Seven days cricket a week is too much.'

Graveney was not a man who existed solely for Test cricket. The stimulus of playing for Gloucester or Worcester was enough. Nor did he believe that, given a sound technique, a batsman's ability was extinguished at forty. None the less the advent of the League, with its emphasis on speed over substance, forced him to consider. In the Championship, Worcester also finished twelfth and there were mutterings that a change of leadership was needed. In September the secretary, Lister, reported that paying spectators had dropped from 24,635 to 8435. His comment – 'I doubt if we have ever had a more disastrous season financially' – eerily echoed his Gloucester namesake's in 1960; coincidentally or not, Graveney began and ended the decade as captain of a county on the brink of ruin. He flew to Australia that winter, guest of the Queensland Cricket Association, to consider his future.

While he was there the following appeared in the *Australian Cricketer*:

> Tom Graveney, by almost whatever yardstick, is the senior man in world cricket today. In an age when cricketers retire so much earlier than they used to . . . he is the oldest of any real account. He has also scored, with a tally of 46,339, easily the most runs of anyone playing.
>
> I have no doubt myself that he is the best professional batsman produced since the Second World War. At all events so far as English cricket is concerned he is, with Barrington, Cowdrey, Dexter and May, in the top five: and in point of classic grace and method even in this distinguished field many would put him head of the list.
>
> It is, and always has been, in Graveney's nature to show his strokes, of which he has the fullest range, and to dictate to the bowler where he can. In the era of Hutton and May, as at other times, it was the grafter who was apt to be the man preferred. There was not, sometimes, the wisdom to perceive that the art of batsmanship is a reflection of temperament . . . Can I detect that some Australian readers may be thinking at this point: 'A pity we didn't have Graveney. He'd have done better with us.' If such a thought crosses anyone's mind, let me not be the man to say it's unlikely.

Australia was Graveney's next destination. That winter (despite having his left arm broken by 'Froggy' Thomson) he and his wife accepted an invitation to settle in Queensland. His mood, in the wake of Luton, left him open to offers; Australia had always intrigued him. When Clem Jones, Lord Mayor of Brisbane, suggested a role as player-coach of Queensland, Graveney accepted. The local press gave him a double-column spread. The photograph was large. Gratified, Graveney returned to England to finalise arrangements.

Luton aside, he harboured a secret fear of outstaying his welcome: 'Kenyon's decline had served as a warning to me. I always had the highest regard for Don . . . in my view he was one of the game's outstanding openers . . . but tragically he reached a point where he was scarcely worth his place in the side. I vowed it would not happen to me.'

It was Graveney's fourth decade as a professional. He was, in the *Cricketer*'s words, 'the senior man', veteran of seventy-nine Tests, a former England captain, approaching his forty-third birthday. (That winter two boys passed Graveney's house on bicycles as he swept away fallen leaves. He heard one say in a lowered voice: 'See where that old bloke's gardening? That's where Tom Graveney lives.') Despite Kenyon having 'politely enquired' if he were still available, he knew his Test career was over. He wrote to Worcester announcing his retirement.

That spring his third book, *Cricket Over Forty*, was published. It pulled no punches. The break with Gloucester 'reshaped [Graveney's] life' . . . 'I made my position clear about appearing at Luton' . . . 'My one regret is not playing at Cape Town'.

And this:

> Looking back, I am surprised at the trouble I have got into. Two major controversies would be a lot of strife for a fire raiser, and I certainly don't class myself as that . . . I have never gone around looking for trouble and if I had to nail my disputes to any one defect in my nature, it would be through being too easy going . . . I lived by the conviction that cricket is played and administered by a wonderful bunch of blokes and we are lucky to be in it. It hardly seems an outlook to account for the kind of grief I have had.

After twenty-two years rich in style and substance, Graveney, the perennial man of promise, began his final season. It was a triumph. In sultry May he scored 94 against Glamorgan, 62 the following week off Derby. His form in early and mid season was outstanding. Worcester were ninth, sixth, fifth in the table; they even enjoyed a run of six wins in succession in the Sunday League. (Graveney's highest score was 68 – against Gloucester.)

He celebrated his birthday; a Conservative government was elected; England played a series against the Rest of the World, losing four-one. On 17 June Graveney led Worcester in a fixture against Essex. He scored 12 and 53 not out ('hitting the ball', says Hobbs, 'like a rocket'), declared and saw his side win by six wickets. The first overtures were made for him to reconsider. (Perversely one of his sternest critics urged him to stay on.) Graveney's response: 'I could go on batting for years . . . My eyesight is sharp still and my method is based mainly on playing through the line of the ball, so really there is no reason why I should put any limit on how many more years I could bat. But I doubt if I have got much more fielding in me.'

In private, he insisted he had 'had enough'.

The strange, twilight season, played increasingly in the shadow of Australia, reached conclusion. Graveney arrived at Canterbury on 1 August with a total of 120 first-class centuries. That afternoon he scored 114, full of glorious improvisation; Ames felt he batted like a man out of jail. A fortnight later Graveney's *bête noire*, Yorkshire, arrived at Worcester. He scored 100 of the county's highest total of the season – his final first-class century. Worcester settled to sixth in the table, a place they held at season's end. ('There was a feeling,' said *Wisden*, 'that their position was only the starting point for a thriving young team.') Much of the acrimony of the previous year vanished, dissolved in the awareness that an era was ending. Record crowds attended the county's final match against Warwickshire. Graveney was 43 not out in the first innings; in the second lbw to Gibbs for 12; the match drawn. He left the field on 4 September to sustained applause. In his final season he scored 1316 first-class runs at 62.66, second behind Sobers in the national averages. *The Times* referred to him as 'unique'; *Wisden* as 'an institution'; the county organised a reception at which presentations were made. That evening Graveney walked alone across the shadowed square, his face quiet, heavy and set. It seemed to some that his feet were dragging.

*

In less than a fortnight he, his wife and two children were *en route* to Australia. Immediately they arrived (to a welcoming cable from Miller) Jackie fell ill with jaundice. Graveney was left to arrange places at school and secretarial college for his son and daughter; find a home; acclimatise to his new surroundings. The temperature that Christmas was 100°.

In the midst of this he played cricket. In late October Graveney scored 5 and 56 for Queensland against New South Wales; 2 and 15 against Western Australia, for whom Lock took 4–22 (and the twenty-one-year-old Lillee 1–35.) Graveney's greatest moment in Australia came on 6 December, when he made 98 for Queensland in the semi-final of the knockout competition. (The state went on to lose heavily in the final.) He also played against the England tourists, for whom Boycott made 124, Edrich 120. Sam Trimble, the Queensland captain, apparently to make a point batted for nine hours; the match, unsurprisingly, was drawn. England went on to win the series two-nil, with Graveney at least theoretically available in reserve. He admits to 'mixed emotions' at the prospect – and at playing for Queensland, who failed not only to win a match all year but even to achieve a first innings lead. At season's end they were at the foot of a table headed by South Australia.

From the start Graveney stressed that he regarded himself more as a coach than player. After three matches he realised he was incapable of fielding for long stretches in temperatures exceeding 100°, and said so.

'During that first season it became apparent I didn't measure up to Jones's expectations . . . In retrospect, I think I was too old for Australian-style cricket and it niggled Jones that he had chosen a man who, as he saw it, could not deliver the goods.'

As for money, the shadow of Graveney's life, he knew he could expect to be disappointed any minute. After travelling 1200 miles up the coast to Cairns he became involved with Mineral Securities. They promptly collapsed. Graveney's efforts in insurance also failed. By spring 1971 he was forced to the conclusion that, like it or not, both his past and present were bound in cricket, a fact recognised by his award of honorary membership of MCC that June. He still received fan mail from England and read of the series of mishaps affecting Worcestershire that led to their fielding no fewer than four captains (and, incidentally, winning the Sunday

League). He even received informal enquiries about returning, and, under other circumstances, might have considered it. But Graveney that spring knew the brooding edifice of age. Heavy and greying, he coached his charges by strength of will. For the first time he felt old.

From April to October he trained the various Queensland Elevens, including the schoolboys. In contrast to the state side the standard of junior cricket was outstanding. (It remained so, says Graveney, until the boys were old enough 'to hold a driving licence and impress a girlfriend with their prowess on a surfboard'.) Lou Cooper, secretary of Queensland Cricket Association, praised his 'inspirational' work. Even Jones was impressed. Graveney regards this as the most satisfying part of his life in Australia.

That November he played his final innings for Queensland. At the last minute he was rushed to Melbourne to captain in place of the injured Trimble. True to his fortunes at the time, Graveney lost the toss and Queensland were trapped on a drying pitch. Batting eight he scored nought and 21 not out; Queensland lost by an innings. He left the field on 14 November determined not to return. That season the state was again fifth in the table.

For a year he remained as coach. His wife had recovered; his son and daughter absorbed Australia. Graveney renewed his friendship with Lindwall, Archer, Mackay; went with Peter Burge to the trotting track; found time even to watch and coach cricket. Graveney's original plan had been to remain indefinitely in Australia. The difficulties with Jones, and finances, forced him to reconsider. Even then, the end came as a shock.

> I arrived at the ground one morning to contact the chairman of selectors to discuss the Colts team, due to play in Sydney. I told Jones's secretary that I intended to use his office to make the call, as it was secluded and away from the noise of typewriters and callers in the outer office.
>
> No sooner had I put the call through than Jones stormed into the room and, as he tried to pull the phone from my hand, demanded, 'What right have you to use my office?' My right, as I saw it, was that it was in the service of Queensland cricket.
>
> The row ended with my stalking out of the room and slamming the door in his face . . . That afternoon I contacted the chairman to tell him I wanted to end my contract and return to England at the first opportunity. Neither he, nor any of the officials, tried to stop me . . .

The echo of Graveney's final word on Gloucestershire ('The executive made no effort . . . to enable me to stay') is irresistible. None the less, the insult was sufficient for him to pack and leave Australia within three weeks. The family arrived in England on 3 December 1972. Graveney had an offer to play for Derbyshire, which he refused. He spent a month coaching the Worcester Seconds, but realised his – and the players' – hearts were not in it. His life as an active cricketer was over. A chapter was ended.

8

The Constant Enigma

Help came to hand in the form of Trevor Bailey. (Of cricket's strengths, not the least is the association of former players the world over.) Bailey arranged an appointment with a squash club at Westcliff-on-Sea. For nine months (during which the county club made an approach) Graveney was employed as manager and sometime accountant. He enjoyed the first, finding the latter no more enticing than in 1944; keeping the club's ledger was, he admits, among the least alluring jobs of his life. He also snapped an Achilles' tendon whilst on court. The result was that, within a year, Graveney was travelling for a local shoe company. The grief of bookkeeping was as nothing compared to the ennui of sales. Both he and the family yearned to return to Cheltenham. Again cricket provided the means. Frank Thisleton, chairman of Gloucestershire, mentioned that the tenancy of a pub at the gates of Cheltenham racecourse might be available. It was. In early 1974 Graveney became landlord of the Royal Oak, Prestbury, where, in his own words, 'every night was party night'.

He played cricket. Following the demise of the International Cavaliers, former players were recruited by the Whitbread Wanderers, a precursor of the Courage Old England XI. Graveney captained intermittently; hit, according to Evans, 'at least one vintage fifty'; coached at Dean Close School. His batting confirmed his thesis that he could go on for years, but he had no illusions about returning. In March 1977 he was flown by the Australian Cricket Board to the Centenary Test at Melbourne. (The home team, remarkably, won by the same margin as 100 years before.) He roomed with Len Coldwell; met Bradman, Miller, Lindwall; enjoyed Australia as never before. Of the England XI, only four had overlapped with him; one, Randall, was born the year Graveney débuted. That June, at home in Cheltenham, he turned fifty.

To Graveney's surprise he missed the game – the camaraderie, the banter, the inner satisfaction of a well-played innings, even the glamour of being a sporting figure – more than he thought possible. It hurt to be remembered only for what he once was. Graveney endured life at the Royal Oak. Writing of this era in 1983, he said: 'It hurt most when I was behind the bar, when all around me the talk was of sport. Memories flooded back, and a wall of loneliness seemed to surround me. I realised I was no more part of the game than the men in cheerful argument on the other side of the counter.'

All that changed in May 1979 when Graveney was contacted by Christopher Martin-Jenkins. Following the World Cup that summer England were due to play a four-Test series against India. Would Graveney, as a former tourist of the sub-continent, lead a discussion on Indian cricket for the BBC? He would. The winter of 1951–52 had left a sufficient impression for him to talk, non-stop, for an hour. (Among Graveney's observations was that 'Indians basically play each other, any ensuing success being entirely coincidental.') When Martin-Jenkins played back the tape he commended Graveney's 'naturalness' on air. They were joined by Peter Baxter, producer of cricket radio. Had Graveney ever considered commentary? He had, he had. So Baxter asked the next question. Was he available?

Graveney shook hands and returned to professional cricket. It was that simple.

The player of genius, on whom fate seemed to have bestowed almost infinite gifts, had done it again. It is not the least of Graveney's talents that he seems to have given and taken in equal measure. In April he was a country publican, associated with glamour and style, yet whose achievements lay exclusively in the past. In June he was professionally employed in the game he loved.

It had changed in his absence.

> Nowadays the players have been given advantages, ranging from financial rewards to being able to take wives on tour, but I am not sure all the changes have been for the best . . . I can well understand a modern player finding it hard to adjust to the county system which we were brought up in . . . The early discipline was particularly valuable

> to a young player, and helped to keep his feet on the ground. The old custom of a senior looking after a junior, making certain he understood etiquette and convention and took care of his appearance, was always appreciated in retrospect and, along with county loyalty, formed the foundation of the professional game. Of course all that is regarded as outdated now.
>
> The oldest players were always conscious of their seniority . . . As a junior, I remember being responsible for carrying the baggage from Cheltenham to the next game at Dover. Play ended at 6.30 p.m. and, when the team arrived at Paddington, the rest grabbed their overnight bags and left me with the job of transporting the cricket kit down the platform and across London in two taxicabs. I reached Dover at 4.30 a.m. and, within an over, I was at the wicket to help Charlie Barnett start a second-wicket stand of 181. My contribution was 73. We then fielded while Kent made 434 and Les Ames 212.

So; Graveney was a member of the Old School, of knowing one's place, of mutual respect. So was Hutton. An understanding of their relationship is central to understanding Graveney as a Test cricketer. In 1951, Hutton was pre-eminently the senior England batsman; veteran of 53 Tests, thirteen centuries; thirty-five to the débutant Graveney's twenty-four. The following year he assumed the England captaincy and in his *annus mirabilis*, 1953, rebuked Graveney for frivolity at the wicket. The next winter, in Australia, he appeared to have 'given up' on the younger player, convinced (in Graveney's words) that he had no 'guts' – a judgement he never wholly lost.

In August 1990, the week preceding his death, Hutton said of Graveney: 'He could play . . . I never doubted that. At the beginning, I think, he was nervous – perhaps overawed at playing for England. I told him to get his head down. He didn't strike me as a grafter, someone who could bat all day. Eventually I ran out of patience with him . . . But he could play. No doubt of that.'

As to when Hutton 'lost patience' with him, Graveney is precise: Sydney, 1954. Having lost the first Test, England rescued the second owing largely to Statham and Tyson. Graveney's contribution was 21 and 0, after which he says, 'My sole use to Len was as a stand-in for other batsmen.' When Graveney 'stood in' in the fifth Test he scored 111, an innings described by Miller as 'about the best of the tour'. By then it was too late. (In his autobiography, Hutton's description of the match is limited to the weather conditions and score.) The captain's mind was made up. Graveney 'wasn't a grafter'. He couldn't bat all day. He could play.

As with Hutton, so with May. He, too, favoured the grafter, the stalwart, the batsman-as-sheet-anchor. In 1956 Graveney missed arguably the most dramatic Test ever through injury, following which he scored 200 in a county match and ended the season top of the national averages. He was not selected for the winter tour of South Africa. Again, it seems, a case of lost patience.

The first phase of Graveney's career was thus dominated by two men for whom, at critical times, he was found wanting. His reputation became proverbial, accepted – a self-fulfilling prophecy. Possibly he sub-consciously played up to it. (The constant enigma.) But much was simply a matter of Hutton's and May's own prejudices; their distrust of a player who actively *enjoyed* himself on the field.

Graveney:

> Len and I were just not each other's cup of tea . . . My approach to cricket was far too carefree for his taste . . . I always held the opinion that it was a game to be enjoyed regardless of the pressures. Len tended to treat it as if it were life or death.

And again:

> As with Hutton, I didn't really hit it off with May because my attitude was too casual for his liking, but that did nothing to lessen my admiration of him as a batsman . . . Peter could be a real tiger in the field, ticking off anybody if he thought they were giving less than total effort and concentration. Yet for a man who came alive the moment he strode on to a pitch, he was strangely shy and uncommunicative away from it. That was his weakness as a captain.

Simultaneous with May's period as captain was Allen's as chairman. Allen played his cricket for Eton, Cambridge, Middlesex, England. (His closest schoolfriend was David Bowes Lyon, brother of the Queen Mother.) Throughout the 1920s he alternated between cricket and the City. In 1932 he toured Australia in the most infamous series in history; four years later he led England against the same country. After service as an Intelligence Officer (being awarded the MBE and US Legion of Merit) he returned to captain England in the 1947–48 series in the West Indies, an appointment even his biographer considered 'a tour too much'. He did not play his last first-class match until just short of his fifty-second birthday. Following his term as chairman, Allen served as treasurer, then president of MCC, re-wrote *The Coaching Book* and was still active at the time of his death in 1989. He left behind a considerable fortune in both England and Australia.

It would be churlish to imply that Allen's differences with Graveney stemmed from a difference of 'class'; less so to say that Allen was most comfortable – in turn inspired comfort – in company of men like May, Cowdrey, Sheppard, Dexter, all of whom in varying degrees prospered under his chairmanship. Obviously, too, Allen concurred that 'the proper and consistent means of assessing a Test cricketer . . . is in the Ashes.' (Allen retained special affection for the Antipodes. He was born in Australia, against whom he played more than half his twenty-five Tests.) It can be further assumed that Graveney's record against the Old Enemy to 1955 – seven Tests, 301 runs, average 30 – did little to inspire confidence in the incoming chairman. On the 1954–55 tour, as stated, Graveney had been declared deficient in 'guts' by his captain and, both by word and deed, these things have a habit of taking root. Graveney, more than most, was on trial in the summer of 1956. He started by scoring 30 for MCC against the tourists at Lord's; 8 and 10 not out in the first Test; in the second 5 and 18, in the second innings chasing a half-volley wide of the off-stump. ('I had failed and I could feel the cold shivers rippling up and down my spine.') After being dropped at Leeds Graveney scored 90 against Surrey, 156 against Middlesex, returned to the Test side and immediately withdrew, injured by Statham in a county match at Blackpool.

Genuinely? Statham, interviewed in 1989, left no doubt: 'That sort of accident, where the hand is jarred against the handle, is among the most painful.' At the close Graveney promptly sought out Washbrook, who in turn arranged for the batsman to see a specialist the following afternoon, the day prior to the Test. His report was unambiguous: 'You're in no state to play.'

The events that followed can be quickly recalled: Oakman's dramatic dash to Manchester; Graveney's unflinching handshake with Allen and May; his subsequent omission from the tour of

South Africa, a decision denounced by Barnett as the 'worst crime against an attractive player'. Graveney's bewilderment (as recently as 1982, at a dinner in honour of Allen's eightieth birthday, he was 'tempted to confront' his former chairman – but didn't) can be offset by two facts: when Graveney first told Washbrook of the injury, he assumed Washbrook, in turn, would inform his fellow selectors. He didn't. The first Allen knew of it was when Graveney, visiting the specialist, failed to appear in the nets prior to the Test. Hence the need to convey Oakman by police escort from his home in Hastings. (In parentheses, the parallel with the Luton Affair in 1969 is inevitable: there again, Graveney assumed full consultation among the selectors only to find that Bedser, like Washbrook, had kept their conversation to himself.) Allen, an orderly man, was thus confronted with a crisis on the eve of a vital Test and, imperfectly briefed, can be supposed to have thought himself 'let down' by a player already prone to let down with the bat.

Not that the chairman condemned Graveney out of hand. He genuinely had reservations. Allen's guiding principle (as quoted by Swanton) was 'When in doubt, go for class.' Little Graveney had achieved in his presence to then suggested any such quality. In 1953 the batsman had flattered to deceive; in the following two home series he remained exasperatingly in chrysalis – capable of outstanding genius, yet lacking the depth of experience to bat through two, three or more sessions in a Test. More pertinently Allen, combining a visit to the Australian stock market, had seen that part of the 1954–55 series exactly coinciding with Graveney's nadir as a player: the second Test, in which he scored 21 and 0, and the third and fourth, in which he was dropped. By the time Graveney scored 111 at Sydney Allen was *en route* to London and his appointment as chairman. This, together with Hutton's report of the player's inability to 'graft', to 'bat all day', meant that Allen's patience with Graveney was at best finite. In 1956 it snapped. His subsequent omission from the tour of South Africa was the first major crisis of Graveney's career, the point at which Hutton's, May's, Allen's perception of him found expression. While their influence – and that of their successors – prevailed, Graveney was always a luxury, an extravagance to be discarded in times of hardship. The selectors were adamant; everyone had their place until an exotic like Graveney, a genius with a talent for disappointing, challenged their thinking. He found himself separate, segregated; set apart. 'At times,' he says, 'my Test career was a misery.'

Hutton and May were two of the three England batting giants of the era. The third was Compton. 'Denis', says Graveney, 'was the natural genius of English cricket . . . He was handicapped by recurring knee problems and past his best by the time I knew him, yet still had the ability to turn a game on its head.' In June 1949 Graveney scored 96 of a Gloucester total of 246 against Middlesex, the moment, Compton says, 'when Tom arrived'. The two were friends thereafter. Early in his career some drew comparison between Graveney's *laissez-faire* technique, his flair for improvisation, and Compton's. Both were regarded with suspicion by Hutton. Had Compton not occupied his niche in the nation's affection, he too might have suffered the vagaries known by Graveney. (In fact, due to the War, he played in one fewer Test.) In varying ways and by differing means, he, Hutton and May remain the three outstanding batsmen of Graveney's era.

At the next level – 'the good to very good' – he rates Cowdrey, Barrington, Dexter, Boycott. The first had the talent to be as good as May. Yet Cowdrey, too, deceived. 'To those who saw him score his first century at Melbourne, he remains an enigma,' says Graveney – no small accolade. On a pitch which defeated Hutton, Edrich, May and Compton on the first morning, Cowdrey, twenty-two, scored 50 out of 69 and 100 of 158 against an attack including Lindwall, Miller, Archer, Benaud, Johnston. Here, says Graveney, was unbridled genius.

And yet:

> Like all who watched him, I wondered why Colin never played as well again. At least I never saw a comparable performance, though I acknowledge several innings of the highest quality. He was an enigma . . . I was never able to understand why a batsman who could play at his Melbourne level, even if only once in his career, should want to fiddle around with the weight of his bat, change his grip, be bothered by his stance, and so on. Surely there was no cause for him to worry with technical experiments like a mere mortal . . . With talent like his, proved in the infant days of his Test career, you stay as you are. You just go out and play, and thank God for bestowing gifts not given to ordinary mortals.

Barrington and Boycott were 'eye-catching players when they started, who became stockpilers of runs and stifled their own talent'; the latter developing a fetish about not getting out to the extent that:

> Once, in the West Indies, he made an astonishing statement: 'My job's to see the shine off the ball.' He left it at that. For a player of his talent to be reduced to one mundane responsibility, albeit important, was nothing short of ridiculous. A Boycott letting himself go would have numbered among the immortals.
>
> Geoff was a victim of his self-imposed bondage, his own complex moods. The carryings-on over the captaincy at Yorkshire were equally bizarre and, to an outsider like myself, looked like a family squabble which should have been avoided. I know what it is like to be kicked out of the captaincy at county level, and I sympathised, but after eight years without tangible success Boycott had no divine right to the job. If he felt as strongly as he apparently did, he should have taken a leaf out of my book and left with as much dignity as he could muster, started afresh with a new club, and made up his mind to enjoy what was left of his career.
>
> Yorkies have a different approach to cricket, as I learnt from Hutton.

Finally, Dexter:

> Like Cowdrey, Ted was a gift to the establishment . . . His background was right; he was a glorious striker of the ball; an elegant strokemaker; a veritable throwback to the Corinthian age. Yet Dexter had too many conflicting interests to be a successful captain. He loved the horses, dabbled with politics, had commercial connections, and practised golf as much as cricket . . .
>
> The county circuit was too humdrum and demanded too much discipline for a man with his free-ranging ideas. Ted was a theorist. One of his ideas, nourished by Alan Davidson, was that leg-spinners were the bowlers to fiddle wickets on good pitches. Fine, if leg-spinners were available. Ted looked around his team in Australia and his eye alighted on Barrington and me. Barrington, yes; Graveney, emphatically no. The result was that Ken, an occasional bowler, was hammered all over Australia . . . another of Ted's pet ideas.
>
> On that tour he had a lot of good advice from Cowdrey, which he ignored, while Bedser acted as a sort of valet-secretary. With a firmer hand on the tiller we could have brought back the Ashes. We deserved to.

Of bowlers: Graveney, like everyone, admired Bedser – a man who took sixty-nine wickets in two successive Ashes series – who spearheaded England's attack for a decade – made invaluable tail-order runs; who indirectly ended Graveney's Test career. The bull head dripping with sweat, body rocking, the piston action and follow-through; this, says Graveney, was cricket at its best. (Does he bear a grudge? Hardly – Graveney could no more dislike Bedser than dislike cricket.)

Trueman was a bowler – and personality – of whom you didn't know what to expect. He frequently didn't himself. Trueman's 'fiery' persona was forged in the Caribbean in 1953–54 when, as Graveney says, 'He wasn't half as bad as the press suggested. But he was still bad.' (Graveney, Trueman and Lock were at various times in the tour threatened with expulsion. Of the three, only Graveney played in Australia the following winter.) As a bowler, Trueman was 'often wild, relying mainly on sheer pace and hostility . . . But he gradually brought accuracy and change of pace and direction to his attack. The Trueman yorker was a deadly and spectacular sight to see, and in later years he perfected the art of swing bowling and used his bouncer more sparingly . . . Like me, he improved with age.' Improve as he did, neither Trueman – nor Bedser – was the most impressive England bowler of Graveney's career. That prize was Statham's. Their friendship dates from the 1951–52 tour of India. In five Tests Statham took a total of eight wickets (his colleague Tattersall collected twenty-one), but ensured for ever his reputation as the stalking-horse of England cricket. 'Brian', says Graveney, 'was the unsung hero . . . A classical pace bowler whose accuracy set batsmen up for Trueman or Tyson . . . The latter were more hostile, but lacked Statham's efficiency . . . The most complete English bowler of my time.' One, incidentally, who accounted for Graveney's wicket most often. Over the years he developed a reputation as 'Statham's bunny', admitting as much on television in 1989: 'Every time I played him he either used to make me feel terrible or get me out . . . I think Trueman bowled me three times in twenty years. Brian did it every time we met.'

Laker.

When Graveney made his début in 1948, county pros – Emmett, Barnett, Crapp – advised him to 'go after' the off-spinner. Laker, they said, had no heart. No one doubted his ability (that season he took 104 wickets; the next 122) but his application was questioned – a charge refuted by Graveney: 'He could be waspish with his opinions and fell out with a number of people . . . You either admired Jim and liked him or admired him and disliked him.' (Graveney liked him.) 'He was the classic spinner of his era – a model action and rarely straying from a line and length. He always gave the ball a real tweak and non-striking batsmen could hear it as it left his hand . . . Jim spun the ball sharply in any conditions and there has rarely, if ever, been a bowler better equipped to exploit helpful wickets . . . As he went on he got better and better.'

Laker's England career, like Graveney's, ended acrimoniously. In January 1959 England, two Tests down in the series, entered the fourth at Adelaide needing to win. Their chances of doing so were halved when, on the eve of the match, Laker dropped out: a chipped finger was diagnosed, though some in the team suggested the same affliction on Laker's shoulder. England lost the Test, the Ashes, and Laker announced his retirement. 'Good riddance', was the comment of one England batsman. Graveney demurs. 'Jim over the years had problems with his finger which developed arthritis . . . Towards the end he could barely grip the ball. I think the problem had more to do with man-management', an epitaph that might serve Graveney himself. Whether in recognition of one 'difficult' player by another, he remains Laker's staunchest ally. 'Quite simply,' he says, 'the best.'

Equally effective, on his day, was Lock, 'the most competitive spinner ever'. Lock was an orthodox left-armer who varied his pace from leaden to electric (the latter involving the use of a noticeably bent arm). He 'hated batsmen' and, until the arrival of Edmonds, was the only spinner known regularly to employ the bouncer. Graveney remains 'mystified' by Lock's omission from the Australian tour of 1962–63 (the previous winter he took 22 wickets in India); a half-decade later Lock arrived as a replacement in the West Indies, scored 89 in the fifth Test and fielded tigerishly. Later still he was playing like a débutant for Western Australia. Lock's attitude to cricket was most evident in his catching. Rarely content to take half-chances he added flourishes – somersaults, cartwheels – for effect; a flying head-butt in the dressing-room counted as 'hello' by Lock's standards. To this day a spectacular stop at short leg recalls one player. 'The so-and-so,' says Graveney.

For much of his first-class career, Keith Andrew was wicketkeeper-in-waiting. In twenty years he played two Tests. For many on the circuit, Andrew was peerless – unerringly accounting for Graveney's wicket – but lacking the impish genius of Godfrey Evans. Evans was a one-off. He never flagged. His appearance as Carmen Miranda was inevitably the *pièce de résistance* of shipboard parties. Colleagues are still reduced to tears at the memory of his rendition of 'The German Band', a community song in which Evans mimed, apparently simultaneously, a dozen musical instruments.

Graveney:

> For sheer exuberance, enthusiasm and match-winning brilliance, Evans was unique . . . He was, without a doubt, the most exciting wicketkeeper of all time. Whether he was plucking a spectacular catch out of the air, or whipping off the bails in a lightning movement, Godfrey was a joy to watch. He was fearless behind the stumps and would stand up to men like Bedser without losing any skill or composure . . . Evans was also an accomplished batsman, as I witnessed at Lord's in 1952.

Asked to elaborate on Evans's 98 before lunch that day against India, Graveney shrugs: 'I can't remember. I was laughing too hard.'

'Perhaps', he says, 'because of the post-match discussions we used to have over a pint, I'm unable to resist picking teams.' Pressed to do so, Graveney nominates an England XI, 1951–91, thus:

Hutton
Boycott
May
Compton
Cowdrey
Botham
Evans
Laker
Trueman
Lock
Bedser
Twelfth man: Dexter

'Near-misses', travelling reserves, include Statham, Tyson, Appleyard, the Edriches, Barrington, Wardle.

A footnote on Bailey: 'I prefer Botham as an all-rounder, but

Trevor in his way was invaluable . . . He put immense thought and intelligence into everything he did, a quality which, reinforced by his quiet determination, ensured maximum efficiency. I could never steel myself to play the type of "barnacle" innings for which he was famous, but I admired him for doing so. He adopted a style to fit England's needs.'

Overseas, Graveney nominates six bowlers operating in pairs. In 1950, his third season, he was confronted by Ramadhin and Valentine. That summer Ramadhin took 135 first-class wickets. By the time West Indies reached Cheltenham in August he commanded almost morbid respect. Ramadhin took 8–15 and 5–36, including the wicket of Andy Wilson, who, in the second innings, ' . . . determined to get off the mark, and cautious with it, put his bat over his shoulder as the ball pitched outside off-stump, confident it was the leg-break. It wasn't. Wilson was virtually in shock – and he was a wicketkeeper, well versed in the arts of watching a bowler's hand.'

Valentine, meanwhile, announced his arrival in Test cricket by taking 11 wickets on début. He finished the series with 33. More orthodox (as who wasn't?) than Ramadhin he delivered spin, like Laker, audible to the batsman. In later life both bowlers were 'found out' – most notably at Edgbaston, 1957, when Ramadhin bowled 98 overs in an innings, in the latter stages of which he floated about like a sleepwalker. But in 1950 they were, to all purposes, unplayable. West Indies won the series three-one and altered their status in world cricket for ever.

Next season England beat South Africa by the same margin. The tourists' attack was led by Cuan McCarthy, a twenty-two-year-old who confirmed Hutton's assessment of being 'faster than Lindwall' by promptly hitting him over the heart. That was as nothing compared to the South Africans' bowling in 1955. Heine and Adcock were 'the most aggressive attack – bar none' Graveney ever faced. He and Kenyon opened the batting for England in the second Test. The first ball was dug in, bounced, and missed Kenyon's head by an inch. Heine took 5–60 that innings. In the next, at Old Trafford, Graveney encountered the most hostile bowling and Cowdrey 'the worst going-over' of their careers. The South Africans played to win – or, failing that, not to lose. Their level of fitness was outstanding. Cricket didn't happen to them as it did to others.

Many applauded, Graveney not among them: 'By the end of 1955, I came to the conclusion that in their ruthless desire to be world beaters, South Africa had forgotten that basically cricket is a game to be enjoyed . . . ' He has 'grudging admiration' for the shock tactics employed. No more.

The reverse applies to Lindwall and Miller. The former remains 'the best – the most complete – fast bowler ever'. At Lord's, 1953, Graveney scored 78 on the second evening. Next morning Lindwall bowled him fourth ball. The dismissal prompted Cardus to suggest that 'Graveney set his alarm an hour earlier', and did much to establish his reputation as laid-back, lazy. The truth, as Compton notes, is different. The previous day, 66 overs of the England innings had been bowled. The new ball was due. Lindwall, perversely, refused it. His aim was to 'rattle the batsman'. He did. Graveney took the field that morning uneasily aware that 'Ray was planning something'; the problem was: what? (The bowler's repertoire included, *inter alia*, the yorker, in-swinger, out-swinger, bouncer and slower ball.) It was the yorker. Graveney cheerfully concedes that this was a case of matter-over-mind. 'All the time I was batting, I was thinking,' he says. 'And while I was thinking, Ray bowled me.' He was that good.

At the other end Miller, an artist in improvisation. Certain batsmen feared him more than Lindwall. He was always at them, bowling at different angles, different speeds, giving the impression he never knew what to do next (confirmed by Miller himself.) 'Keith', says Graveney, 'was on a par with Botham as an entertainer . . . He was at his most dangerous when shaking off a hangover, or impatient to get to the races.' At Lord's, 1956, Miller gave the 'greatest bowling exhibition' of Graveney's career. Joking, laughing, running off a perfunctory mark, Miller took 10–152 and cost Graveney his Test place for the first time since 1952. In the second innings Miller (who could be 'kidded' by Bailey into a rash shot) employed some elementary psychology of his own: exploiting Graveney's penchant for the drive, he switched to round the wicket, delivered a half-volley wide of off-stump . . . and saw Langley pocket the catch. The silence that greeted him was, says Graveney, deafening. He played no further Tests for a year.

Other bowlers whom Graveney admired include Mankad, Fazal Mahmood, Hall, Gibbs, Archer, Johnston, Benaud, Davidson.

Surprisingly, he nominates Bruce Dooland, who played three Tests for Australia, as 'the best leg-break and googly bowler I saw' (Dooland twice did the double for Nottinghamshire); ahead even of Benaud, who had greater control but 'never attempted to buy wickets . . . preferring to close a game up like a left-armer'. In bowling, as batting, Graveney's preference was for the colourful, the conspicuous. If, like Dooland, they were also 'difficult', so much the better.

Of batsmen, his greatest regret is 'never seeing Bradman'. (In his four visits to England he only once, in 1930, visited Bristol. The match ended in a tie.) Débuting as Bradman retired, Neil Harvey was, says Graveney, 'a joy to watch . . . even when chasing his shots to the boundary'. He was the Astaire of cricket, flexible and fluid. Harvey batted with animal grace. At Sydney, 1954, he scored 92 of an Australian total of 184 (Tyson 6–85); this and Cowdrey's 102, says Graveney, were the innings of the series. (Some nominate his own 111 in the fifth Test.) A half-decade later England encountered Norman O'Neill, twenty-one, who scored 71 not out on his début at Brisbane; reminiscent of Compton, says Graveney – 'the ball *sounded* so good off his bat.' O'Neill eventually scored 2779 runs, average 45, in 42 Tests, and could have done more. 'He was among the most naturally gifted batsmen ever. Unfortunately, he was the least intelligent.'

Between 1973 and 1976 one England player scored four centuries against West Indies, prompting Lloyd to describe him as 'the best, on his day, in the world'. On his day because Amiss, like Graveney, could be wilful – not least in Australia where he ended the 1974–75 series with an average of 19. Another analogy: both scored eleven Test centuries and over a hundred in all. Amiss, like Graveney, fell out with his county when, after signing for World Series, it was announced that he would not be offered a contract until the Packer crisis was resolved. Graveney sympathised: 'Anyone who can bat like Dennis in the Caribbean has my vote.' In the Caribbean Graveney and Amiss are still regarded as the most fluent English players of their day. They in turn nominate one West Indian. Between his début (watched by Graveney) and swansong (by Amiss), Sobers scored 8032 Test runs, took 235 wickets, 109 catches. In 1966, when both batsmen appeared for England, Sobers scored three centuries in four Tests. In the fifth, which England won, he made nought. 'Garry', says Graveney, 'was a big-match performer . . . a master of invention with a sound technique and flair for improvisation.' More surprisingly, he rates Sobers 'among the best new-ball bowlers ever – better than Hall or Griffith'. England batsmen of the late 1950s and 1960s were 'scared witless' when Sobers failed to score – an inevitable prelude to his taking wickets. 'We knew, every Test, Garry would do something with either bat or ball – or both. He was the most stylish player ever.' The feeling was mutual.

Finally the trinity of Weekes, Worrell, Walcott. The first 'continually looked to be on the offensive' and with his devastating cut earned the admiring sobriquet 'butcher'. Weekes had the broadest bat, and among the broadest grins, in cricket. The most uncomplicated and unassuming of the three; 'With Everton,' says Graveney, 'what you saw was what you got.' His near-namesake Walcott was 'less effervescent', with a tendency to be suspicious of open praise. He was the engine of West Indies cricket. To drive the ball out of the ground is a relatively rare feat; Walcott could do it off the back foot. Animally strong, he hit the ball from a crouch; one was reminded of a half-open blade – or flick-knife. Completing the trio, Worrell ('the Perry Como of cricket') brought determination to winning personal charm. Early on he was intimidated by other batsmen. Substitutes are always haunting cricketers' lives. Worrell learnt the game in the Lancashire League and was equally at home socially in Burnley or Bridgetown. He lasted longer than the others because, says Graveney, he was 'technically superior'; he played through the line. In 1963, age thirty-nine, he was still the outstanding West Indies tactician. That summer he asked Dexter if England were 'joking' by omitting Graveney.

Under the same terms of reference, Graveney names his World XI 1951–91, as follows:

Hutton
Barry Richards
Viv Richards
Compton
Harvey
Sobers
Dooland
Evans
Lindwall
Laker
Bedser
Twelfth Man: Miller

A party of seventeen would include Worrell, Benaud, Gavaskar, Trueman, Knott. As to whether he himself would merit inclusion, Graveney is ambiguous. 'I was a very good player, not a great one.' After a pause: 'Except on certain occasions. Then I was great.'

Barry and Viv Richards: the two pre-eminent bats since Graveney's retirement – 'Not that I'd necessarily want to be stranded with either of them'. Others whom he watched and admired include Zaheer Abbas, Javed Miandad, Imran Khan, Kapil Dev, Azharuddin, Greenidge, Haynes, Hadlee, Crowe, Pollock, Bland, the Chappells, Border – the last of whom 'stuck with it when the going was rough'. Graveney admitted years ago that he admires anyone with patience.

Meanwhile, in England:

> Cricket will never be able to meet the debt it owes to Botham . . . He had the talent of genius and there is not an England side since 1946 which would not have welcomed him with open arms. Ian's impact would have been as great in any era, and it is a measure of his standing that he was thought to have 'failed' when returning figures that other all-rounders would kill for.

Having said which:

> I never understood why Botham was made captain; or saw him being tied to the cares of office. With respect, I doubt if he had much to do with managing himself, let alone ten others . . . I never pictured him as a forward planner, a tactician in the mould of Brearley or Illingworth . . . Ian, quite simply, was out of his depth. Significantly, I never saw him smile once when he was captain.

A month after ceasing to be, Botham gave evidence of his (then) genius as a bowler. The occasion was the fourth Test against Australia at Edgbaston. The tourists began their second innings needing 151 to win in two days. Willis, 'bowling . . . as if the devil were at his heels' (*Wisden*), removed Dyson and Hughes; still Border remained. The score rose to 105–4. At this stage Botham entered into conference with Brearley.

'How are you, Guy?'

'Why do you ask?'

'No reason. You just look tired.'

'Tired?'

'Fancy a bowl?'

'Watch me,' said Botham.

He proceeded to take five wickets for 1 run. Australia collapsed and lost the Test by 29 runs. For the second successive match England contrived to win after appearing badly beaten. '*That*', says Graveney, 'was Ian's finest hour' – and, incidentally, Brearley's.

Playing in the same Test with almost ghostly reticence (he scored 0 and 23) was David Gower. Not the least of Gower's cares has been his constant comparison to Graveney. The two, according to the *Telegraph*, are 'the great enigmas of the modern game'; not only for the style of their batting but in their 'seemingly casual approach to it'. Gower is on record as admiring Graveney, and a number of those who saw both at their peak testify to the influence. (Graveney never perfected the leg-side flick which brought Gower so much pleasure – and pain.) Brian Johnston admits to an almost eerie sense of *déjà vu* when watching the younger player. Swanton calls the resemblance notable.

All the more credence, then, to Graveney's own view. He acknowledges the 'special place' occupied by the highly gifted, the enigmatic. He sympathises: 'Gower was, and is, a "touch" player, relying on his eye and an inherent sense of style. I admire that. The only trouble is it leaves a batsman in his thirties without a solid technique to fall back on. Players like Barrington, myself and, to an extent, Cowdrey got better as we got older. Gower got worse.'

The same applies to Botham; though not, strangely, to Gooch, who in cricketing senility 'lowered his stance and learnt to play straight again'. (Graveney still rates Gooch in the third tier of modern English batsmen, behind that occupied by Cowdrey, Barrington, Dexter, Boycott and himself.) Another in the class is Gatting: 'A battler whose strength was a knowledge of his own weakness . . . He could have done more.' (Gatting's celebrated comment following the Shakoor Rana saga – 'They've been at it for thirty years' – was in fact Graveney's. He relinquishes the copyright.) In short: touch may be fine, but not at the expense of technique. 'Look at Compton,' says Graveney. And wistfully: 'If only we could.'

For the future he has hopes for Atherton, Smith, the Bicknells, Ramprakash, Tufnell. Johnson, the Nottingham middle-order bat, has 'class' says Graveney, adding superfluously, 'Not that that necessarily ensures selection.' Others include Afford, Bailey, Hussain, Moles, Hugh Morris, Roseberry, Thorpe – and, incredibly, Alan Butcher, thirty-eight, who 'until recently was playing the best cricket of his life' (Butcher, who no one would describe as a 'touch' player, does have 'technique'); few, or none, of whom may in future appear in a side selected by Dexter. 'I rate Ted,' says Graveney, 'but not as an administrator.' Illingworth, for one, has 'greater appreciation of the way cricket works'.

Which is?

Graveney's first and foremost conclusion: 'There are simply too many matches, particularly Tests. In the fifties we played twenty-eight three-day fixtures, four or five Tests, and toured two winters out of three. A top pro played 110 days a summer . . . Today they average 130, in a variety of one, three, four and five-day formats. It doesn't allow players to settle into a groove . . . A batsman out of touch in Tests isn't likely to find it in the Sunday League. It seems we've confused quantity for quality.'

The answer? A Championship of seventeen four-day matches for each county, 'to be played during mid-week when attendances are at their lowest'. Weekends would be reserved for the single-innings competitions. Warming to his theme, Graveney would 'actively explore' devoting certain weeks exclusively to Tests: 'They already hog the scene, devouring all the time on TV and radio and all the space in the newspapers, not to mention removing the leading players . . . If a clash could be avoided, the Championship would be immeasurably stronger and be given fresh status without detracting from Tests.'

One-day cricket, Graveney acknowledges, is here to stay: 'I have no problem with the sixty-over format' (having played in the first Gillette Cup final); 'but three one-day competitions, including the Sunday League, is one too many . . . The fewer the overs, the less like cricket it becomes.'

The result:

This goes back to the dark ages, but it is an inescapable fact that when Hutton, Compton, May *et al* reached 50, the next target was a second

> 50, and after that fresh guard was taken as if the innings was starting again.
>
> Compton tells of a blast from his captain [Hammond] when exuberance got the better of him after scoring a century in his first Test against Australia. He was twenty years old at the time and England had already scored more runs than seems possible in these days, but instead of praise Denis was rocketed. [Compton scored only 102 which, in the captain's view, was deficient.] God knows what Hammond would have said to those who all too often get out on the wrong side of 50, having got over the most difficult part of an innings.
>
> For my part, if I got out other than to a good ball which would have defeated me at any time, I was furious with myself. 'Laid-back' I may have been, but the attitude wasn't ingrained as it is today.

The format has also bred a generation of bowlers whose brief is to absorb, not attack. Two technical changes have encouraged this:

> The hard leather used in the manufacture of cricket balls has developed a sort of swing bowler whose sole aim is to restrict runs . . . When I first went to The Oval in 1948 the shine would be off within ten overs and, unless the bowler had genuine pace, accuracy, the rare skill of Alec Bedser, or gave the ball a definite tweak, he stood no chance. Today much of the work is done for him.
>
> Another factor has been the lush condition of the outfields which, nourished by fertilisers, tend to keep the shine on the ball; this in turn encourages the medium-pacer who, with one or two exceptions, is useless at Test level, particularly abroad. The difference that conditions make can be startling. Bowlers who are outstanding in England can be flops when taken away from pitches producing movement off the seam. Ken Higgs was an example. In 1966 I stood in the slips and saw him create problems for batsmen of the calibre of Sobers, Nurse, Butcher, Kanhai, Hunte. He finished with 24 wickets. Eighteen months later, in the Caribbean, he couldn't get into the side . . . Everyone said he was a 'great' bowler, but he wasn't. Great bowlers can bowl in all conditions, not just those they're familiar with.

For those possessing genuine skill, or pace, Graveney has nothing but praise. His is not among the voices raised for the restriction of short-pitched bowling: 'I knew exactly what it was like to see a potentially lethal missile hurtling towards my head at a speed fast enough to land a motorist in the dock . . . However dangerous and emotive the bouncer may be, it ought not to give any batsman worthy of the name undue trouble, provided he is in the right position and keeps his nerve' – presuming, of course, the delivery is legal. Griffith was an exception.

More pressing is the matter of over-rates. Graveney's formula for a programme of seventeen four-day matches would – reluctantly – include a stipulated daily quota of overs; reluctantly because 'the players cannot be trusted to maintain a reasonable rate', and the discretionary powers of umpires have proved inadequate.

On umpiring generally:

> I find myself among the establishment ranks, if only because I fear the popular cures of so-called neutrals, electronic aids or a third official would, in the end, be worse than the disease . . . I never went on a tour without encountering umpiring problems of one sort or another, and no matter how well briefed beforehand, even the most disciplined team can be upset by contentious decisions; some manage to accept it stoically as an occupational hazard, but cricket needs to concern itself with the growing practice of pressurising umpires by incessant and cynical appealing. Pakistan are the masters of this. As a batsman I deplore the shouts from all directions for leg-before, when only the bowler and wicketkeeper are in a position to appeal.

While noting the 'increased pressure' such tactics create, Graveney restates his praise of umpires generally, with one exception:

> The public may not know it . . . but, more and more, umpires are making compensatory decisions – giving a batsman out merely to amend an earlier mistake. This happens frequently in Australia. Rather than righting a wrong it is, in fact, creating another one . . . The effect of the original decision can never be reversed. It all depends when, and in what circumstances, the mistake was made.

Graveney was present at Lord's when, in 1980, the umpires were offered police protection in the Long Room. The incident seemed to epitomise the decline in standards affecting both players and spectators, whose root he identifies as 'lack of discipline' at the top:

> A lot of cricket's problems would disappear with strong and purposeful captaincy, and I am bound to think the appointment of

> team managers might be considered superfluous . . . The fact is that if a county has a good captain it does not need a manager . . . As well as determining tactics, the captain should be personally responsible for discipline. When I was in charge no one was in any doubt where they stood.

Except, of course, Graveney himself. More than thirty years on he remains hurt (at best), bitter (at worst) by his treatment at Gloucester. Where, he asks, did he go wrong? He seems genuinely perplexed. Graveney, after all, captained by instinct. He had no gift for management, but even his critics concede he was true to his nature. ('It wasn't his fault,' says Brown.) He was in turn described as 'serene' (Swanton), 'severe' (Cardus.) The same equation applied to, among others, Hammond and Compton. It was Graveney's tragedy that at critical times he was considered as a batsman too serene, as a captain too severe. 'Confused?' he says. 'At times I didn't know what was wanted of me.'

Bitter? In black and white, the facts look stark. Nobody cared about Graveney so long as he was an errant genius, no more challenging than a Simpson or Edrich, but when he made a bid to play at a higher level he aroused powerful emotions. (All batsmen-captains are remembered first for their captaincy, then their batting.) The Gloucester Affair changed Graveney. It hardened him. Today he visits Bristol only under sufferance. Nothing in the county's later history – their dismissal of Ken Graveney and his son David as chairman and captain respectively – has changed that. 'Three sackings in the family is too many,' says Tom. To Gloucester the Graveneys were as good as a circus. They say so themselves.

David's troubles were exacerbated when, in 1990, he acted as player-manager of Gatting's rebel tour of South Africa. For his sins he received a largely notional ban from Test cricket, causing his uncle to write:

> As a simple cricketer I abhor the intrusion of power politics into the game, and I am certainly not in favour of racial discrimination. [D'Oliveira to this day recalls Graveney shaking with rage when, on tour in Rhodesia, Weekes was refused a drink.] I want to see all cricketers everywhere allowed to play the game of their choice without being accused of supporting repressive regimes, or of taking

blatantly extreme stances either way . . . I want to see an end to the sickening hypocrisy and double standards of governments who use sport and cricket for their own ends. An impossible middle-of-the-road position? Perhaps – but the alternative is to see the greatest of all games torn to pieces.

Graveney's largest fury is reserved for politicians:

To me the worst aspect is the intervention of so-called world leaders, starting with Mr Vorster . . . We cry to heavens about the iniquities of apartheid, call on sportsmen to sever all links, yet continue to trade and invest in South Africa . . . So while speculators grow rich it is a 'crime' for even a county pro to spend six months coaching whites, blacks and browns. At least Guyana thought so when they banned Jackman and stopped a Test in 1981.

In batting, certainly in captaincy, Graveney could be oblique, sometimes given to Delphic utterances in the manner of Hammond or Hutton. As a man he is nothing if not direct. ('Straight' is the most frequent response when colleagues are asked to describe him.) His views on South Africa have the merit of bluntness. He was genuinely saddened by the loss of Pollock, Procter, Richards to Test cricket. As a professional it depressed him that restraints existed on cricketers' rights to play where they chose. It was, he says, a simpler game in his day.

Sportsmen like myself can only put a toe into the deep-swirling waters of international politics. Cricket is caught up by the tides of big business, race, prejudice and intolerance, and the question is: Can the game survive such intolerable pressures? If I had an answer I would be an oracle, but I believe the readmission of South Africa was overdue. The danger of outlawing them indefinitely would be to invite them to regress and to undo all the recent achievements. On that score I do not totally condemn the unofficial tours by Gooch and Gatting, though I didn't like the way they went about them.

It should also be clearly understood that England and Australia in particular made sacrifices, both financially and personally, in standing by the principle of multi-racial cricket in South Africa. Frankly, knowing the passion for the game in India and the West Indies, I would not care to be a politician in either of those countries whose action led to further loss of Tests and tours. To me it is unthinkable

> that bigotry could yet bring about a breakdown in world cricket, but in the last twenty years we came perilously close to it.

And now, with greater objectivity, himself: How did Graveney personally react to the South African crisis and its aftermath? He deplored it. An earnest, brooding, heart-struck man, he worried about matters other cricketers took for granted. He seriously feared for the game's survival. He fought prejudice intuitively, because it offended him. He refused to be used as a spokesman, preferring to express his views through personal deed and word. D'Oliveira calls him 'about the best friend I have'. Speaking of Graveney he becomes strongly agitated. 'No one', he says, 'did more for me at the time of the crisis.' For a while the families – Tom and Basil, Jackie and Naomi, their two identically aged sons – were inseparable; much of this took the form of simple kindness, away from the gaze of press and public who saw only two professionals, obviously revelling in each other's company. For morale, the two wives often sent each other flowers. When Jackie wrote, she enclosed copies of fan letters from supporters. She concealed the hate mail that also came in. Then there was other pressure, for Graveney to align himself with the radical left. Typically he refused. 'Those loudest in their condemnation of visits by unofficial teams, with their cries of "blood money", should reflect that they might not have taken place had an official multi-racial side toured South Africa earlier . . . Cricketers play cricket, and no amount of legislation can stop them. It's as simple as that.'

On the subject of overseas players Graveney is categorical:

> If English cricket is to be jealous of its standards and fair to itself, it has to be an English game for English players. The era of foreign domination has to end, and counties become self-reliant. The influx of imports has not only chipped away at the foundation of England's national side, but led to a blasé public . . . In the past cricket followers anticipated with relish the arrival of touring teams and the big foreign names. The opening fixture at Worcester was an occasion. Nowadays it is possible to see the world's leading performers any day of the week in county cricket. Familiarity has bred, if not contempt, a little indifference. Some of the magic, some of the curiosity value, has gone. It was a sign of the times when one national newspaper did not even report the arrival of the Australian side in England.

So: Graveney stresses the manufacture of product, not the manufactured product. He demands 'good habits', technical and temperamental, in young cricketers, so much so that critics have accused him of obsession. He insists. Ever since touring Graveney has been intrigued by other systems. Cricket overseas seems gaudy, wild by comparison. He questions the work of the NCA (managed by his old adversary Andrew), knowing it faces an uphill battle:

> Too many schools omit cricket from the sporting syllabus, for two reasons. First, pitches and facilities are either not available or not up to scratch. Second, it is far easier to set boys to run around a field, or to play football the whole year round . . . Astonishingly some of the leading physical education colleges, Loughborough included, do not have cricket on the curriculum as a compulsory subject . . . The result must be that countless sports masters have been appointed with little or no knowledge of cricket, and an extra burden placed on national coaches . . . Nor is there any justification for teaching softball or rounders in preference to cricket, if only because the chance of continuing those activities after leaving is remote.

Result: potentially good, even great, cricketers are lost through lack of amenities. Contrast the situation in Australia where, says Graveney, the facilities have to be seen to be believed. (He calls the wicket at the Church of England School, Brisbane, among the best in the country.) His own coaching by Tulloch and Carter, and his exposure to cricket both in Bristol and overseas, were vital in extending his style. Critics have referred to Graveney's 'flawed' genius, his 'inflexible' manner, yet few question his commitment as a coach. Lou Cooper, then secretary of Queensland, described him as possessing 'infinite patience' and 'treating each case on its own merits'. Even today a winter's evening finds him in Taunton, Northampton or native Newcastle at the request of a club or college; few are ever refused. Don Wilson, former MCC head coach (the man whose bowling deprived Worcester of the Championship in 1962), describes Graveney as a 'natural communicator . . . always ready to listen to a youngster and respond with genuine interest'. The point is echoed by a master at Dean Close, Cheltenham, who calls Graveney 'the best coach I've seen . . . whose chief asset is an obvious love affair with cricket'.

Graveney confirms it. He loves cricket. Why else would he have played for derisory wages, forsaking his wife and family for tours undertaken in anything but luxurious conditions? Been praised for being Graveney and criticised for playing in Graveney's way? If every life has its characteristic difficulty – one theme developed thousands of ways – then Graveney's was his ability to infuriate and exhilarate in equal measure. His weakness as a captain – as a man – was his refusal to adapt, to adjust his own characteristics to the demands of others. Hence his success with the undemanding young. A child of ten will be answered by Graveney with more patience than, at times, were Milton, Mortimore or Cook; a club cricketer urged to 'play straight' as once Hutton urged Graveney himself. He feels most alive among cricketers and most lively amongst the young. His travels give him no cause to retract the view that, even in diminished numbers, 'excellent cricketers' are still being produced. Graveney's advice to any player, notwithstanding the flaws in the modern game – 'appalling' manners, 'political meddling', 'unnecessary' contrivances (including the helmet) – is uniform: 'Cricket is the greatest game on earth. Given it all to do again, I wouldn't change. Not one thing.'

Graveney made his début as a radio commentator in June 1979. One of his first assignments was the World Cup semi-final between Pakistan and West Indies at The Oval. Twenty thousand spectators were present. Graveney was paired with former colleagues Trueman and Bailey ('Lucky,' he says, 'me') and a fortnight later another former team-mate, Laker, asked if he were 'interested' in moving to television. As usual, fortune, good or bad, seemed to have sought him out. Graveney took all of a minute to agree.

He took less than that to regret it when, moments before appearing live, a studio manager upset a scalding cup of coffee over his arm. 'By the grace of some guardian angel, I instinctively pushed the microphone down and by the barest possible margin my painful expletive escaped being picked up. Had it come across I fear my first word, though sensational, would have proved my last, and I might have made it into the *Guinness Book of Records* heading a column under the title: Brief Television Appearances.'

After that things improved. Working with Laker, Benaud and Peter West allowed Graveney to develop what came naturally and discard what did not. Letters from viewers praised his 'laid-back' yet 'authoritative' style, qualities also apparent in Graveney personally. Early in his new career Benaud advised him to 'talk just as you are to me', adding that 'naturalness is what commentary is all about'.

The point echoed a theme in Benaud's book *On Reflection*:

> The televising of cricket is quite different from that of other sports where the action is very fast . . . Cricket tends to meander along, although there may be some high points in the day. Usually you are required not to give a running commentary, as is the case on radio, but to provide comments at what you hope is exactly the right time . . . I believe you should only talk when you can add to the picture on the screen.
>
> It is nigh impossible to get the right balance. You have, sitting out there, children, mothers and fathers, some of whom may not have seen a cricket telecast before or may be watching it in their first season. Then there is the person who might play club cricket, knows a lot about the game and requires a midway commentary. Finally, there is the one who considers he knows everything about the game and a lot more besides, and wants to be told nothing.
>
> Television cricket commentaries are by far the most difficult of any, mainly because you have to try to strike a balance of conversation with the person to whom you're talking through the lens. That person needs to be a blend of everyone I have listed, requiring all the information available and, at the same time, needing none, so from that you may appreciate it is a difficult job.

Benaud concludes by commending Graveney's sincerity on the air, a quality also communicating itself to the audience. (Laker, too, believed that 'being oneself' was the key to successful broadcasting.) Ironically, Graveney found himself praised for the very virtues for which once he had been damned – notably the relaxed manner which had so irritated Hutton. During the dramatic 1981 series Graveney could be heard at intervals adding his unique deadpan comment: 'My word, Richie'; after a spectacular back-foot six, 'Hmmm'; and (throaty chuckle), 'He actually *looked* at it that time.' His characteristic approach to batting ('I played every innings essentially the same way') soon extended to commentary, for which he felt equally calm whether reporting a provincial one-day match or a sold-out Test at Lord's. Graveney was born to be relaxed. His weakness as a player became his strength as a pundit.

His new role also allowed him to take fresh guard on old issues:

> I have heard television berated because of the replays of dismissals and the instant examination of umpires' decisions . . . The truth is that, more often than not, umpires are shown to be right. If anything, television has provided certain proof of the generally high standard of English officials . . . one reason I do not believe in a future of instant play-backs on a huge screen.
>
> Umpires should, though, be relieved of the responsibility of decision-making in the often contentious matter of the fitness of grounds . . . Let them control the match, and pass on the onus of starting or resuming play to another authority, be it the managers of the teams or a neutral observer.
>
> I welcome the idea of a referee to levy punishments for indiscipline or behaviour calculated to bring the game into disrepute. The mere presence of such an official should cool some of the hot-heads who, sadly, have been getting away with it too long.

How good a broadcaster is Graveney? According to Benaud 'a natural', whose only flaw was an early tendency to over-elaborate, a point made by Graveney himself: 'Television, with events unfolding before the viewer, demands more discipline from its commentators than radio. The temptation to talk too much is strong for the beginner. Viewers do not need to be told what they can see for themselves, and the art is to observe and inform without being over-technical. Stating the obvious and the overworked cliché can be irritating. The close-ups give the armchair spectator an insight denied even to those with the best seats on the ground.'

Off-camera Graveney's comments are anodyne – 'cracking', 'marvellous', 'super' – punctuated by lunging demonstrations, left arm cocked, head over the ball – 'through the line, see . . . through the line'. Graveney took the view that cricket is a simple game, simply explained ('Keep still . . . bowl straight . . . hold your catches') and something of this clarity is evident on the air. His correspondence is as large now as in his pomp, much of it gratifyingly from those with little or no previous interest in the game.

> The cameras have put all-seeing eyes on the behaviour of players and crowds . . . I recall times when I returned from abroad to find the

public highly sceptical of riots and incidents on the field. Local officials were wont to cry that it was all highly exaggerated. After an interval even the Georgetown riot of 1953–54 – when bottles and other objects were hurled on to the pitch – was played down as the invention of 'foreign' correspondents. No longer can authority hide behind a smokescreen of denials.

Undeniably television has also brought its problems to cricket. More would-be customers stay at home and watch Tests on the screen . . . But this in itself provides an opportunity for hundreds of thousands to learn something of the game, its players and personalities. After a quarter of a century playing cricket, I want to share something of its beauty with others. If television allows me to do that, it's been a worthwhile profession.

Graveney is essentially benign, and his comments are made benignly: 'a wonderful talker, a good improviser, champion critic', said Arlott. To be dissected by Graveney is a kind of privilege. Even his views on fellow broadcasters are lenient. Benaud is peerless, Illingworth guileless – Jack Bannister ambitious. His sole censure is reserved for Boycott: 'A much better player', says Graveney, 'since he retired.' He can watch a batsman for ten minutes and know whether or not he can play. He believes in honest criticism, but none was ever made because he was Tom Graveney. ('I try', he says, 'to help.') More than one first-class player has approached him and been answered with genuine care. His credo on batting is simple and simply stated ('Players get into trouble because they fail to stay in line'). He has contributed to coaching books and videos and advised a number of England batsmen before facing the West Indies:

Modern players are inclined to hook, even if the ball is outside the off stump. This is folly. Hooking on or around off stump is both hazardous and strictly unprofessional, for if the stroke is fractionally mistimed there is a real danger of the ball being deflected into the face.

Reg Simpson was a master of short-pitched bowling. His method was disarmingly simple. He swayed out of line and allowed the ball to fly harmlessly by. When I batted with him for England I recognised him as an expert in dealing with the bouncer . . . Simpson could hook, but only when he was satisfied everything was right, including the pace of the pitch . . . otherwise he blandly discouraged any form of intimidation by weaving six inches one way or the other and not

> offering a stroke. When players like Graeme Hick ask for advice in facing the likes of Marshall, Ambrose and Walsh I immediately refer them to Simpson – though sadly not all take the point.

As for artificial aids:

> The helmet, for me, is unnecessary . . . Ironically it probably encourages short-pitched bowling. Bowlers think they are absolved from responsibility for accidents, and that, as the helmet protects the head and face, they have a licence to let it rip. I can well imagine the helmet acting as a red rag to a bull to certain bowlers . . . I can only guess what Trueman's reaction would have been.

In summary:

> As a critic, I try to stress the simple truths of batting without being pompous . . . It comes down to two or three basic rules that worked fifty years ago and will work fifty years from now. Long after I am forgotten the game will essentially be the same as when I played it.

The game does not forget him, and never will. In 1991 Graveney was offered a vice-presidency of Worcester; invitations to clubs and committees followed. In addition to commentary he appears regularly at first-class fixtures for pleasure. He adjudicates Man of the Match awards and is active as an after-dinner speaker. He has built up a reputation not only as a player but as an observer, a kindly and ironic critic whose views are sought by cricketers everywhere. Typically, he has done little to court this; it was the style and manner of his batting that fascinated his followers, and at a distance of twenty years fascinates them still. In an age of declining standards, standards conferring the illusion of greatness on technically inferior players, Graveney stands as a reminder of all that is natural and uninhibited. He is now, even to the generation that can never have seen him, the first among all the great names associated with style and glamour. That, more than the mere facts of his career, serves as his epitaph.

'I loved playing,' he says. 'Why else would I have done it?' In 1944 Graveney was faced with the sombre prospect of finding a job. He considered accountancy before joining the army. But for the influence of his brother he might have stayed there – but influence him he did. Ken Graveney, whose playing days, beset by injury, were restricted to a score of matches between 1947–51 and a brief period as captain in 1963–64, described it as a 'once-in-a-lifetime chance', adding that 'the army will always be there . . . but cricket only knocks once.' In 1948 Gloucester were undergoing penitence. Not for the last time they suffered from captain trouble, appointing an amateur with scant regard for men like Barnett, Crapp, Emmett. Both brothers confirm that the dressing-room atmosphere at the time could be tense. Tense himself, the younger Graveney was in awe of those whose names he knew chiefly from the pages of magazines. He was diffident. He was shy. His first first-class innings was nought. From there things deteriorated until on 16 June, his twenty-first birthday, he was dropped. At this stage few in Bristol, Graveney included, had much hope; few outside it had heard of him. Had the England selectors not chosen that moment to drop Hutton and, incredibly, include Emmett, it is arguable that his career would have been caught short. In the event Graveney returned and scored 64 not out. In the following month he made 600 runs. By season's end *Wisden* was praising his 'graceful right- handed strokeplay'. He was awarded his cap. Gloucester were convinced.

Was Graveney? The life of a junior pro in those days was arduous. He watched. He waited. He fetched and carried. He was paid £4 a week. Graveney had no commercial interests and in the winter he batted on the splintered floor of the indoor school. The next season, 1949, he scored 1784 runs and four centuries. He found himself accepted by his fellow professionals. He was greeted warmly by Compton and without insult by Edrich. On Midsummer Day he scored 96 against Middlesex, the match he 'arrived' as an England prospect. His horizons were expanding; experience was broadening his youthful exuberance, and two congested seasons taught him adaptability as fast as he could learn it. It is a measure of his growth that, in 1950, his 1892 runs were considered 'not to have made the progress anticipated' (*Wisden*). The next season, his fourth, he was selected for England.

Comfortable, in the midst of life, Graveney developed a love affair with cricket. Even on retirement he did not cut himself off as others have. He was happy to play for the Wanderers, Old England, in occasional overseas matches, for charity. Even today something of the machinery survives. In 1990 he appeared for the President of MCC's XI at Lord's. He flowed into the drive like something from another age; like Tom Graveney. 'He can still play,' said Snow, who bowled at him. 'I saw him coming forward and dropped it short . . . He drove me off the back foot, the so-and-so.' In the dressing-room Graveney was happy, effusive, tired, introducing his son. And where were his wife and daughter? Applauding from the stand.

Graveney's family have known the vicissitudes of cricket. From 1952, the year he married, to 1970, the year he emigrated, he toured overseas eighteen times; that in addition to his county contract. In the calendar year 1954 Graveney was free of cricket for exactly a fortnight. His wife states that their daughter, born that spring, was for years apprehensive of the 'strange man' appearing at intervals between tours. Graveney's family were with him and about him as an essential part of his career; if they are seen here from his perspective, that is only because for the moment it is his perspective that matters. Abandoning his infant daughter for six months, in the last five of which he played barely a dozen innings; shielding his newborn son from the prying eye of the media; committing his wife to two decades of virtual widowhood; such things affected him no less than they would a man expressing himself through words or music. If, as Bailey suggests, the key to Graveney's 'relative failure' as a Test batsman lay in his 'unconscious resentment . . . of the need to restrain himself', might not other unconscious factors have counted equally? It is known that a number of Graveney's most sorry innings coincided with sorrowful news from home. Conversely, he visibly brightened at the sight of wife, daughter or son watching from the stand, and in June 1960, following the last's birth, he scored 135 of the best runs imaginable. Graveney's life away from the field, whether during his active career or after it, is his concern in the way that the man of words or music's is not. That is why I have concerned myself little, though he concerned himself much, with his family, his home and friends, his life away from cricket. For twenty-five years cricket *was* his life, and by his own admission it was only on retiring that his family and he returned to normal. Graveney is touchingly grateful for his wife's patience, forbearance, even her admiration. He needed security; she gave it to him. On his return from Queensland he professed not to miss the merry-go-round of professional cricket. He did, though, profoundly miss the social side – 'the camaraderie, the banter, the inner satisfaction of a well-played innings, even the glamour of being a sporting figure' – and knew full well the stories of successful players who, through no fault of their own, had become embittered ex-players. It was Graveney's wife who, with less cause than most, encouraged him to return. ('What a waste to have someone like you behind the bar.') She persuaded him to write to the BBC, with the eventual response by Martin-Jenkins and all that followed. She also realised early on (her cousin, after all, played professionally) that cricket essentially is a club – a view echoed by Graveney, who adds, 'You might not want it every day, but it's comforting to know it's there.' It is this understanding of the game – the mistress of so many players' lives – that has finally, after four decades, broadened and strengthened the Graveneys' marriage. In August they celebrate their fortieth anniversary.

He gained weight – he could hardly have lost it – after retiring. Always a conservative dresser he sometimes inclines to double-breasted jackets, giving him the look of a giant bird. His nose, too, is beaklike. Graveney's hair is flecked with white, his face richly tinted. His movements are angular, as if controlled by motors of varying voltage. This June he turns sixty-five. When Graveney smiles certain muscles – muscles some people never develop – become visible. He still lives in Cheltenham, a retiring, unobtrusive figure, playing golf, collecting stamps. No one understands better the value of fame. Besides the neutral expression that he wears at home, Graveney has two others, forward and reverse, that he uses for all human dealings. The former is reserved for fans, for friends, for autograph hunters nudged forward by nervous fathers. The latter is for those occasions when Graveney considers himself put on or used. He seldom uses the second expression – being respected more now than as a player – but when he does his face comes to a complete stop, his mouth tightens, his eyes seem to recede. You might then get the impression that Graveney, though physically there, was no longer present. As for getting through to him when this happens – one might as well get through to Mount Rushmore. Graveney might respond with 'Yes', 'No', or, more cryptically, 'We'll see'. He long ago decided that fame has its drawbacks –

dealing with troublemakers and strangers, receiving proposals, playing golf with businessmen and sponsors who, translating their professional style on to the course, outflank him and win. And always the same question as, veteran of 79 Tests, 122 centuries, lauded and fêted in every country where cricket is played, he hears, 'Where did it all go wrong?' He reviews his career modestly, but in the conviction that at times he was better – far better – than the public knew. He is hurt by his failure against Australia, or to play in South Africa. ('To this day, I don't know what I did wrong'). In full maturity Graveney is inclined to be generous to his critics ('At times I did give the wrong impression') while maintaining that 'Cricket taught me to appreciate players' strengths and tolerate their weaknesses', a courtesy denied himself. He is pleased at the honours and recognition; pleased, generally, when the press remembers him; pleased even to be the subject of a biography. He looks on himself today as a sort of monument, appreciated not merely for his elegance, 'but for having been around so long'.

He has. Graveney's first Test was under a man who had known Bodyline; his last included recognisably modern players like Boycott, Underwood, Knott. No one but Cowdrey had his depth of experience, and (excluding his last call to Australia) Cowdrey's Tests were played over seventeen years to Graveney's eighteen. In the public's eye they, and later Barrington, became associated as a unit. Of the three it is arguable Graveney was the most naturally gifted; unarguably he scored the fewest Test runs. Luck, circumstance and his own temperament may have contributed; so too the fact that Graveney, an inept captain, was captained ineptly. In Tests only Cowdrey encouraged him to be natural, and Cowdrey's pomp coincided with Graveney's as a batsman. His early cricket was played under the austere gaze of Brown, Hutton, May, men by whom 'the grafter was apt to be preferred'. He was held up by them and reached maturity years behind schedule. Had Graveney played under a Benaud or Brearley, had his county been led by a man like Surridge – had someone been appreciative of *his* strengths and tolerant of his weaknesses – Graveney's name might today be mentioned in company of Hutton's and Compton's. Nothing actual ever fits expectation and expectation itself is a source of disappointment. When Graveney failed it was too often seen as failure, not a prelude to success. To appreciate him took control. It took composure.

His memories are so numerous that not even he can name best and worst. Was it his first first-class season, out for nought to a student who promptly returned to cricketing obscurity; his second, wherein in the same fixture he scored 108; his fourth, in which he played for England; *Wisden*'s likening him to Hammond; the disappointments of Australia and the Caribbean, of not touring South Africa; his return; the Gloucester affair; his début for Worcester and recall to England; the Championship years, in which, he says, 'I had a feeling I was the best in the country'; the hundredth hundred; his return and captaincy of England; Luton; Australia . . . His return? Or is Graveney's abiding memory that 'cricket was a way of life as much as a way of living', causing him to forgive, if not forget, all? His own view of himself is simpler than others'. He gave us things faster than we could discard them.

In reviewing post-War English cricket, most (Graveney included) nominate three pre-eminent bats. There are those who think his name sits among them. Gover, who played with Hammond, who knew Bradman, Fingleton and McCabe, who bowled at or coached batsmen from Chapman to Chappell, has no doubt; Graveney was of the best. (Gover is also convinced that Graveney has been unfairly compared to Hammond, not least because the latter's 'sheer strength' was incomparable.) Cowdrey calls him the 'great man' of his generation. John Murray, who played his early cricket alongside Compton and Edrich, agrees that 'Tom was as good as any . . . and, on his day, better', adding that Graveney's 165 at The Oval was peerless. D'Oliveira describes him as 'the master'; Bailey as 'a very fine batsman, who with maturity became a great one', writing of Graveney in 1968:

> At Romford a few years ago the wicket was so green that it would have served as a natural advertisement for an artificial fertiliser and the ball moved about in a most bewildering fashion. It was a seam bowler's paradise and Gloucester were removed for 153, of which Tom contributed exactly 100. In their second innings they were all out for 107. Once again Tom was the highest scorer with 67, and indeed was unlucky to be out caught down the leg side . . . It was a classic example of how to bat under really difficult conditions, a triumph of technique and application, which only a great player could produce.

Finally the views of two men, pre-eminent in the playing and reporting of cricket, neither of them over the years uncritical of Graveney.

Hutton:

> There weren't many better. I knew as soon as I saw him he "had" it, and he had. All Tom lacked was confidence.

Cardus:

> If some destructive process were to eliminate all we know about cricket, only Graveney remaining, we could reconstruct from him every outline of the game . . . every essential character and flavour contributing to cricket.

It is often the simplest truths that illuminate the hardest arguments. Graveney played in Graveney's way and to know this was to appreciate him. His story is one of promise, frustration, despair, dignity, fulfilment. It is the story of cricket.

Statistical Index

Peter Wynne-Thomas

Test Match Record for England

	M	*I*	*NO*	*Runs*	*HS*	*Avge*	*100*	*50*	*Ct*
v Australia									
Home 1953	5	7	0	169	78	24.14	0	2	4
1956	2	4	1	41	18	13.66	0	0	1
1968	5	9	1	337	96	42.12	0	2	4
Home Total	12	20	2	547	96	30.38	0	4	9
Away 1954–5	2	3	0	132	111	44.00	1	0	4
1958–9	5	10	1	280	54	31.11	0	2	5
1962–3	3	5	1	116	41	29.00	0	0	6
Away Total	10	18	2	528	111	33.00	1	2	15
Total v Australia	22	38	4	1075	111	31.61	1	6	24
v South Africa									
Home 1951	1	1	0	15	15	15.00	0	0	0
1955	5	9	0	219	60	24.33	0	1	9
Total v South Africa	6	10	0	234	60	23.40	0	1	9
v West Indies									
Home 1957	4	5	1	472	258	118.00	2	0	1
1966	4	7	1	459	165	76.50	2	1	5
1969	1	1	0	75	75	75.00	0	1	1
Home Total	9	13	2	1006	258	91.45	4	2	7
Away 1953–4	5	10	3	265	92	37.85	0	2	8
1967–8	5	8	0	261	118	32.62	1	1	9
Away Total	10	18	3	526	118	35.06	1	3	17
Total v West Indies	19	31	5	1532	258	58.92	5	5	24
v New Zealand									
Home 1958	4	5	0	119	37	23.80	0	0	2
Away 1954–5	2	3	1	86	41	43.00	0	0	2
1958–9	2	2	0	88	46	44.00	0	0	2
Away Total	4	5	1	174	46	43.50	0	0	4
Total v New Zealand	8	10	1	293	46	32.55	0	0	6
v India									
Home 1952	4	5	1	191	73	47.75	0	2	2
1967	3	5	0	251	151	50.20	1	1	2
Home Total	7	10	1	442	151	49.11	1	3	4
Away 1951–2	4	8	2	363	175	60.50	1	0	1
Total v India	11	18	3	805	175	53.66	2	3	5
v Pakistan									
Home 1954	3	4	0	150	84	37.50	0	2	3
1962	4	4	0	401	153	100.25	2	1	8
1967	3	4	0	216	81	54.00	0	2	1
Home Total	10	12	0	767	153	63.91	2	5	12
Away 1968–9	3	4	0	176	105	44.00	1	0	0
Total v Pakistan	13	16	0	943	153	58.93	3	5	12
Total at Home	48	70	5	3115	258	47.92	7	15	43
Total away	31	53	8	1767	175	39.26	4	5	37
TOTAL	79	123	13	4882	258	44.38	11	20	80

Test Match Summary

Opponent	*M*	*I*	*NO*	*R*	*Hs*	*Ave*	*Ct*
Australia	22	38	4	1075	111	31.61	24
South Africa	6	10	0	234	60	23.40	9
West Indies	19	31	5	1532	258	58.92	24
New Zealand	8	10	1	293	46	32.55	6
India	11	18	3	805	175	53.66	5
Pakistan	13	16	0	943	153	58.93	12
TOTAL	79	123	13	4882	258	44.38	80

Test Record for England

Batting and Fielding

		M	*I*	*NO*	*Runs*	*HS*	*Avge*	*100*	*50*	*ct*
1951	v South Africa	1	1	0	15	15	15.00	0	0	0
1951–52	v India	4	8	2	363	175	60.50	1	0	1
1952	v India	4	5	1	191	73	47.75	0	2	2
1953	v Australia	5	7	0	169	78	24.14	0	2	4
1953–54	v West Indies	5	10	3	265	92	37.85	0	2	8
1954	v Pakistan	3	4	0	150	84	37.50	0	2	3
1954–55	v Australia	2	3	0	132	111	44.00	1	0	4
1954–55	v New Zealand	2	3	1	86	41	43.00	0	0	2
1955	v South Africa	5	9	0	219	60	24.33	0	1	9
1956	v Australia	2	4	1	41	18	13.66	0	0	1
1957	v West Indies	4	5	1	472	258	118.00	2	0	1
1958	v New Zealand	4	5	0	119	37	23.80	0	0	2
1958–59	v Australia	5	10	1	280	54	31.11	0	2	5
1958–59	v New Zealand	2	2	0	88	46	44.00	0	0	2
1962	v Pakistan	4	4	0	401	153	100.25	2	1	8
1962–63	v Australia	3	5	1	116	41	29.00	0	0	6
1966	v West Indies	4	7	1	459	165	76.50	2	1	5
1967	v India	3	5	0	251	151	50.20	1	1	2
1967	v Pakistan	3	4	0	216	81	54.00	0	2	1
1967–68	v West Indies	5	8	0	261	118	32.62	1	1	9
1968	v Australia	5	9	1	337	96	42.12	0	2	4
1968–69	v Pakistan	3	4	0	176	105	44.00	1	0	0
1969	v West Indies	1	1	0	75	75	75.00	0	1	1
Total		79	123	13	4882	258	44.38	11	20	80

Bowling

			O	*M*	*R*	*W*	*Avge*	*BB*
1951–52	v India	6b	1	0	9	0		
1953–54	v West Indies	6b	8	0	59	0		
1954–55	v Australia	8b	6	0	34	1	34.00	1–34
1956	v Australia	6b	6	3	6	0		
1957	v West Indies	6b	5	2	14	0		
1962–63	v Australia	8b	7	1	34	0		
1968–69	v Pakistan	6b	6	0	11	0		
Total		6b 8b	26 13	5 1	167	1	167.00	1–34

8b = 8-ball overs; 6b = 6-ball overs

All First-class Matches

Batting and Fielding

	M	*I*	*NO*	*Runs*	*HS*	*Avge*	*100*	*50*	*ct/st*
1948	24	38	4	973	114	28.61	1	6	11
1949	31	55	1	1784	159	33.03	4	8	23
1950	33	56	4	1892	201	36.38	3	9	21
1951	29	50	3	2291	201	48.74	8	8	11
1951–2 (India)	19	32	7	1393	175	55.72	6	3	4
1952	28	50	7	2066	171	48.04	6	10	13
1953	31	57	6	1816	211	35.60	4	10	16
1953–4 (WI)	8	14	3	617	231	56.09	1	3	14
1954	25	38	4	1950	222	57.35	5	14	21
1954–5 (Aus and NZ)	15	22	3	855	134	45.00	4	0	20
1955	28	51	2	2117	159	43.20	5	8	31
1955–6 (WI)	4	6	0	373	154	62.16	2	0	1
1956	31	54	6	2397	200	49.93	9	8	25
1956–7 (India)	2	3	0	284	153	94.66	2	0	1
1956–7 (WI)	3	6	1	329	92	65.80	0	3	5
1957	32	53	5	2361	258	49.18	8	7	35
1958	28	47	6	1459	156	35.58	2	8	25
1958–9 (Aus and NZ)	19	30	4	1229	177*	47.26	2	8	18
1959	19	30	5	1062	155*	42.48	1	9	11
1959–60 (SA)	3	5	2	343	102*	114.33	2	1	1
1960	31	54	6	1625	142*	33.85	2	11	27
1960–1 (SA)	4	7	0	177	105	25.28	1	0	1
1961	4	7	2	330	152*	66.00	2	0	2
1961–2 (World)	8	13	3	813	116*	81.30	2	6	7
1962	29	48	6	2269	164*	54.02	9	8	30
1962–3 (Aus)	11	18	4	737	185	52.64	2	2	13
1963	28	50	7	1492	100	34.69	1	11	21
1963–4 (Pak)	4	6	1	500	164	100.00	2	2	4
1963–4 (Jam)	3	4	1	175	108*	58.33	1	0	0
1964	30	51	7	2385	164	54.20	5	16	26
1964–5 (Rhod)	2	4	1	192	136*	64.00	1	0	0
1965	28	45	9	1768	126	49.11	4	11	10
1966	24	40	6	1777	166	52.26	4	7	20
1966–7 (Barb)	1	2	0	41	31	20.50	0	0	1
1967	26	42	4	1668	151	43.89	4	10	15
1967–8 (WI)	11	17	2	389	118	25.93	1	1	17
1968	21	34	4	1130	107*	37.66	1	10	14
1968–9 (Pak)	6	6	0	317	106	52.83	2	0	1
1969	21	33	7	963	110*	37.03	1	5	12
1969–70 (Aus)	2	2	1	15	15	15.00	0	0	2/1
1970	21	34	13	1316	114	62.66	2	9	18
1970–1 (Aus)	4	7	1	102	56	17.00	0	1	2
1971–2 (Aus)	1	2	1	21	21*	21.00	0	0	0
Total	732	1223	159	47793	258	44.91	122	233	550/1

* *Signifies not out*

All First-class Matches

Bowling

		O	M	R	W	Avge	BB	5i
1948		16	1	53	0			
1949			did not bowl					
1950		13	2	51	0			
1951		7	1	33	0			
1951–2 (India)		42.4	7	182	6	30.33	4–67	0
1952		71.5	8	249	10	24.90	3–26	0
1953		94.3	19	324	19	17.05	5–28	1
1953–4 (WI)		16	6	71	0			
1954		156	34	415	10	41.50	1–11	0
1954–5 (Aus)	8b	6	0	47	1	47.00	1–34	0
(NZ)	6b	9	3					
1955		105.3	22	374	11	34.00	3–18	0
1955–6 (WI)		14	1	59	1	59.00	1–47	0
1956		88.5	30	252	4	63.00	1–5	0
1956–7 (India)			did not bowl					
1956–7 (WI)			did not bowl					
1957		60.2	7	216	5	43.20	2–27	0
1958		11	0	46	0			
1958–9 (Aus)	8b	18	0	107	1	107.00	1–39	0
(NZ)	6b	3	1					
1959		24	9	49	1	49.00	1–3	0
1959–60 (SA)			did not bowl					
1960		56	10	182	3	60.66	2–24	0
1960–1 (SA)			did not bowl					
1961		1	0	4	0			
1961–2 (World)		1	0	4	0			
1962		16	2	52	1	52.00	1–52	0
1962–3 (Aus)	8b	9	2	36	2	18.00	2–2	0
1963		15.3	2	66	1	66.00	1–22	0
1963–4 (Pak)		18	2	87	2	43.50	1–32	0
1963–4 (Jam)			did not bowl					
1964		2	1	1	0			
1964–5 (Rhod)			did not bowl					
1965			did not bowl					
1966			did not bowl					
1967		3	0	10	0			
1966–7 (Barb)			did not bowl					
1967–8 (WI)		4	2	3	0			
1968			did not bowl					
1968–9 (Pak)		6	0	11	0			
1969			did not bowl					
1969–70 (Aus)			did not bowl					
1970		14	1	53	2	26.50	2–10	0
1970–1 (Aus)			did not bowl					
1971–2 (Aus)			did not bowl					
Total	6b	869.1	171	3037	80	37.96	5–28	1
	8b	33	2					

8b = 8-ball overs; 6b = 6-ball overs

Gloucestershire First-class Matches

Batting and Fielding

	M	*I*	*NO*	*Runs*	*HS*	*Avge*	*100*	*50*	*ct*
1948	23	36	4	960	114	30.00	1	6	10
1949	28	49	1	1656	159	34.50	4	8	21
1950	31	52	4	1772	201	36.91	3	8	19
1951	25	43	3	2139	201	53.47	8	7	10
1952	20	37	5	1515	171	47.34	5	7	10
1953	20	38	3	1391	211	39.74	4	6	11
1954	19	29	4	1748	222	69.92	5	12	18
1955	19	34	1	1403	128	42.51	3	6	19
1956	22	38	3	1821	200	52.02	6	7	19
1957	22	37	3	1600	134	47.05	6	5	32
1958	21	37	6	1186	156	38.25	2	7	21
1959	19	30	5	1062	155*	42.48	1	9	11
1960	27	46	6	1452	142*	36.30	2	9	23
Total	296	506	48	19705	222	43.02	50	97	224

**Signifies not out*

Bowling

	O	*M*	*R*	*W*	*Avge*	*BB*	*5i*
1948	16	1	53	0	–		
1949			did not bowl				
1950	13	2	51	0	–		
1951	7	1	33	0	–		
1952	71.5	8	249	10	24.90	3–26	0
1953	74.1	17	239	16	14.93	5–28	1
1954	154	34	407	10	40.70	1–11	0
1955	105.3	22	374	11	34.00	3–18	0
1956	72.5	25	213	3	71.00	1–14	0
1957	37	5	105	3	35.00	2–27	0
1958	11	0	46	0	–		
1959	24	9	49	1	49.00	1–3	0
1960	56	10	182	3	60.66	2–24	0
Total	642.2	134	2001	57	35.10	5–28	1

Worcestershire First-class Matches

Batting and Fielding

	M	*I*	*NO*	*Runs*	*HS*	*Avge*	*100*	*50*	*ct*
1961	2	3	1	191	152*	95.50	1	0	2
1962	23	40	6	1666	164*	49.00	6	7	21
1963	27	48	6	1452	100	34.57	1	11	21
1964	29	50	7	2375	164	55.23	5	16	26
1964–5 (Rhod)	2	4	1	192	136*	64.00	1	0	0
1965	28	45	9	1768	126	49.11	4	11	10
1966	20	33	5	1318	166	47.07	2	6	15
1967	20	33	4	1201	113*	41.41	3	7	12
1968	16	25	3	793	107*	36.04	1	8	10
1969	20	32	7	888	110*	35.52	1	4	11
1970	21	34	13	1316	114	62.66	2	9	18
Total	208	347	62	13160	166	46.17	27	79	146

**Signifies not out*

Worcestershire First-class Matches *cont.*

Bowling

	O	*M*	*R*	*W*	*Avge*	*BB*	*5i*
1961				did not bowl			
1962	16	2	52	1	52.00	1–52	0
1963	15.3	2	66	1	66.00	1–22	0
1964	2	1	1	0			
1964–5 (Rhod)				did not bowl			
1965				did not bowl			
1966				did not bowl			
1967	3	0	10	0			
1968				did not bowl			
1969				did not bowl			
1970	14	1	53	2	26.50	2–10	0
Total	50.3	6	182	4	45.50	2–10	0

Worcestershire Gillette Cup Matches

Batting and Fielding

	M	*I*	*NO*	*Runs*	*HS*	*Avge*	*100*	*50*	*ct*
1963	4	3	0	191	93	63.66	0	1	0
1964	1	1	0	1	1	1.00	0	0	2
1965	1	1	0	40	40	40.00	0	0	0
1966	3	3	1	66	26	33.00	0	0	3
1967	1	1	0	9	9	9.00	0	0	1
1968	2	2	0	119	74	59.50	0	1	1
1969	1	1	1	61	61*	–	0	1	0
1970	2	2	1	47	27*	47.00	0	0	0
Total	15	14	3	534	93	48.54	0	4	7

**Signifies not out*

(Graveney did not bowl in Gillette Cup Matches)

Worcestershire John Player League Matches

Batting and Fielding

	M	*I*	*NO*	*Runs*	*HS*	*Avge*	*100*	*50*	*ct*
1969	12	12	1	236	48	21.45	0	0	1
1970	15	14	2	271	68	22.58	0	1	5
Total	27	26	3	507	68	22.04	0	1	6

(Graveney did not bowl in John Player League Matches)

First-class Centuries

**Signifies not out*

1	114	Gloucestershire v. Combined Services (Gloucester)	1948
2	108	Gloucestershire v. Oxford University (The Parks)	1949
3	139	Gloucestershire v. Nottinghamshire (Trent Bridge)	1949
4	132	Gloucestershire v. Surrey (The Oval)	1949
5	159	Gloucestershire v. Somerset (Bristol)	1949
6	197	Gloucestershire v. Nottinghamshire (Bristol)	1950
7	115	Gloucestershire v. Glamorgan (Gloucester)	1950
8	201	Gloucestershire v. Sussex (Worthing)	1950
9	201	Gloucestershire v. Oxford University (The Parks)	1951

First-class Centuries *cont.*

10	107	Gloucestershire v. Leicestershire (Bristol)	1951
11	146	Gloucestershire v. Surrey (The Oval)	1951
12	113	Gloucestershire v. Nottinghamshire (Trent Bridge)	1951
13	128	Gloucestershire v. Warwickshire (Bristol)	1951
14	104	Gloucestershire v. Oxford University (The Parks)	1951
15	103	Gloucestershire v. Nottinghamshire (Bristol)	1951
16	105*		
17	101	MCC v. Combined Universities (Bombay)	1951–2
18	101	MCC v. Services (Dehra Dun)	1951–2
19	109*	MCC v. Pakistan (Lahore)	1951–2
20	123	MCC v. Pakistan (Karachi)	1951–2
21	175	England v. India (Bombay)	1951–2
22	102*	MCC v. Ceylon (Colombo)	1951–2
23	158	MCC v. India (Lord's)	1952
24	171	Gloucestershire v. Sussex (Bristol)	1952
25	104	Gloucestershire v. Worcestershire (Worcester)	1952
26	105	Gloucestershire v. Cambridge University (Bristol)	1952
27	113*	Gloucestershire v. Somerset (Bristol)	1952
28	166*	Gloucestershire v. Leicestershire (Leicester)	1952
29	124	Gloucestershire v. Oxford University (The Parks)	1953
30	126*	Gloucestershire v. Leicestershire (Bristol)	1953
31	211	Gloucestershire v. Kent (Gillingham)	1953
32	110*	Gloucestershire v. Somerset (Bristol)	1953
33	231	MCC v. British Guiana (Georgetown)	1953–4
34	177*	Gloucestershire v. Glamorgan (Gloucester)	1954
35	125*	Gloucestershire v. Northamptonshire (Northampton)	1954
36	111*	Gloucestershire v. Essex (Gloucester)	1954
37	107	Gloucestershire v. Somerset (Taunton)	1954
38	222	Gloucestershire v. Derbyshire (Chesterfield)	1954
39	134	MCC v. Tasmania (Launceston)	1954–5
40	111	England v. Australia (Sydney)	1954–5
41	101	MCC v. Canterbury (Christchurch)	1954–5
42	102	MCC v. Wellington (Wellington)	1954–5
43	104	Gloucestershire v. Somerset (Taunton)	1955
44	101	Gloucestershire v. Northamptonshire (Kettering)	1955
45	128	Gloucestershire v. Worcestershire (Worcester)	1955
46	101	MCC v. Yorkshire (Scarborough)	1955
47	159	T. N. Pearce's XI v. South Africans (Scarborough)	1955
48	154	E. W. Swanton's XI v. Barbados (Bridgetown)	1955–6
49	117	E. W. Swanton's XI v. Trinidad (Port of Spain)	1955–6
50	112	MCC v. Yorkshire (Lord's)	1956
51	152	Gloucestershire v. Middlesex (Lord's)	1956
52	133	Gloucestershire v. Somerset (Bristol)	1956
53	100	Gloucestershire v. Essex (Romford)	1956
54	190	Gloucestershire v. Leicestershire (Bristol)	1956
55	156	Gloucestershire v. Middlesex (Gloucester)	1956
56	200	Gloucestershire v. Glamorgan (Newport)	1956
57	124	Players v. Gentlemen (Scarborough)	1956
58	101	T. N. Pearce's XI v. Australians (Scarborough)	1956
59	153	C. G. Howard's XI v. Cricket Club of India (Bombay)	1956–7
60	120		
61	101*	Gloucestershire v. Middlesex (Lord's)	1957
62	111*	Gloucestershire v. Worcestershire (Bristol)	1957
63	122	Gloucestershire v. Warwickshire (Bristol)	1957
64	106	Gloucestershire v. Warwickshire (Edgbaston)	1957
65	101*		
66	258	England v. West Indies (Trent Bridge)	1957

First-class Centuries *cont.*

67	134	Gloucestershire v. Somerset (Bristol)	1957
68	164	England v. West Indies (The Oval)	1957
69	156	Gloucestershire v. Essex (Bristol)	1958
70	114	Gloucestershire v. Northamptonshire (Gloucester)	1958
71	177*	MCC v. Western Australia (Perth)	1958–9
72	108	MCC v. Northern and Central Districts (Hamilton)	1958–9
73	155*	Gloucestershire v. Nottinghamshire (Trent Bridge)	1959
74	100*	Commonwealth XI v. Combined Transvaal XI (Pretoria)	1959–60
75	102*	Commonwealth XI v. Invitation XI (Johannesburg)	1959–60
76	135	Gloucestershire v. Derbyshire (Chesterfield)	1960
77	142*	Gloucestershire v. Middlesex (Cheltenham)	1960
78	105	Cavaliers v. Invitation XI (Johannesburg)	1960–1
79	152*	Worcestershire v. Cambridge University (Fenner's)	1961
80	124	Col. L. C. Stevens's XI v. Cambridge University (Eastbourne)	1961
81	112*	International XI v. Rhodesian XI (Nkana)	1961–2
82	116*	International XI v. New Zealand CA President's XI (Auckland)	1961–2
83	117	Worcestershire v. Pakistan (Worcester)	1962
84	119	Worcestershire v. Middlesex (Lord's)	1962
85	110	MCC v. Pakistan (Lord's)	1962
86	147*	Worcestershire v. Middlesex (Worcester)	1962
87	164*	Worcestershire v. Somerset (Worcester)	1962
88	153	England v. Pakistan (Lord's)	1962
89	115	Worcestershire v. Northamptonshire (Kidderminster)	1962
90	114	England v. Pakistan (Trent Bridge)	1962
91	106	Worcestershire v. Hampshire (Worcester)	1962
92	122*	MCC v. South Australia (Adelaide)	1962–3
93	185	MCC v. Victoria (Melbourne)	1962–3
94	100	Worcestershire v. Derbyshire (Worcester)	1963
95 96	164 107*	Commonwealth XI v. Pakistan (Lahore)	1963–4
97	108*	Cavaliers v. Jamaica (Kingston)	1963–4
98	122*	Worcestershire v. Yorkshire (Scarborough)	1964
99	109	Worcestershire v. Leicestershire (Worcester)	1964
100	132	Worcestershire v. Northamptonshire (Worcester)	1964
101	106	Worcestershire v. Essex (Leyton)	1964
102	164	Worcestershire v. Nottinghamshire (Worcester)	1964
103	136*	Worcestershire v. Rhodesia (Salisbury)	1964–5
104	104	Worcestershire v. Essex (Worcester)	1965
105	105	Worcestershire v. Warwickshire (Edgbaston)	1965
106	126	Worcestershire v. Leicestershire (Worcester)	1965
107	104	Worcestershire v. Hampshire (Bournemouth)	1965
108	109	England v. West Indies (Trent Bridge)	1966
109	109	Worcestershire v. Surrey (The Oval)	1966
110	165	England v. West Indies (The Oval)	1966
111	166	Worcestershire v. Essex (Worcester)	1966
112	113*	Worcestershire v. Warwickshire (Edgbaston)	1967
113	151	England v. India (Lord's)	1967
114	108	Worcestershire v. Sussex (Worcester)	1967
115	101	Worcestershire v. Warwickshire (Edgbaston)	1967
116	118	England v. West Indies (Port of Spain)	1967–8
117	107*	Worcestershire v. Leicestershire (Leicester)	1968
118	106	MCC v. Ceylon (Colombo)	1968–9
119	105	England v. Pakistan (Karachi)	1968–9
120	110*	Worcestershire v. Warwickshire (Edgbaston)	1969
121	114	Worcestershire v. Kent (Canterbury)	1970
122	100*	Worcestershire v. Yorkshire (Worcester)	1970

Notable Wicket Partnerships

2nd wkt	266	with P. E. Richardson	England v. West Indies (Trent Bridge)	1957
	259*	with R. T. Spooner	MCC v. Pakistan (Lahore)	1951–2
	256	with C. T. M. Pugh	Gloucestershire v. Derbyshire (Chesterfield)	1960
3rd wkt	318	with J. F. Crapp	Gloucestershire v. Kent (Gillingham)	1953
	314	with M. J. Horton	Worcestershire v. Somerset (Worcester)	1962
4th wkt	402	with W. Watson	MCC v. British Guiana (Georgetown)	1953–4
	271	with B. L. D'Oliveira	Worcestershire v. Essex (Worcester)	1966
5th wkt	344	with M. C. Cowdrey	MCC v. South Australia (Adelaide)	1962–3
8th wkt	217	with J. T. Murray	England v. West Indies (The Oval)	1966

** Signifies unbroken partnership*

Index